An
Economist
at Home and
Abroad

Praise for *An Economist at Home and Abroad*

'This book is a gripping account of the life of an accomplished scholar, policymaker and public intellectual. The writing is clear, simple and honest. The canvas is large, the players varied and the settings range across India and abroad but the author's Indianness comes through beautifully. Shankar provides rare, frank and valuable insights into a wide range of policies, institutions and processes in India. Above all, it is a gentleman's account of the complexities he encountered in life and work in India and overseas, while also giving a retrospect and prospect for the Indian economy at this critical juncture.'

—**Dr Y. Venugopal Reddy,**
Chairman, Fourteenth Finance Commission, and former governor,
Reserve Bank of India

'In this wonderful book, Shankar Acharya displays to the full his decency, perspicacity and intellectual honesty. Shankar was, above all, a distinguished public servant in his years as chief economic adviser to the reforming government of the 1990s. But it is as a commentator on the Indian economy that he excels: he is the best. He ends his book with a sobering warning on India's current prospects. Pay attention. He is right.'

—**Martin Wolf,**
Chief economics commentator, *Financial Times*

'I found Shankar Acharya's book riveting. The sheer width and depth of a fascinating seventy-five years woven with intricacy, insight and perspective of history. He shares his wide travel experiences, his twenty-three years in the West, his Indian journey both as a child and later back home. His lively account of his twelve years as our chairman makes banking seem exciting. A great read at home and abroad!'

—**Uday Kotak,**
Managing director and CEO, Kotak Mahindra Bank

'A delightful book by a key insider who was chief economic adviser for a record eight years during the reforms, straddling three governments. He understates his own role, which was considerable, and which he left before his normal retirement because he wanted to sample academic life. His regular op-eds have brought truly high-quality commentary on economic issues to a wide audience. But the book is not just a detailed account of economic policy and performance. It touches lightly on those issues while providing a fascinating account of what it was like to be an insider at a key moment in India's economic history and of the subsequent seamless transition to academia. A charming account covering professional, personal and social life.'

—**Montek Singh Ahluwalia**,
Former deputy chairman, Planning Commission

'This lucidly written memoir, smoothly combines the personal with Acharya's role as an influential policymaker, and takes the reader on an engaging journey through the period charm of newly independent India, the unexpected contrasts between life as a student in Britain and the US, a globe-trotting job and finally back in India at a pivotal moment of change. The larger story, hence the importance of the book, is that Acharya was one of the accomplished economists who left well-paying careers overseas to return home to relatively modest government incomes and housing, in order to steer public policy in new directions. It's a story well worth telling, not just because it recounts an intelligent insider's well-considered views on both policies and personalities, but also because it is a timely reminder that at least some of the now-demonized members of Lutyens' Delhi, admittedly privileged, also represented the best possible breed of public-spirited civil servants.'

—**T.N. Ninan**,
Columnist and former editor of *Business Standard*

An Economist at Home and Abroad

A Personal Journey

SHANKAR ACHARYA

HarperCollins *Publishers* India

First published in hardback in India by
HarperCollins *Publishers* in 2021
A-75, Sector 57, Noida, Uttar Pradesh 201301, India
www.harpercollins.co.in

2 4 6 8 10 9 7 5 3 1

Budget group 1996 photo from *Backstage: The Story Behind India's High-growth Years*,
published by Rupa Publications, reproduced with permission.
Kotak board photo reproduced with permission from Kotak Mahindra Bank

P-ISBN: 978-93-5422-739-4
E-ISBN: 978-93-5422-782-0

Typeset in 11.5/15.2 Bembo Std at
Manipal Technologies Limited, Manipal

Printed and bound at
Thomson Press (India) Ltd

In memory of my parents, Bejoy and Nilima, who gifted me life, values and education.

For my wife and life partner of 54 years, Gayatri, daughter, Maya, son, Nikhil and other close relatives and friends, who enriched my life in so many ways and made it so worth living.

Contents

Preface

THIS BOOK WAS BIRTHED by the global Covid-19 pandemic of 2020, and its associated features of the lockdown and, later, the self-isolation recommended for the elderly. I expect quite a large number of books were started during this prolonged period of partially voluntary 'house arrest', though perhaps not all were finished. For me, there was a limit to the hundreds of hours I spent watching Netflix, Amazon, YouTube and webinars, and reading books, newspapers and endless streams of jokes, information and trivia on WhatsApp. After about three months, around June 2020, the creative juices began to churn and propelled me from the lounge chair in front of the TV to my desktop.

There were other prods to embark on these memoirs. Quite a few friends and family members, for quite some time, had been suggesting I write a book. Among those who were more insistent, were our daughter, Ta, who wanted to know more about the first forty years of her parents' lives; old friend Isher Ahluwalia, who set an astonishing example by completing her own life story in the last few months of her tragically shortened life; childhood friends, Ravi Bhoothalingam and Pabi Wadhawan, who wanted to revisit our early years in Delhi of the 1950s; and Indian Council for Research on International Economy Relations (ICRIER) colleague and friend, Amita Batra, who wanted to know more about the lives of an earlier generation of middle-class professionals in India.

So, from the middle of June, I sat down before my desktop for a few hours every day and started this act of remembering, aided by some photo albums, a bit of Google research and Ta's prodigious memory of the four most recent decades. As chapters rolled out, I circulated the drafts among close family members and friends, and received tremendous encouragement to continue with the enterprise. Remembering, writing and sharing became a rewarding daily activity, which gained momentum and generated the necessary discipline to persevere. Initially, I simply intended to put my memories together in a document for a few dozen family members and friends—for our mutual benefit and entertainment. Perhaps halfway through the manuscript, I began to get serious encouragement and recommendations from this 'inner circle' to aim for eventual publication.

As my writing progressed, I leaned towards accepting this recommendation—though with some trepidation. Everyone has a life story to tell. But only a small minority of these stories are interesting for those outside a limited circle of family and close friends. I ventured to think that mine might just slip into that select category for a few reasons. First, thanks to parental circumstances, I attended school and university across three different countries (India, Britain and America) on three different continents, which meant that my formative years were intrinsically cross-cultural. Second, for over twenty-three continuous years, from my early teens to my mid-thirties, I lived, studied and worked outside India. This meant when my wife and I returned to India, in the early 1980s, we had the benefit of looking at our home country from the outside—but now faced the challenges of reintegrating into our own society and regenerating our original roots. Third, during those twenty-three years in an English boarding school, Oxford, Harvard and the World Bank, I formed an eclectic set of friends—quite a few of whom later became prominent in India, UK, Myanmar (formerly known as Burma) and Sri Lanka. Fourth, while I had trained as an economist, I was fortunate to pursue and experience a variety of occupations: A decade in the World Bank, as an economics scholar back in India, as a senior adviser to the Union Government during two decades of serious economic change and policy reforms, as a regular columnist for one of India's best financial papers and as chairman of the country's fastest-growing private bank for a dozen years.

Taking all this together, I dare to think that this personal account of my life journey might just hold some interest for a wider set of people outside my immediate family and friends. I certainly hope so.

1

Childhood Snapshots

A DISTINCTIVE FEATURE OF my childhood—and indeed, of my life till my mid-thirties—was its peripatetic nature. Every second or third year, we would find ourselves living in a different place. This was quite common among children of families where the parents, usually the father, worked in India's elite civil services. My father (Bejoy Krishna Acharya, henceforth referred to as Baba) was in the Bengal cadre of the Indian Civil Service (ICS), 1936 batch. It was only much later that I understood that this nomadic life was not the norm, at least as far as the vast majority of humanity was concerned. Most people spent their childhoods in the town or village where they were born. Most had a 'family home', which often anchored much of their lives. But that was not the case for my brother, Sanjoy (six years older, whom I call Dada), and me.

I was born in our government-provided house in Heysham Road in Kolkata (then Calcutta) on a Sunday in October 1945. For obvious reasons, I have no memory of the place. Nor was I aware

1

that I had arrived on this planet just weeks after the greatest global war to date had ended, and just two years after the Great Bengal Famine had killed perhaps some 2 million people—thanks, in large measure, to the deliberate British policy of commandeering nearly all railway rolling stock for their war effort against the Japanese on India's eastern front, to the exclusion of grain shipments to areas of harvest failure in Bengal.

With Acharya as our family name, my parents thought it would be a good idea to name me Shankar. After all, Shankaracharya had a certain historico-cultural resonance in India. When I was around five years old, and suffering from a bout of sibling rivalry, I complained that Dada had a middle name, Kumar, and I agitated for some parity. My parents relented, and inserted Nath as my middle name, thus spoiling their original plan. Much later, I also realized that my childish contention had been a bad idea. So I slowly dropped the use of Nath, but could not do so entirely as too many legal and identification documents now had it enshrined.

My earliest—and faintest—memory, greatly reinforced by a couple of surviving snapshots, was of being on a lake in a boat. Apparently, this was in Tripura, a small princely state in the north-east of India, where Baba was posted as Acting Dewan in late 1947, during Sardar Patel's tremendous enterprise of integrating India's 500-plus princely states into the Indian Union. The lake was part of the Maharaja's luxurious Neermahal palace and estate, about 50 kms from Agartala, where Dada assures me that the bathrooms had bidets and gold-plated taps. The Acting Dewan and his family were housed in the east wing of the Kunjobon Palace in Agartala. I also have faint memories of two much-squished soft toys of a puppy and a bunny, called Khedi and Penchi. These, I am reliably informed, one day fell into the lake at Neermahal. The palace staff were mobilized and searched diligently using long boat hooks among the ubiquitous water lilies, managing to rescue Khedi, who gave me comfort for a few more years. Penchi was irretrievably and tragically lost forever.

From Tripura, we moved to Darjeeling, where Baba was posted as District Magistrate (DM) for a year or so. Fifty years later, on a private visit to the city, I visited the DM's office to see his name, B.K. Acharya, inscribed on the board behind the DM's desk. Oddly, I have almost no memories of Darjeeling from my time there. Based on parental accounts, I recall only two events. First, I was given a small guinea pig as a present, which I managed to almost suffocate to death by hugging it excessively. The other matter, of greater significance, was my father's success in negotiating an amicable end to what might be called the 'first Gurkha rebellion' without a single shot having been fired. He had to face down armed leaders of the movement and work out a deal with them, supported only by the local police—quite an achievement for a thirty-five-year-old.

In 1949, we were in Delhi for a year, with Baba posted as a Deputy Secretary in the Ministry of Civil Supplies, a significant ministry in those years of post-Partition food distribution and rationing. We were allotted two rooms in the stately Western Court on Queens Way (now Janpath), along with several other young officers and their families. I was sent to Miss Hartley's kindergarten school for my first experience with formal schooling. I think I was dropped to school and picked up by either by my father or mother in our car.

I have a clearer memory of the car, a 1948 Chevrolet, purchased by my father from his share of the sale of his paternal home on Harrison Road, Kolkata. I probably remember the car because of a close encounter I once had. One day, on the way to school, my father (or mother) had to brake suddenly. I was in the seat next to the driver and was thrown forward against the dashboard, cutting open my lip. This was decades before seatbelts became standard issue in cars.

I don't recollect much of what we did in school or of my interactions with the other children. Except for one traumatic incident. As the months passed, my parents noticed that I became very reluctant to go to school, and had even started throwing up on the way there. Investigations revealed the following. At school, wearing my shorts and shirt, I used to be seated next to a Sikh girl with striking double-looped pigtails, who developed a proclivity to pinching my thighs—whether motivated by strong affection or sadism, or simple bullying, I never found out. I bore this trial timidly and stoically, until the vomiting syndrome developed and my parents intervened and took the matter to the class teacher. The teacher's solution was simple and effective: Change the seating. Luckily, there were no lasting scars as far as my attitude to the opposite sex in later years was concerned.

Back at Western Court, we had no lack of playmates in the children of other young government officers. One of them, Gautam Datta, I got to know better later in life as a friend. In the evenings, all four of us in my family often played board games such as ludo and snakes and ladders. There was no TV and we did not own a radio. On weekends, we would sometimes go on picnics with a few other families to 'distant' places like Hauz Khas and Qutb Minar.

In 1950, we were back in Kolkata, ensconced in the large house allotted to the DM of Howrah. I completed standard one at St. Thomas school there, winning my first school prize. In Kolkata, this time around, I began to relate more to some of my relatives, especially my mother's family, spread over eight small flats in her father's house (my Dadu's) on Darga Road, near Don Bosco school. My special favourites were my uncle, Bhaiya Mama, and his wife, Minu Mami. They were childless, and showered affection on Dada and me. Dadu, who had lost his wife when my mother was only seven, was a benevolent presence in the household. He had retired from the Indian Education Service. For many years, he had been principal of Patna Science College, from where my mother, Nilima, earned her physics degree in the mid-1930s, probably one of the first female graduates in physics in the country.

On Baba's side, it was his elder brother, Ajay, a gynaecologist, my older cousins, Jayanta-da and Atashi, and my paternal grandmother, or Thakurma, who lived with them in their home in Shebak Baidya whom we spent time with. Thakurma had been widowed since 1936 and observed strict white sari attire and a spartan, Vaishnavite diet. To us she was always very affectionate and indulgent. Dada and Atashi were only two years apart, and were quite chummy; I was six–eight years younger and in no way a peer. My close cousin-friend came from the line of my Pishima (Baba's sister, but fifteen years older than him). Pishima, Usha Haldar, was also a widow (of another ICS officer) and lived with her only child, my cousin Lakhi-di, and her husband, Mohit Mukherji, a senior Railways officer. Lakhi-di's only child, Nandita, was actually my niece, but two years older than me because of the big age gap between my father and Pishima. From those early years, Nandita and I developed a close friendship, which has endured for seven decades now.

Sometime towards the end of 1950, Baba moved to the West Bengal government's Ministry of Civil Supplies and we shifted to a government flat in Ekdalia Place. Those two Kolkata years, 1949–51, were my years of closest contact with the Bengali language and culture. I had developed an early fondness for reading in both English and Bengali, and recall spending many hours enthralled by the Ramayana and Mahabharata in Bengali. I saw them as unmatched adventure stories, with strong overtones of good vs evil. Mama and Mami indulged me by allowing me to read out loud from these fascinating epics whenever I spent some days with them. Sadly, my written Bengali skills peaked at the age of six! It was during my holidays with my Mama and Mami that I also learned to play carom and became quite good at it. And I also loved the very special chicken cutlets that Mami often cooked for us.

At cousin/niece Nandita's home, the preferred game was Chinese checkers. She and her family lived in one of those spacious quarters allotted to senior officers in the railways, with large grounds in which their dachshund, Fritz, would roam freely. Family dynamics were generally warm, but with undercurrents of tensions and jealousies, which I was largely ignorant of at that stage, but came to understand slowly as the years unfolded. During visits, aside from Chinese checkers, we would often play word-making with those little cardboard letters, and other games. Nandita and I also began to share a love of books, especially Enid Blyton and Richmal Crompton.

Sometime in 1951, we made a long and interesting car trip to the Damodar River Valley Project, where we visited a number of new dams and power stations, including those at Maithon, Panchet and Tilaiya, the barrage at Durgapur and the Bokaro complex. Whenever I come across the old, once-popular phrase 'temples of modern India', the images of these dams come to mind.

In 1951, our family 'went international', in a manner of speaking, when Baba was posted as Deputy High Commissioner to Dhaka, the capital of East Pakistan, on loan to the fledgling Indian Foreign Service (IFS). Our three years there were a whole new chapter in our lives, partly because East Bengal was both different and familiar at once, and partly because I grew from six to nine years of age there, gradually absorbing more about the world outside of home and school. We lived in a charming old mansion, Baitul-

Aman, with spacious gardens and a separate building for official entertainment, on the road to the old airport. The entrance was manned by armed guards from India.

I was admitted to the Holy Cross Convent school, meant mainly for girls, but taking boys up to the age of ten. Dada was dispatched to the famous boarding school in Darjeeling, St. Paul's, on the top of Jalapahar Hill. This made me an 'only child' at home, with both its pluses and minuses. I don't recall much about school in Dhaka other than a close friend, Ashfaq, who often came over to play after school, provided he got permission from his parents, which was sometimes denied to moderate fraternization with the enemy! Some sixty years later, I met the Bangladeshi High Commissioner in Delhi, Tariq Karim, at a dinner, and our conversation soon established that we had been classmates at Holy Cross in the early 1950s!

The Indian mission in Dhaka was quite large, especially on the consular side, and there were fairly close interactions among the families of senior officers. Sometimes, in small groups, we would head out for weekend trips on board steamers and launches 'up river' on the vast rivers and tributaries of the enormous delta of the Ganges and Brahmaputra. For Baba and his officers, these trips combined work with pleasure. For the spouses and the children, it was pure fun. It was on these trips that I watched my parents play bridge and learnt the rudiments of the game. The riverine scene was a wonderland, as we watched the crew navigate perilous shoals and batten down the hatches when monsoon storm clouds gathered menacingly. At the confluence of the Meghna and Padma, the distance between the banks was several kilometres, and the waves whipped up by a storm could threaten even steamers, let alone the much smaller launches. In the many decades after, despite substantial world travel, I have never encountered again the sheer grandness of the rivers of Bengal.

On the longer trips in the bigger boats, the families would gather on the upper deck before sundown to socialize. Often Baba, who had a lovely baritone voice, would lead the group in river songs of Tagore, like 'Kharo bayu boye bege ... ' and the great Bhatiali/Baul folk songs of Bengal like 'O amar daradi ... ' Unfortunately, those musical gifts escaped me entirely, though luckily Dada got some of them. Which is why, at eighty-plus, he still sings in small local choirs in Canada, where he has been long settled.

After a year or so in Dhaka, I was rudely uprooted from this pleasant existence and sent off in March 1953, at the tender age of seven, to begin the academic year in the junior school of St. Paul's in Darjeeling. Dada was settled in the senior school, and became a guardian of sorts. I say 'of sorts' because interaction between the junior and senior schools was not permitted, except for limited outings on Sundays. March was not a pleasant time to start school atop Jalapahar at 8000 feet, with cold winds whipping through the playgrounds and other open areas where we assembled for various daily activities. Moreover, us juniors had to wear shorts as our uniform, which exposed our knees and thighs to the freezing cold. The fantastic views of the glorious Kanchenjunga mountain from our dormitory windows were not adequate compensation for the many hardships of boarding school life at that altitude! I was frankly miserable, and two months into the first three-month term (or semester), I wrote desperate letters home (in Bengali, to avoid routine censorship by the typically Anglo-Indian 'misses' who ruled our lives) asking to be returned home to Dhaka. My pleas must have been sufficiently pathetic, because my parents took me home after my first term ended around June.

The remaining year and a half in Dhaka proceeded much the same as the previous ones had. As the only child at home, I was sometimes taken to events where eight-year-olds don't normally figure. For example, I recall a semi-formal lunch given by the avuncular English Governor of East Pakistan, Sir Thomas Ellis, for just our family. While having soup from fine china bowls, my melba toast snapped and flew halfway across the room. Ellis was a perfect host and pretended not to notice. When the soufflé dessert arrived, I was nervous about the fine bird's nest on top. The Governor assured me that it was made from caramelized sugar and was quite delicious. He was right. On another occasion, my mother took me to the famous Dhaka Club to play housie-housie (bingo or tambola) with the ladies. To keep me occupied, I was given a typical slip with numbers. Much to my delight, and to applause from the ladies, I won the first round. Unfortunately, my subsequent encounters with games of chance have been far less successful.

The saddest incident I can recall is when one of the nicer guards at Baitul-Aman fell down from the large jackfruit tree in our garden and broke his neck.

During this period, we made a couple of trips (by road, boat and elephant-back) to Kaoraid, about 80 kms north of Dhaka. This little town (or big village) was the seat of the old Gupta zamindari, a well-established and progressive family of Brahmo Samajis (a nineteenth-century reform movement within Hinduism, founded by Raja Ram Mohan Roy) into which my Thakurda, Pran Krishna Acharya, had married in 1894. He himself came from a modest, sometimes impoverished, rural background in Pabna district, and had made it to Kolkata through sheer intelligence and application, winning scholarships all the way to earning his medical degree in Calcutta Medical College and becoming one of the city's top three doctors, with a large charitable practice. He was also a leading member of the Brahmo Samaj in Kolkata. His ashes are buried in the family graveyard of the Kaoraid Guptas, which includes some other well-known figures, like Sir K.G. Gupta and the poet–lyricist Atul Prasad Sen.

My childhood memory of the place is blurry, of a large semi-abandoned mansion with a small Brahmo mandir, with an adjacent graveyard filled with tombstones. When I visited the place fifty years later, on a private trip, the mansion was not to be seen, but the mandir and graveyard remained, tended to by the sole remaining family of Hindu-Brahmos in a fairly prosperous village of about 4000 Muslim residents. The school I visited, originally founded by the Guptas, was large, well-kept and full of bright-eyed students. The elderly government principal spoke warmly of the educational initiatives and charities of the Guptas in the long-gone decades … But perhaps he knew I had a family connection.

During the Dhaka years, we made frequent trips to Kolkata, partly for Baba's work and partly to meet with relatives. On one of those occasions, the parental story goes, a younger cousin of Baba's, who worked in the creative side of a well-known advertising firm, approached my parents for the 'loan' of their younger son (that was me) for a few months to play a key role in a feature movie he was making — his first such venture. He thought I would suit the part well. My parents, concerned about disrupting of my trajectory in school, declined politely. The film was *Pather Panchali*, the role was of Apu and the cousin was Satyajit Ray! Probably just as well, as I may have scuttled Ray's stellar career as a movie director, without establishing mine as a screen actor. The boy who played the role of Apu did a fantastic job.

In retrospect, I can only marvel at how sheltered my life was during those Dhaka years. I had no inkling or understanding of the powerful political currents that were swirling around in the province and its capital. After all, those were the years of surging Bengali language nationalism and the rise of the Awami League, led by Abdul Bhashani, culminating in the League's sweeping defeat of the Pakistan Muslim League in the 1954 provincial elections. Later, I learnt that my father, with his finger on the East Bengali pulse, had predicted the victory against the convention wisdom prevailing in the Ministry of External Affairs (MEA) in Delhi and our High Commission in Karachi. This brought him to the attention of Pandit Jawaharlal Nehru, who persuaded him to make the switch from the domestic civil service cadre to the IFS.

Our stint in Dhaka ended towards the end of 1954, and we were promptly dispatched to Cambodia, a country which had just been reborn following the 1954 Geneva Accords signed after the historic defeat of French colonial forces by the Viet Minh led by the famed General Vo Nguyen Giap at Dien Bien Phu in Vietnam in May that year. Baba was tasked with opening the Indian diplomatic mission there, initially as a Legation headed by a minister, rather than by a full ambassador. Dada continued into his final, Senior Cambridge year at St. Paul's, and I accompanied him into the fourth and final year of junior school. This time, I was two years older and was determined to see the full year through.

It went off reasonably well. I did well scholastically and, though I did not make any life-long friends there, I was not miserable. My class teacher liked me and, for some reason best known to her, nick-named me 'baby mongoose'. On Sundays, Dada would pick me up from the junior school and we would take the shortcuts downhill to Darjeeling town, usually to spend the day with some distant cousins, the Boses, including their sixteen-year-old son, Arup. The Boses were nice to us, treating us to tasty home food, a real pleasure after the institutional fare served up at school. Darjeeling was a very pleasant, uncrowded place to wander around in those years, with magnificent views at every corner. When the school chapel bell began to toll, we would scramble up the shortcuts on the path to Jalapahar and arrive in time for the 6 p.m. evensong service, as required.

During the brief inter-semester breaks, Dada and I counted on the generous hospitality of Mama and Mami, who would time their visits to Takdah, some 30 kms away. There, we had access to Dadu's holiday home, comprising five small cottages, each named after his wife and progeny. We would typically stay with Mama and Mami in one of them. The cottages were really in the wild, with just a couple of provision stores and a few other country homes nearby. We loved the little treks up and down the pine-covered hillsides, returning tired and happy at sunset to burn off the leeches which inevitably clung to our legs. In the evenings, we would play cards, sing songs or tell stories in the light of petromax lanterns (there was no electricity in Takdah in those years). Some years later, the Indian Army requisitioned these cottages for their purposes.

The school year ended in December and I returned to Kolkata. In a few days, I boarded a flight with my parents to Phnom Penh with a brief stopover in Bangkok. My recollection of Bangkok in early 1956 was of a poor, populous Asian city—with roughly the same standard of living as Kolkata, if not lower. For some reason, Dada joined us a few days later.

My few weeks in Phnom Penh were quite action-packed with new sights and events to take in. I recall the first India Fair being held then. It was opened by the young Crown Prince Norodom Sihanouk. At that function, I was given the honour of presenting him with a welcoming ivory chess set on behalf of the India Fair. There is a photo of me in a pair of trousers and a white shirt, with my tie a little askew, making the presentation to the immaculately attired, suave young prince bending down graciously to accept it, with my parents looking elegant in *bandhgala* and sari looking on smiling. Coterminous with the India Fair was the dispatch by our government of a prototype of the first trainer aircraft built by Hindustan Aeronautics Ltd, the HT-2. At a special air show, the plane went through its aerobatics in the presence of Cambodian dignitaries. I was thrilled, but I don't know if the Cambodian government ordered any.

Then there was the enthralling two-day trip to Angkor with Dada and my parents. Delhi had already given me a taste for old and magnificent ruins. But Angkor exceeded all expectations. My memories of the visit are reasonably good, mainly because I had been gifted a Brownie box camera for my tenth birthday. So I took a few snapshots of Angkor with it. When you look through a camera lens you see things differently, especially if you can only take a few shots because of the costs of film and printing. The short trip was special for another reason. Baba had done his homework well, and educated the rest of us on how the Angkor ruins had been found by a French botanist chasing rare butterflies, and about the strong links of the Khmer culture with contemporary Indian civilizations of our eastern–southern coast. He told us how the name Mekong came from Ma Ganga, Angkor Thom from Nagar Dham and so on. All this came back to me when my wife, Gayatri, and I made a marvellous five-day excursion from Delhi to Siem Reap, the town near Angkor, in 2003.

Our Cambodian interlude ended in early 1956 when Baba was transferred to Delhi as a Joint Secretary (JS) in the MEA. In those days, there were only five or six such positions, as compared with more than thirty now. So, JS's had considerable personal contact with the external affairs minister, at that time Pandit Nehru, as well as a great deal of responsibility. After a few weeks in some temporary accommodation, we were allotted a bungalow on Sunehri Bagh Road, 1A. Actually, it was half a bungalow, with the other half fronting on York Road (now Motilal Nehru Road). For the initial eighteen months, the occupants of this other half were Rabi Dutt and family. Rabi kaka, as Dada and I called him, had been Baba's classmate in Hare School and Presidency College in Kolkata, and his batchmate in the ICS. It was good to have old friends as neighbours, especially for me, as I formed a close and enduring friendship with their only child, Parvati (aka, Pabi), who was two years older than me. We both loved Enid Blyton books, of which Pabi had a large collection, especially the ones for young girls (the Malory Towers series, etc.!). Incidentally, after I got married to Gayatri, I learned that her mother had been a classmate of Pabi's mother, Lily Dutt, in Gokhale School in Kolkata! About eighteen months into our stay at the bungalow, the Dutts moved to their own new house on Kautilya Marg and we took over the front part of the bungalow.

Dada was admitted to St. Stephen's College, while I was sent to St. Columba's school, near Gole Market, joining standard four. While Dada took the university special bus each day, I went by a horse-drawn tonga in the morning for a 7.30 a.m. start (8.30 in winter), and was picked up by Ma in our brand-new Fiat Millicento (1100) after school. After that we would swing by South Block to pick up Baba for his lunch break and drive home. Often, we would see Pandit Nehru walk to his car to be taken home for lunch. There was no security to speak of then. Once, when we (including Dada) were waiting in the parking area for Baba, Nehru's sister Vijaya Lakshmi Pandit walked up to our car and said, 'Ah! You children have come up to pick up your father?' My mother, I think, was so flattered to be mistaken as our sibling that she did not disabuse Mrs Pandit of her error.

My recollection of those three years in Delhi was of a happy time. Baba was fulfilled at office, working with a relatively small group of talented officers to help shape and implement Nehru's foreign policy. Ma made good friends with some wives of peer officers, and they would often drive to Connaught Place for window shopping (or a little more!) and cold coffee at Alps or Gaylord's. Her closest friend was Arati Lahiri (Arati Mashi to us), who was an earthy and fun-loving scion of the Mymensingh rajas. Her husband, Shishir, was director general of India's lighthouse system and was sometimes referred to as 'Lighthouse Lahiri'! Their somewhat Bohemian artist daughter, Archana (aka Tutu), was a friend of Dada's. In the evenings, couples would drop by or my parents would go to their homes for a beer or nimbu pani, some pakoras or *moori* and lots of 'adda'.

In the autumn and spring evenings, they would play badminton on our lawns, with us youngsters also joining in sometimes. And on winter weekends, of course, there were the fun-filled picnics with two or three other families in places like, Qutb Minar, Tughlakabad and Hauz Khas. After partaking of parathas, puris, dum aloo and some mithai, the parents would doze off and chat on the *satranchis*, while we youngsters would run around, exploring the various ruins. Tughlakabad Fort was a special favourite of mine. Gymkhana Club was also a frequent destination, with full use being made of the library by all of us. Then there was swimming on summer weekends (and sometimes, on weekdays) as well as group lunches on the lawns on Sundays. And occasionally, there would an adventure film at Plaza or Rivoli.

With government salaries being modest, there was not much money around for us. For example, I remember the sense of occasion we felt when our first small Philips radio was bought (for Rs 175) and carefully housed in a cloth cover. Or when I was given my first full-sized bicycle on my twelfth birthday, on which I rode around much of New Delhi. But I have no recollection of feeling hard up or of the lack of money blighting family conversations over meals. Perhaps we were protected by our parents. More likely, all our basic needs were taken care of, and we lived full and satisfying lives among family and friends.

Much more than before, these Delhi years were enriched by good friends—either at school or through family connections. My school friends included Ravi Bhoothalingam (later president of Oberoi Hotels in the 1990s), Ajit Shetty (later Baron Shetty of Belgium) and Sunil Sud (later a senior Indian Administrative Services officer). Aside from Pabi, friends made through parental connections included Sumantra Nag, Sujit Dutt, Inderjit Chatterji and his younger sister, Devika (aka, Twinky), who later married my brother-in-law, Chandrashekhar (aka Shekhar) Dasgupta (later the Indian Ambassador to China and the European Union, and recipient of the Padma Bhushan for his services). The practice of 'day spending' on holidays was quite common in our circles, and I have happy memories of such extended exchange visits to the homes of Ravi, Sumantra and Inderjit. In the late afternoons, I would often cycle down to what is today called Rabindra Nagar to play games with some of these friends. A more stately destination was 5, Race Course Road, the house allocated to Foreign Secretary Subimal Dutt, to play cricket with his son, Sujit. Tragically, at the age of sixteen, Sujit died from a stomach infection contracted in Moscow, where his father was then our Ambassador.

Now, more than sixty years later, I remain good friends with both Ravi and Pabi.

As a day school, St. Columba's was pretty good, with able teachers among both the founding Irish Brothers clan and the lay appointees. Classes tended to be big, with each 'section' having up to fifty students. In our section, four of us tended to vie for first place each year: Ravi, Sunil, a boy called Suresh Rao and myself. The five-hour school day allowed for only one fifteen-minute break, during which we gobbled up whatever was in our lunch box, if we could manage to protect the stuff from the diving kites which perched on the roofs of the school buildings. Sometimes we returned in the late afternoon for extra-curricular sports. The teachers I remember include: Brother Rigney, Mr Mascarenhas and Mr Pillai (who went on to join one of our intelligence services). Then, of course, there was our Hindi teacher, nicknamed Bulldog (I can't recall his actual name), who was quite fierce and readily wielded the flexible rubber truncheon he carried, especially on some of us non-Hindi speakers.

Interestingly, neither at school nor at play, do I have any recollection of being conscious of the caste of my peers. Brought up as I had been in a fairly committed Brahmo Samaji household, I had no knowledge of caste, other than what I read in our school textbooks. Nor did I know that family names correlated with caste. It simply wasn't an issue of identity in the way linguistic differences clearly were (Punjabi versus Tamilian versus Bengali, etc).

During these three years in Delhi, my relationship with Dada was warm but not especially close. On most days we inhabited different worlds—he in his college, I in my school. We came together in the evenings as part of a family unit, for example, over dinner, or to play badminton together or to listen to Baba reading out from some book by Tagore or some other Bengali author. Looking back, the last activity was perhaps part of Baba's conscious effort to keep us connected to our Bengali roots. Dada and I were probably closest on family trips, either on visits to relatives in Kolkata, or on the several memorable road trips we undertook in our little Fiat to Agra, Nainital/Ranikhet, Gwalior/Khajuraho and Kashmir. In Khajuraho, I recall sneaking in a snapshot of one of 'those' erotic friezes! Many years later, I have revisited all these places with my own family, stirring up some of the memories of earlier visits.

These were also years in which one became more conscious of the wider world, including that outside India. I have clear memories of the Suez Crisis in 1956 and feeling partisan sympathy towards Nasser as the old colonial powers of Britain and France dropped bombs on Egypt. Non-alignment and Panchsheel were real to us, even if we understood these matters only dimly. Basic patriotism was taken for granted. Rightly or wrongly, we felt that India was progressing at home and abroad.

Sometime in 1957, Baba took over the East Asia division (including China), and it was on his watch that cartographic investigations revealed the road China had built across the Aksai Chin to connect Sinkiang and Tibet. Other intrusions followed, and so did the difficult Barahoti conference, where Baba was a key member of our official delegation and he came back fuming about the intransigence of the Chinese. I recall his speaking about the need to forget 'Hindi–Chini bhai–bhai' and recognize the harsh ground realities, which called for a much stronger defence capability on our northern border. Krishna Menon was then the Defence Minister and was not yet persuaded to this view. According to a fellow Joint Secretary in Defence, Menon once said, 'Tell Acharya I will make him a general, but he must not make notings on defence ministry files!'

Then there was Abdul (Rahman), who had served as Man Friday to Baba since 1937. He hailed from Rangpur in East Bengal, but rarely returned there for visits to avoid the eternal land disputes among his quarrelling sons. With one or two gaps, he served with us till the late 1960s. Not to be forgotten was our dachshund, Badshah, who joined our household as a puppy and was a much-loved member. When we moved to Europe in 1959, he was billeted with the Lahiris, but did not live long after an injudicious attack on a neighbour's Alsatian four times his size.

Our trip to Kashmir in the summer of 1958 brought the first hint of romance to my life. In Gulmarg and Pahalgam, we teamed up with the famously beautiful Delia Chaudhuri (born Palit) and her younger daughter, Joya (with some of her mother's looks), who was also twelve. They used to live in 7, York Road. Though we had no real social exchanges, I sometimes saw her walking across our gate as she returned home from her school bus drop. In the pleasant environs of Kashmir, I began to develop some confused romantic interest in her, which led nowhere then. The only hint I had of some possible reciprocation was a phone call one afternoon, soon after our return from Kashmir, from a close friend of hers (later identified as Dipika Jha, aka Pikoo, whom I only met face to face in 1982) pretending to be Joya and identifying herself as my 'girlfriend'. That conversation, which Pikoo now does not recollect, ended in peals of girlish laughter at their end, and complete confusion and embarrassment on mine.

Those were years during which I read widely and eclectically, with my book list ranging from Biggles and Zane Grey to Winston Churchill's six-volume history of the Second World War and Sigmund Freud's *Interpretation of Dreams* (the last mainly for the sexy bits!). Ravi was also a bit of a book worm, and sometimes, we could be found perched on the branches of a large frangipani tree in our garden, buried in our respective novels. It was during this period that I was presented with an air gun and became quite a good shot, targeting Baba's empty cigarette tins and, on one occasion, a street lamp on York Road. On a couple of occasions, I accompanied Baba and a few of his friends for early morning 'shikars' to the shallow marshes at Okhla, where they 'bagged' small game like ducks and pigeons. That's when Baba taught me to fire his shotgun, and I managed to nail a couple of pigeons and doves 'for the table'.

Not only was our family happy in those Delhi years between 1956–59, it was also the last time that all four of us actually lived together. It would never happen again. In mid-1959, I entered a boarding school in London, while Dada went to an engineering college of London University. We would join our parents for our academic holidays at their successive diplomatic postings in Prague, Rabat (in Morocco), Ottawa, Rio de Janeiro and Islamabad. But it just wasn't the same as living together all year round. Basically, for both Dada and me, living most of the year away from our family began at a relatively young age of thirteen. We both adjusted to the challenge reasonably well, but perhaps we also lost the nourishment and protection of parental love and security a bit too early in our lives.

2

School in London and Home in Prague

IN THE SPRING OF 1959, Baba was posted as India's ambassador to Czechoslovakia and Romania, concurrently, with Prague being the headquarters of the mission. Czech was not a lingua franca. The nearest English-speaking nation, where Dada's and my education could continue best, was England. So that's where we ended up, with our High Commission in London facilitating Dada's admission in the West Ham College of Technology and mine in Highgate School, both in London, the former in the east and the latter in the north of the city.

Thus began my first encounter with and my long sojourn in the West. When we sailed from Bombay one May morning, little did I know that it would be another twenty-three years before I would return to live in India. At that time, I recall having very mixed feelings about England: It was the source of a lot of books (and some comics) I had read, and the main language of communication with peers at school and outside; but there were also some anti-colonial and anti-racist sentiments I had imbibed from my Bengali reading, family tales, and from our newspapers and magazines, where it was a prevalent theme. This duality persisted for many years, waxing and waning with the complex currents in ambient world affairs and my own personal experiences of living in England and, later, in the United States.

At a simpler level, I felt a great sense of adventure in going abroad, mixed with considerable apprehension. Sometime in May, we boarded the *SS Iberia* of the P&O line for the fifteen-day journey across the Indian Ocean, the Red Sea, the Mediterranean and a part of the Atlantic, to the Tilbury Docks on the Thames, 25 miles from London. The journey itself was full of adventure and novelty as the passenger liner sailed west. I remember the enormous repasts served at meal times, the variety of entertainment available, the pitch and roll of the seas, some lovely sunsets, the flying fish in the Red Sea, the sand dunes and camels less than 50 metres away as our ship threaded through the recently reopened Suez Canal, and, of course, the ports we called at, including Aden, Naples and Gibraltar. We were allowed to disembark for a few hours at these ports. We did so in Naples, for a quick visit to Pompeii, in the shadow of the mighty Vesuvius volcano. The great Rock of Gibraltar was an impressive sight, which I remember, perhaps because the memory was reinforced by a separate visit in 1963.

Then there was the fancy dress ball aboard the ship one evening. Lacking anything better, Ma dressed me in one of her saris, with a bit of lipstick and a bindi, and the sari pulled over my head to hide my short hair. At the ball, a young Englishman came across to ask me to dance and, sportingly, did not withdraw his request when informed of my sex. I can't recall whether we actually pirouetted across the floor!

The weather cooled appreciably as we entered the Atlantic and swung north towards England, skirting the coasts of Spain and France. When we arrived in Tilbury, there was the predictable grey sky and cold drizzle. We were met by staff from the London High Commission, who escorted us to a hotel. After a few days in London, we caught a flight to our destination, Prague. Our new home, the Ambassador's residence, was at No. 7, Šárecká, a few kilometres from the city centre, but within walking distance of a tram stop.

The house stood three–storeys high (complete with a basement), framed by poplar trees, at the end of a narrow, cobbled uphill drive from the entrance gate. It was an old house which had belonged to a nobleman before it was requisitioned in 1948 by the new Soviet-backed Communist government after the war. It was a fate common to many properties that had belonged to aristocrats and the gentry before the Second World War (WWII). The ground floor had the formal entertainment rooms, the first floor had three main bedrooms and a study, and the second floor, which was really an enlarged attic, was where we had a spacious table tennis room. In the front of the house was a large stone goldfish pond, which Dada and I turned into a small swimming/wading pool during a couple of summers. The upward sloping back garden sported the statue of a somewhat scantily clad woman.

Since Dada and I were due to report to our respective educational institutions in London in early September, we had three full months to settle down and explore Prague and its environs. Architecturally, Prague is undoubtedly one of the most beautiful European capitals, with the river Vltava coursing picturesquely through the city under lovely old bridges. Furthermore, unlike nearly all other European capitals, it was neither bombed nor shelled during the Second World War, thanks to the famous Munich Agreement of 1938 (promising 'Peace in our time' that Britain's Neville Chamberlain had boasted about so emptily), which handed over a large part of Czechoslovakia to Hitler on a platter without a single shot being fired.The one blot on the horizon was a massive Stalin statue on a hill, towering over one stretch of the river.Years later, it was taken down.

If the city was stunningly beautiful, it was startlingly lifeless in those years, 1959–62. The Communist regime since 1948 ensured it remained this way, and certainly during our three years there during the somewhat Stalinist rule of President Antonín Novotný. There was no café life, something so characteristic of other European cities. And the shops were devoid of consumer goods, even some simple groceries. Indeed, we were obliged to drive each month to either Vienna in Austria or to Nuremburg in West Germany (each about 300 kms away) to do some of our basic consumer goods shopping! In the process, of course, we got to know those cities quite well too.

After presenting his credentials to the President in Prague, Baba was obliged to do the same in Romania, to which he was accredited as well. So, we undertook a 1400 km–long, but enjoyable, car trip in our official Buick to Bucharest, with stops on the way in Bratislava and Budapest, the capital of Hungary.Among some of my notable memories were the profusion of bullet holes pockmarking so many buildings in Budapest, which had seen fierce intra-city fighting during the Hungarian uprising of 1956 that was ruthlessly put down by Soviet forces.Another memory was of the surprising relative backwardness of the Romanian countryside, with many rural folk walking barefoot by the roadside. Bucharest in those days was a poorer and less pretty version of Prague, and did not tempt one for repeat visits.

On this 2700 km round-trip, we stopped for meals and refreshments at many small towns in Czechoslovakia, Romania and Hungary. We would usually attract a fair bit of friendly attention from local citizenry for two reasons: Our shiny American

Buick and sari-draped Ma. Both big Buicks and saris were rare in those parts at that time. Some of the local folk, inferring that we were Indians (*Indichke*), would burst into some rendering of '*Awara hoon*'! Raj Kapoor and his movies were a big hit in central Europe then. Ma's fluency in French and German helped us a lot during this and other European trips. Actually, in these central European countries, German was often a second language, but rarely acknowledged as such because of the memories of the brutal Third Reich.

Back in Prague, we utilized the summer weather to make frequent weekend excursions to some beautiful nearby castles, like Karlštejn and Kokořín. Forty-four year later, in 2000, when Prague hosted the autumn Annual Meetings of the IMF and World Bank, I successfully tempted our then executive director at the IMF, Vijay Kelkar, to slip away with me from the meetings for a few hours to revisit Karlštejn.

Prague itself, especially the Old Town, was a wonderful city to explore by tram and foot, especially the top sights like Prague Castle, St. Vitus Cathedral, the old Týn Church in the Old Square, the beautiful fourteenth-century Karlův Most (Charles Bridge) with its eye-catching statues, the Waldstein gardens, the spacious central Václavské Náměstí (Wenceslas Square), and so on. In those tourist-free years, the Czechs were friendly and curious about foreigners, since strict entry and exit controls made the species rare. I also remember the innovative 'Laterna Magika' productions, an early form of multimedia, which mixed film and real actors, along with clever lighting and music. I am told it still functions to date.

The comforts and privileges of an ambassadorial home ended for Dada and me in early September, when we boarded a train from Nuremberg to Ostend, from where we crossed the English Channel by ferry and then took a train to London. Dada arranged some 'digs' near his college, while I became a boarder at Highgate School, billeted in School House, the largest of the four 'Houses' for about 200 boarders. Highgate also took around 400 dayboys (yes, all boys then), making a total student body of about 600. Nearly all the students were British and white. There was not a single black student and only three brown ones: Two older Pakistanis and me, all three boarders in School House.

The challenge for us three was to get accepted by the monochromatic school body, especially the fifty or so in School House. Ali came from a conservative Muslim background, and his approach was to be completely reclusive. Even I don't recall any significant interaction with him. Zafar Hilaly, who had already been there for two years, was also a diplomat's son; his father, Agha Hilaly, was Pakistan's Ambassador in Moscow and was known to Baba as an ICS colleague from his pre-Partition years. Zafar was already 'assimilated' by the time I arrived to join the fourth form (the one before we took our GCE 'O' levels, equivalent to Senior Cambridge in India then), helped no doubt by his considerable skills in boxing and 'fives'—a game somewhat like squash, except one uses gloved hands instead of a racquet.

I don't remember having a considered strategy, but I may have instinctively played to my scholastic strengths. It helped to come first in seven out of eight subjects in my first term (in the eighth, divinity, I came second) in my section of thirty-five to forty boys, since Highgate was quite results-oriented. In time, I also came to represent my House in fives and became a moderately proficient medium-pace bowler, playing inter-school matches in our third Eleven. Perhaps, above all, it helped that my command of the English language was strong. What changed within months, as part of an unconscious and instinctive assimilation process, was my accent, which went from 'Delhi English medium' to 'pukka Angrez' swiftly.

All this did not mean I was wholly protected from overt instances of racism from my fellow students. I remember being called 'blackie' on at least two occasions, once by an unknown student on the football field and once by an aggrieved 'friend' towards the end of a friendship. On the whole though, my personal experience of racism in school was insignificant. Where I came across far more instances of racism were in my forays outside the school precincts, among the general public. While I was mostly protected by my accent, clothes and English public schoolboy demeanour, I noticed, all too frequently, how less-equipped brown and black people were served last (and sometimes gruffly) in shops, buses and railway ticket offices. The behaviour of immigration officers at Heathrow airport towards incoming semi-literate Punjabi immigrants from India was often gratuitously rude and obstructive. All this bothered me and made me uncomfortably conscious of the colour of my skin. This sensitivity and discomfort remained with me throughout my eight years in England, whenever I strayed outside the cloistered environs of school and, later, Oxford University.

Looking back, it is easy to understand, though not condone, the latent sense of superiority and racism among large sections of British whites in those years. They were only a few years past their two centuries of colonial domination, during which their small white nation had ruled nearly half the (largely brown and black) world. The exhaustion from the Second World War had greatly diminished the country's relative role on the world stage, though it took decades for the associated psychological consequences to be absorbed across the population. It also must be said that a large proportion of the British, perhaps a majority, were not racist even in those years. Furthermore, as the years passed, Britain progressed, sometimes unsteadily, towards the ideal of a genuine multiracial society.

Life at Highgate was full: Early waking, a wash daily, but bathing only twice a week (when shirt, socks and underwear changes were put on the bed by our matron); breakfast sitting on benches at rows of tables in the main dining hall of the school; putting on caps and walking 400 yards along and up Hampstead Lane to the main school buildings at the top of Highgate Hill for classes from 9.15 a.m. to 12.45 p.m., with a fifteen-minute break in the middle; back down the hill to the dining hall for lunch at 1 p.m. and back up to the main school for two more hours of classes between 2 p.m. and 4 p.m. (except on Wednesday and Saturday afternoons, which were devoted to sports); back to School House for some relaxation in the library or to the common room or for special activities, followed by supper around 6 p.m. in the dining hall; then prep (homework) time between 7 p.m. to 8.30 p.m., followed by assembly for announcements and a few minutes of prayer/pep talk led by a monitor, with the housemaster presiding; finally, a bottle of milk, brushing of teeth, etc., and into our respective dormitory beds for 'lights out' by 9 p.m. (10 p.m. for sixth form students, that is, those doing the two years between the 'O' levels and 'A' levels).

In winter, the short days ended early, with darkness by 4.30 p.m., while in the months of May, June and September, the days were long, with twilight lingering till 10 p.m.

The quality of teaching in Highgate was almost uniformly excellent. The teachers were experienced and knowledgeable, and knew how to engage productively with adolescent boys. I owe a big debt to George Sellick, also the housemaster of School House, for biology, C. Topham, my later housemaster in Waiting House, for physics, and Crichton, for the engaging way he taught chemistry. They nurtured my love of science. 'Practicals' in our labs were an important part of our science instruction, perhaps reflecting the long British tradition of empirical discoveries in the physical sciences. Alan Palmer was a brilliant teacher of history and an author of several books, including his popular *Penguin Dictionary of Modern History*, which is still available on Amazon! He encouraged class presentations by his students, and was favourably impressed by mine on the Jallianwala Bagh massacre. It was quite normal for Highgate to send ten or twelve graduating students to Oxford and Cambridge each year—a pretty good record for a single school.

Come rain or shine, we played sports every Wednesday and Saturday: Cricket and tennis in the summer and early autumn; football, fives and athletics in winter and spring. I enjoyed cricket and fives, but was a reluctant participant in football in the cold, wet mud, or in the exhausting long-distance runs on Hampstead Heath in the drizzling rain. Perhaps it built character! There was also swimming in the summer term in temperatures not welcomed by shivering subcontinental lads. Luckily, that one was optional!

Sunday was our day off to lounge around or visit family and friends in town. In my first couple of years, I would take the 'tube' (underground/metro) to a station near Dada's digs in the East End and spend a few hours with him. Usually, we would have a bite somewhere and then go to Leicester Square in the West End to see some cartoon movies, which were the only ones open under the 'Sunday closing' regulations then prevailing. Then a dash back on the tube to Highgate to return for evening chapel service. After a few months, I managed to win another hour of freedom by being excused chapel on religious grounds. Looking back, I am deeply grateful to Dada for giving up so many Sundays to provide brotherly affection and companionship to me. Few twenty-year-olds would have done this for a kid brother. For me, this regular caring link with family was extremely important during my first couple of years in Highgate.

The other invaluable family links were, of course, the twice-a-year visits to home in Prague over the longer inter-term breaks, three–four weeks over Christmas/New Year and two months

(July–August) in summer. That's when our family got back together to renew bonds and, especially in the summer, go touring Europe in Baba's freshly acquired duty-free Mercedes 190. It's the one in which he taught me to drive at the age of fifteen. Our first European winter was in 1959–60. Prague, typically, had serious central European winters, with lots of snow and ice, which totally transformed the urban landscape in strange and beautiful ways. We went out wearing fur caps and earmuffs and sweaters and jackets. Luckily, the house had good, old-fashioned central heating that kept us warm. That first winter we drove to Černá Hora (Black Mountain), where I had my first, and only, experience skiing. It consisted mostly of sliding a few feet on skis and then toppling over … And then doing it again and again!

In the summer holidays of 1960, the four of us made a marvellous car trip north through both the Germanys (East and West) up to Denmark, crossing at Malmö into Sweden, due north towards Norway, across to Stockholm and then back down through West Germany to Prague. It was a great adventure for us, with Baba and Dada sharing the driving. Our first stop was the still shattered, and once beautiful, city of Dresden in East Germany, where sustained 'terror bombing' by British and American heavy bombers over two days in February 1945 had triggered a deadly 'firestorm' (when extreme heat ignites the oxygen in the air), which incinerated much of the city and killed more than 70,000 civilians. There was no significant military target in Dresden. Everyone remembers Hiroshima and Nagasaki, but what happened in Dresden is a comparable atrocity.

We drove on to fascinating Berlin, deep in East Germany, but divided into West and East Berlin, because at the end of the European war in June 1945 the Red Army and the Anglo-American armies raced to carve up the capital city of the Third Reich. We stayed a couple of days in prosperous, glittering West Berlin, but made a day trip to the poorer Eastern sector, with its still-broken buildings, unrepaired to remind the population of the horrors of war, not to mention the other reason—of an economy faltering in the coils of the Soviet-controlled system. Later, when I read the classic spy novels by John Le Carré and Len Deighton, their texts evoked my own childhood memories of this remarkable city.

As before, Ma's wonderful command of German was an enormous help on our trip. She herself had visited Germany in the 1930s, when Dadu had brought her and a younger sister on a trip from Patna. Her linguistic skills became particularly valuable when, with Dada driving, we suffered a collision with a late-braking truck in Hamburg. Luckily, our sturdily built Mercedes 190 remained roadworthy after some quick repairs, even if we were much shaken. The police very kindly gave us a quick tour of Hamburg while our car was being repaired. In those days CD (diplomatic) license plates carried some value! Then on to Copenhagen, followed by the crossing to the Scandinavian peninsula at Malmo. In Oslo, we marvelled at the famed Kon-Tiki balsa wood raft in a museum. It was with this raft that the intrepid explorer Thor Heyerdahl and his crew had proved in 1947 that South American inhabitants could have journeyed to the Polynesian islands in the south Pacific many centuries ago. Balsa had very special meaning for Dada because of the many balsa wood model planes he had built painstakingly in his little room in 3 York Road.

From Oslo, we wended our way further north to the picturesque little coastal town of Kragerø, where Baba's old ex-girlfriend from his London student years now lived with her family. They were extraordinarily welcoming and hospitable. It was the first time that I partook of a smorgasbord buffet. And it was also the first time that I saw jellyfish in the clear sea inlets. From Kragerø we drove due east to visit beautiful Stockholm, spending a couple of nights in the famous Grand Hotel. Our Ambassador, Madanjit Singh (poet, painter and photographer), was our knowledgeable guide. Thence the long journey home through Denmark and West Germany.

Back in Highgate, as the years passed, I steadily acquired familiarity, seniority and confidence in my habitat. I did well in my eight 1961 GCE 'O' level subjects, and opted to specialize in physics, chemistry and mathematics for my 'A' levels in sixth form. Soon, I became a house monitor, entrusted, along with some peers, with some basic 'governance' of younger boys in School House. My group of friends also changed from the typical sporty, public school types to a more intellectual, socially and politically aware set. We read the morning newspapers in the common room, talked about Biafra, the Sharpeville massacre in South Africa and nuclear disarmament. The more literary among us read lots of books, and three of us (Steve Martin, Michael Minton and I) formed a pretentiously titled 'Eliot Society' for discussing books.

And, of course, we discussed sex. The great sexual revolution of the 1960s in the West was in its early stages, but had not left Highgate wholly behind. Sex was not common, but by no means was it absent. There was probably also a lot more boasting than actual practice. My own first experience of kissing a girl had occurred at age fifteen, on a short holiday at a school friend's home in Bradford, Yorkshire. On a couple of evenings, my host, Fred Jowett, invited a few local friends (mostly girls) over for a 'children's supper' (with parents in another part of the large mill-owner's house) and, at an appropriate time, put off the lights to allow a few minutes of free-for-all of kissing and petting. I recall having been 'paired' with an Angela, with whom I dutifully corresponded with for a few weeks afterwards. English public schools were supposed to be notorious for rampant homosexuality. But I didn't see much of it. I knew that one of my friends, David X, was a 'queer' (to use the favoured term of that time), but that didn't bother me and he never propositioned me.

One member of our literary group was a shy and awkward boy called Nicholas Comfort. His father was a gerontologist, psychiatrist and anarchist, who sometimes visited his son, and once gave a little talk to our Eliot Society. I recall him as being a man of wide learning, who, amongst other things, had read Tagore (in translation) and knew about his central role in the evolution of modern Bengali. A decade later, Alex Comfort achieved enduring global fame with his book *The Joy of Sex* and its subsequent editions!

I think it was in the context of the short-lived Eliot society that I got to know Michael Minton (from Grindle House), who, in a few months, became my best friend in Highgate and is, to this day, perhaps my best friend in the world. We still take annual vacations together (pre-Covid-19) in some part of the world, and I stay with his family in Oxford for a few days every year. This wonderful, enduring, sixty-year friendship has been greatly reinforced by the friendship between his wife, Liz, and Gayatri.

As I grew older, my Sunday visits with Dada became less frequent, which must have relieved him, as it allowed him to spend more time with his own friends, including girls. My Sundays were increasingly spent with Mike and his family in their lovely flat near Hampstead Heath, where his parents, Henry and Gwen, were wonderfully warm and hospitable to me. I also got to know his younger brother, Jonathan, and elder sister, Jill. Mike, I and some others would sometimes go into London together to participate in demonstrations campaigning against nuclear weapons at Trafalgar Square and wear their iconic buttons. Another regular destination for my Sundays became the home of cousin/niece Nandita in south London. She was studying in Oxford and her parents had shifted to England to provide her with a home base (Oxford terms only accumulate to twenty-four weeks per year!).

During our free time on weekdays, our group of school friends began to hang around the home of Dawn Lowe-Watson and her family in Highgate village, partly to help with her Oxfam distribution centre for old clothes, partly to smoke freely (though I didn't), and partly to be taken seriously as young adults by a cosmopolitan lady in her mid-thirties. I suspect the smoking venue was a significant reason, the alternative having been the nearby, and famous, Highgate cemetery, which held the remains of many historical figures, including Karl Marx, Michael Faraday and George Eliot. There may also have been some undercurrents of mutual lust. I remember Dawn once telling me that I was the only one of our group of sixteen- and seventeen-year-old schoolboys who had failed to make a pass at her! In retrospect, I wonder if that was a reproach.

Back home in Prague, our social life became more active, both with Prague residents and with friends and official delegations visiting from India. I remember an enjoyable visit by the Lahiris and a separate one from their daughter, Tutu, who was now studying art at the Slade School of Fine Art in London. Among official cultural visits, I recall one by Ravi Shankar and remember him giving a sitar soirée for select guests in our drawing room. Sometimes Baba would also organize showings of special Indian films at our home. One such was the superb one-hour documentary on the life of Rabindranath Tagore made by Satyajit Ray around 1960.

Among the residents, we had a couple of interesting officers in the mission. One was A.K. Damodaran (Damu), who worked hard to pass his exam in Russian, his chosen language for an IFS career. Another was Manohar Lal Sondhi, a very intelligent and pleasant young officer, who became a favourite with our family (including me), often accompanying us on family picnics. Later, he quit the foreign service and join the Jana Sangh, becoming quite a charismatic figure and member of Parliament for New Delhi during the 1960s. He went on to become a respected professor of international relations in Jawaharlal Nehru University (JNU).

There was, of course, the usual round of obligatory diplomatic entertainment. More emotionally satisfying for my parents were their good relations with a few Ambassadors and their spouses from relatively non-aligned countries like Indonesia, Egypt and Yugoslavia. Yugoslavian Ambassador Petrich and his charming wife, Sophie, became quite close friends of my parents. This yielded substantial collateral benefits for me in the form of their rather lovely fourteen-year-old daughter, Jagoda. She and I hit it off well and developed something of a romantic, though chaste, friendship. I recall going with her to a couple of parties among diplomatic kids, including one where I formally guided her to the dining table on my arm. Ma liked her a lot and once dressed her up in a sari; the photo lingers in our family album. In due course, Ambassador Petrich got transferred, but Jagoda and I kept in touch through sporadic letters. A decade later, on a World Bank economic mission to Belgrade, Gayatri and I had dinner with her and her husband. I have sometimes wondered about what happened to the Petrich family in the Balkan turmoils of the 1990s.

With time, Dada came home less and I had more time alone with my parents. I remember taking long evening walks with Baba, the three of us playing cards some evenings and spending time talking to Ma when Baba was in office. She was then learning Russian, adding to her considerable repertoire of European languages. The common Slavic root meant that she now understood more Czech than anyone else in the family. She also started writing some verse in English, including a beautiful poem on the river Vltava, which I can't now find. Ma also introduced me to Western classical music, which we used to listen to on our radiogram. With her children away for most of the year, the linguistic and other barriers to making friends among Czechs and the undeniable emptiness of much diplomatic social entertainment, Ma's life lacked the emotional richness of the Delhi years.

The three of us (sometimes four, when Dada came) continued with our car trips: To Switzerland, Germany and a variety of destinations inside Czechoslovakia. The latter included the famous thermal springs of Karlovy Vary, the astonishing underground stalagmite/stalactite caves near Brno and a couple of iconic industrial units. One of them was the Skoda works in Pilsen (an internationally famous home for beer), which had been bombed out by the Allies as a munitions factory, but had since resumed production of its well-known line of cars. The other was the famous Bata factory in Gottwaldov (formerly Zlín). Many Indians think Bata is an Indian company, but the original factory was founded in Zlín by Tomas Bata in 1894 and still produces shoes, though the company has morphed into a multinational, with headquarters in Switzerland.

Early in 1962, we went on 'home leave' to Delhi. We renewed our contact with all our close friends. I made a special trip to Ranchi, where Pabi's father then headed the National Coal Development Corporation, to meet up with her. Of course, we all went to Kolkata to be with family members. One day, at the Lahiris' home in Curzon Lane in Delhi, I ran into Joya and we had a long conversation, one among sixteen-year-olds, and not the twelve-year-olds of Kashmir. I remember reading out some Rupert Brooke poems to her from a handy collection. Yes, we Bengali teenagers get easily romantic! Though we did not revisit India for another nine years, Joya and I kept in touch through occasional letters.

Shortly after our return from India, we learned of Baba's posting as Ambassador to Morocco and Tunisia, headquartered in Rabat, the capital of Morocco. So my next summer holiday, before my final year of school, was there. Morocco was very different from central Europe. Islam was the religion and Arabic was the language. It was a monarchy, with the rakish Hassan II having recently succeeded his reformist father, Mohammed V.

Rabat was a somewhat sleepy modern capital city on the Atlantic coast, about 200 kms south-west of the much more interesting old town of Tangier, which lies across the Strait of Gibraltar from the southern tip of Spain. Due east were the fascinating old Moorish cities of Meknes and Fez. Close to Meknes lie the ruins of Volubilis, an ancient Roman walled city dating from pre-Christian times, where many colonnades still stand tall. An inscription on one speaks of slaves from Britain toiling there, bringing home the power and reach of the mighty Roman empire.

We saw all these new sights in that first summer in Rabat while settling down in our new home, a fairly nondescript two-storeyed modern building. I made friends with the son (name now forgotten) of the Pakistani Ambassador and we spent a fair bit of time together. But after a few weeks, I found Rabat a bit boring.

Back at Highgate in September 1962, I was loaned out as a monitor by my School House to Waiting House (one for incoming youngsters while they await allotment to a regular House) for a term, later extended at my request for the remainder of that final year at Highgate. There were four of us monitors, including Mike Minton as the head boy. We all got along pretty well, with Mike being a quietly efficient team leader. The new young boys were sometimes rebellious, but the age difference made it easier to exercise our authority when necessary. The housemaster was the kind but firm C. Topham, our physics teacher. And daily proximity deepened my friendship with Mike. It was a harmonious situation for the final lap towards our 'A' level exams in the summer of 1963.

Within a month of shifting to Waiting House, two major geopolitical crises shook our little world … and that of many others. At the global level, the Cuban missile crisis erupted in mid-October and led to a fortnight of Soviet–American confrontation and brinkmanship that only ended on 28 October 1962, when Soviet ships carrying nuclear warheads for their missiles in Cuba turned around in the face of an American naval blockade. I still remember how Mike and I listened to the BBC radio broadcasts in his small room late into the night of 27 October, wondering whether we would live to see the following day. In the middle of that crisis, Sino-Indian border tensions flared into a serious Chinese invasion on 20 October in both the Aksai Chin sector and across the McMahon line in the north-east of India. That war lasted a month, until the Chinese victors withdrew unilaterally in late November, while retaining control of significant chunks of Indian territory. That was a tense month for me, worrying both about the war's outcome, and the safety of relatives and friends back in India.

In the early spring of 1963, I took an entrance exam for some Oxford colleges and was called up for interviews. Based on these, I was offered a seat in Keble College to study physics, but because I was not yet eighteen, my entry had to be postponed till autumn 1964; it was also subject to my 'A' and 'S' level results. I accepted the offer and turned my scholastic attentions to the forthcoming examinations in June. So, of course, did everyone else in our second year of sixth form.

Life in those final months of school was not all about studies. Mike and I hatched a plan to go on a major hitch-hiking trip after the end of school, through France and Spain, all the way to Gibraltar, and on to my 'home' in Morocco. So, after the exams were over and our schooling at Highgate had ended, we began our journey. The trip, planned mostly by Mike, was a wonderful success, and I couldn't have had a better companion and guide for this first intimate exposure to France and Spain. We didn't have much money, but that didn't seem to matter.

We crossed over to Calais by ferry and hitched a ride to Paris, with our rucksacks on our backs. I remember us wandering the streets of Paris late into the night, and visiting Notre-Dame the next morning, as much for a quick nap kneeling in the pews as for seeing this famous cathedral. Then we hitched rides, the French called it 'auto-stop', down the Loire Valley to some of the famed châteaus, such as Chambord and Chaumont. The nights we spent in cheap youth hostels or, occasionally, slept in an empty barn.

Our route took us through Orleans (of Joan of Arc fame) and Tours, with an eastward detour to Mâcon to visit Nandita and Lakhi-di, who were holidaying there with Lakhi-di's childhood friend, Gabrielle. Gabrielle made us feel welcome, and Nandita, Mike and I happily wandered around the environs of Mâcon for a couple of days, including a visit to the heritage home of poet Alphonse de Lamartine, before Mike and I resumed our itinerary towards Albi, the hometown of artist Henri de Toulouse-Lautrec, with the best collection of his striking paintings and posters. We crossed the Massif Central, including an adventurous ride on the pillions of two kind French motorcyclists, and went on to Albi for a day or two. Then, on to the Spanish border. There, we got stuck for long, dreary hours without a ride and finally caught a train to Madrid. Hitchhiking in General Franco's Spain proved very difficult. After a day or two sightseeing in Madrid, much of it spent in the magnificent Prado Museum of Art, we took a train to Gibraltar and crossed over to Tangier. And thence, another train to Rabat, where we surprised my parents and Abdul by slipping in through the kitchen door one afternoon. They knew we were coming, but had no idea when. There were no mobile phones, email or WhatsApp messaging!

Our weeks in Morocco were very enjoyable this time, as I had the company of Mike. We made a memorable family trip down to Marrakesh and a bit further south into the foothills of the Atlas

Mountains, beyond which lay the limitless Sahara desert. We also revisited Casablanca (of Humphrey Bogart fame), and Meknes and Fez. During our time in Rabat, our 'A' level results arrived. Mine were good, above the minimum grades required by Oxford. Mike's were not as good as he had hoped for, but good enough for him to join the London teaching hospital, the Royal Free, to pursue a medical degree, which was what he wanted to do.

During our time in Morocco, I also had long discussions with Baba about how to usefully spend my 'gap year' till autumn 1964. I expressed my desire to learn some philosophy, political science and economics before I got immersed in a physics degree programme. Baba suggested that I do a year-long 'Occasional Student' programme at the London School of Economics (LSE), under which one paid a fee and was allowed to 'audit' five lecture courses for a year, but with no degree at the end. As Baba had done some of his ICS exam preparation work at LSE in the mid-1930s (in those days, the ICS entrance exam had to be taken in London), he was able to activate contact with his ex-teachers and set this up for me. The programme did not offer access to LSE student housing. So, where would I stay during those months? Once again, Baba's old contacts came through. He had spent his two years in London in a boarding house for students and young adults, run by a kind lady called Mrs Ponsford, in 37 Woodlane, Highgate. Lo and behold, she was still around and had a room for me!

So, at August end, Mike and I took a flight from Rabat to London to start our respective post-Highgate School lives. I was two months short of eighteen; Mike had just turned nineteen.

3

London Alone: Interlude

I F HIGHGATE WAS A test of survival and fitness in an alien
habitat at a rather young age, my year in London and LSE was
about growing in several dimensions: Emotional, psychological,
intellectual and cultural. It was not that I achieved great progress
in these matters in that single year, but living on my own as a
teenager in one of the planet's great cities certainly helped the
process along.

In early September, I moved into a small room on the top floor
of Mrs Ponsford's sprawling Victorian house at 37, Wood Lane,
about 100 yards from the Highgate tube station. The room had
a small washbasin, and the other necessary facilities were only a
few steps away. The building probably had about sixteen to twenty
young lodgers, mostly south Asian males and a few English girls.
Most were aged twenty-one to twenty-five, and post-college; I
was easily the youngest. The lodgings were run by the kindly elder
Mrs Ponsford (in her seventies then) and her tougher fifty-ish,
unmarried daughter, Ruth. Breakfast and dinner were provided in

the large dining room in the basement, with all of us seated around a single large table. Dinner was always served at a designated time. Platefuls were ladled out (with minor choices of side dishes) by Mrs Ponsford and Ruth. It was at one of these dinners in November that Ruth shared the latest radio news about US President John Kennedy's assassination. Breakfast was less structured in time and largely on a self-help basis. Lodgers had to fend for themselves at lunch. There probably was a night curfew, but I really can't recall what it was, perhaps 10 p.m. or 11 p.m. Highgate School was about a mile away up Southwood Lane. But now I had no reason or inclination to go there. It was a part of my past.

LSE was easy enough to get to: I could take the Northern Line down to Charing Cross and walk for ten–twelve minutes, or change to the Central Line to go to Holborn for a five-minute walk from there. I probably did both on different occasions. The LSE campus is spread across several buildings, with the central one at Houghton Street, two minutes from Aldwych. That's where I mostly went for lectures after I had sorted out the paperwork and got an identity card of some sort. There were no green spaces or sporting facilities and, especially for an Occasional Student, no real campus life or cohort to relate to. It was just a few buildings one went to for imbibing knowledge. I accepted it on those terms.

In practice, LSE's Occasional Student system was very flexible, and pretty much allowed me to audit any lecture at any time and with no supervisory academic person to report to. The lecture series that drew my interest and attention were: Karl Popper on epistemology, Michael Oakeshott on political philosophy, Lionel Robbins on history of economic thought, S. Ozga on principles of economics, a young American lecturer on American democracy and an unremembered teacher on international relations. It was an eclectic set of choices, but, together with some associated reading, it held my interest and attention. Popper and Oakeshott were particularly good lecturers and inspired me to read widely on their subjects. Popper's classic *Open Society and its Enemies* and his *Conjectures and Refutations* on the logic of scientific discovery made a lasting imprint on my thinking in these areas. Robbins was getting old and tired (he had been a young star in Baba's time!), but there were still flashes of brilliance in his classes. The economics lectures I attended were more run-of-the-mill, but I considered it prudent to persevere.

As the months passed and my liking for these subjects grew, I began to think of switching to the famed PPE (politics, philosophy and economics) degree in Oxford. I had already figured out that modern physics was mostly about higher mathematics, and while I was quite good at mathematics, I was not truly outstanding. The prospect of becoming a second-rate physicist, inventing new kinds of toothpastes in a corporate laboratory for a living, did not appeal to me. So, sometime during that year, I wrote to Keble College asking for permission to shift from physics to PPE when I reported there in October 1964. Amazingly, they agreed and I duly informed my parents, giving them my reasons for the change. They were startled, but quite sporting and supportive.

It was not a case of all work and no play for this Jack. Even though money was tight, London had a great deal to offer. After completing his degree in electrical engineering from London University in 1963, Dada had moved to Rugby to do a two-year graduate apprenticeship with the major British engineering firm AEI. Rugby was easily accessible from London. Besides, I had emotional moorings in Mike and his ever-warm family, and Nandita and her parents. Mike was doing a sort of preliminary year in his medicine degree, and had not yet got swept into the rigours of the full programme. He was a wonderful cultural mentor to learn about London's theatre, music, ballet and museums. With him, I went to a few plays, a couple of memorable ballets at the Royal Opera House (featuring Rudolf Nureyev and Margot Fonteyn), several offerings in the relatively new Royal Festival Hall (including Ravi Shankar and folksingers like Pete Seeger and Joan Baez), and introductory tours of the National Gallery and the Tate.

It was also, unfortunately, the year in which Henry Minton's dormant multiple sclerosis flared up after decades, and slowly and tragically reduced his functionality. It was then that I witnessed Mike's patience and tenderness with his father, and realized that he would make a wonderful doctor. Henry passed away in 1967.

Nandita was already in Oxford, but I saw her often in the vacations, and a couple of times, I hitchhiked up to Oxford to visit her. In those days, that meant taking the tube to Hanger Lane, then the westernmost station on the London Underground, and walking on to the A40 highway to hitch-hike further westwards. On one of the trips, she billeted me for the night in the little flat shared by Deepak Lal and Vijay Joshi, who were already post-graduates and would later become well-known, world-class Indian economists, with major books on India. The other couple I used to visit often that year were the Lahiris, who had moved to London to get treatment for some medical issues Arati Mashi had developed. They were renting a flat, first in Half Moon street, and then in Eaton Square, both pretty fancy addresses. Both the Lahiris passed away in London some years later, within a few days of each other.

As part of growing up, and to make a few pounds, I took up a part-time job as a 'cleaning man' in response to a little index card posted, with other sundry advertisements, on the large notice board at the local post office in Highgate. It involved spending two mornings a week going to a house down our Wood Lane, to vacuum floors and clean the bathtub of an elderly lady living alone. I soon realized that she was perhaps more interested in having someone to talk to than the actual cleaning. I had no problem doing either. Also, when the Christmas season came, I did not rush off to Rabat on the usual holiday with family but stayed behind to put in a fortnight's paid work with the London postal service to help out with the Christmas rush of parcels and cards. This was a standard and readily available temporary employment in those days. In practice, it meant zooming around in a coach filled with bags of post in an area of North London, supervised by a regular postman (who also did the driving), doing deliveries with another young, temporary co-worker. Jack, the middle-aged regular postman, generally let us off early. None of this brought big money, but it was satisfying.

At 37, Wood Lane, I made friends with some co-lodgers. They included Malay Chatterji and Pradip Dutt (a cousin of Pabi's, I found out much later), who were doing chartered accountancy. In fact, after Christmas, the three of us did go down to Rabat for a few days for a Moroccan holiday with my parents. I also befriended two girls, Christine and Mary, who shared one of the larger rooms at 37. Both were from the north of England and were very pleasant. Christine was blonde and particularly attractive, and over time, we became more than friends. One could say I was following established family traditions at Wood Lane! Thoughts of a longer-term relationship did crop up, but I felt I was far too young to make any commitment. Also, I was beginning to dimly understand that teenage hormonal instincts aside, intellectual, if not cultural, compatibility was a necessary condition for any long-term relationship as far as I was concerned. So, when the year ended, we stayed in touch for while (she even came up for a summer ball in Oxford), but not for very long.

Baba and Ma came to London to visit in the spring of 1964 (Baba may have had some official work as well), and they lodged in a vacant room in Wood Lane. There is an iconic photograph of all the Indian lodgers, my parents and I, Nandita and her parents, and

Satyajit Ray, his wife and son (the three were also visiting London at the time) in a large basement room in Wood Lane. The co-lodgers were thrilled to rub shoulders, however briefly, with the world-famous director of Indian cinema. I took the opportunity of the parental visit to ensure they met Mike's mum and dad. My parents had already grown fond of Mike from his visit to Morocco in the previous summer.

The other big 'event' of that academic year was the arrival, and then inexorable rise, of The Beatles. They were followed later by many others, like the Rolling Stones and other popular rock bands. But The Beatles dominated Western pop music in the 1960s and early 1970s in a way none had before or since. If you were not a Beatles fan by 1964, you were regarded as simply weird. I easily escaped that label.

Shortly after my parents returned to Rabat, they learned that Baba was being posted to Ottawa, Canada, as our High Commissioner effective summer, 1964. So once again, it was time to pack and engage in a round of farewells from the local government and diplomatic community. For me, this meant that my summer holidays before joining Oxford would be spent in North America.

On 27 May 1964, Pandit Jawaharlal Nehru passed away, bringing down the curtain on the first era of Independent India. The last eighteen months, after the Chinese invasion, had been a sad twilight of his seventeen-year premiership as the pre-eminent leader of India. But his legacy lived on … And still does today. Lal Bahadur Shastri became his immediate successor. By then, I had read Nehru's *Discovery of India* and *Glimpses of World History*, both written in prison, and felt the loss keenly.

4

College in Oxford, and Home in Ottawa and Rio

S O, IN THE SUMMER of 1964, off we went to Canada. Dada was working and could not join us. We first flew from London to New York, and stopped for a few days there, partly to see the famous World Fair that year and partly for Baba to have consultations with our mission at the UN. For me, the skyscrapers of Manhattan were a wondrous sight. Europe had nothing like it then. The World Fair in Flushing Meadows had about 150 pavilions (including the Indian one) and over a hundred restaurants. Curiously, what lingers in my mind is a little joke about the famous Greyhound bus company, which also ran buses in the enormous Fair. One of them got lost in the maze of pavilions, and the passengers sang, 'Go, Greyhound, and leave the driving to us' to the unfortunate driver! That was the motto of the company.

We arrived in quiet and picturesque little Ottawa, and settled in to our new home at 585, Acacia Avenue in Rockcliffe Park, the very pleasant upmarket neighbourhood for senior diplomats and Canadian government officials. Our next-door neighbour was John Diefenbaker, Leader of the Opposition (Lester Pearson then led the Liberal Government). His dogs had the annoying habit of trespassing on our lawns to discharge their waste. Our house was large and spacious, with a beautiful sun room, and was located on a particularly quiet street. Hans, our official driver, was a taciturn character, who had driven panzer tanks in the Second World War in the Wehrmacht. He had a fetish for cleanliness and kept cleaning the official car whenever he was not driving. Our own new Mercedes 220 arrived soon and I drove it often as I had acquired an international driving licence since our Morocco years.

After settling into the house and our basic routines, we began to explore Ottawa and its environs. In those years, Ottawa was one of the smaller cities of Canada (about 4,00,000 in population), especially when compared to Toronto, Montreal and Vancouver on the west coast. Traffic was usually light, and driving around easy. Across the river Ottawa lay the twin city of Hull in Quebec; the Ottawa river formed the border between Ontario and Quebec provinces all the way down to Montreal at the mouth of the St Lawrence estuary. And a couple of miles beyond was the entrance to the lovely Gatineau Park, with its beautiful little lakes and thousands of acres of pine and silver birch forests. In the fall, the park was ablaze with orange and yellow colours.

As usual, we made weekend trips to other parts of Ontario, like the Thousand Islands National Park, the hugely impressive Niagara Falls, Toronto and Montreal, with its famous McGill University. Either then or later, one of our Montreal visits coincided with an international film festival, with a small contingent that had come from India. At a party given by Baba for them, I recall refilling the whiskey glass of a slightly inebriated Raj Kapoor!

In Ottawa, I made friends with the twenty-ish children of officers in the high commission. The two I spent the most time with were Nalini Goel and Krish Sahai. Nalini, who was studying in Carleton University, Ottawa, became a good friend throughout our Ottawa years. In that first summer of ours, she, Krish and I went around together quite a lot, sometimes joined by some of her Carleton friends. In our second and last year in Ottawa, she became an informal 'ward' of my mother, with whom she got on very well, after her own parents were posted back to India, and she decided to remain and work there. After a few years, she married a Canadian from a successful business family and became a prominent patron of the arts in her later years. Several decades later, with the advent of the internet and email, we renewed contact and our friendship.

At the end of September, I boarded a flight back to London, and in early October, reported at Keble College. At that time, Keble was perhaps the most 'modern' of the men's colleges, less than 100 years old (Keble turned 150 in 2020), designed, unusually, as a set of red brick buildings by architect William Butterfield. I never came to like its looks. As the months unfolded, I realized that the two greatest assets of Keble were its closeness to the beautiful University Parks (fifty yards from our 'lodge') and its proximity to nearly all the women's colleges. I was given corner rooms down one corridor, with the windows opening on the main back garden. 'Rooms' would be an exaggeration, as the bedroom could barely accommodate a single bed, a wooden chair and a little table for a basin and jug. Running water was some twenty yards away.

My principal tutor was the young Keble economics don, Adrian Darby, whose main claim to fame at that time was being the son-in-law of the Conservative leader and Prime Minister for the year October 1963–October 1964, Sir Alec Douglas-Home. Darby was a very bright and pleasant person; he may not have published any economics papers, but was a good tutor and later became a stalwart of the college as bursar for many years. Moral philosophy was taught by Basil Mitchell, and for other parts of philosophy, we were farmed out to different colleges. Paul Hayes was the politics don. Later, after I chose my special papers, I was tutored in 'currency and credit' by the dynamic Peter Oppenheimer in Christ Church, very much a 'TV don' of those years.

In Oxford, tutorials, the primary mode of teaching, were the responsibility of the college, while university departments organized the various lecture series. It was customary, indeed fashionable, for students to pay only limited attention to the latter. Out of curiosity and diligence, I did attend some of these, with mixed results. The great Sir Roy Harrod, of Harrod–Domar growth equation fame, was an elderly gentleman who mumbled into the blackboard about 'warranted' rates of growth and so forth; I stopped attending after two lectures. The even more famous Sir John Hicks, a co-founder of neoclassical economics and (later) Nobel prize winner, was also a mumbler and got equally short shrift from me. What a contrast with another knight, Sir Isaiah Berlin, who lectured to full halls, holding hundreds of students spellbound. He would stare up at the ceiling while whole, perfectly formed paragraphs came rolling out of his mouth on political theory and ideas.

The better, well-attended lecture series also allowed some mingling of students from different colleges (about thirty at that time) in the same discipline. That meant the men, in an unfortunate majority of six to one in those years, could check out their female counterparts, who remained comfortably disdainful, basking in their status of extreme scarcity.

I did my reading and writing in three places, the New Bodleian library (specializing in PPE material), the small college library at Keble, and my own room. We were expected to read widely and deeply, with our tutors offering indicative guidance. In economics, we read contemporary texts by British and American authors (including Paul Samuelson, Richard Lipsey and Gardner Ackley) as well as the classics by the likes of Adam Smith, Alfred Marshall and John Maynard Keynes. In philosophy, we were steeped not only in the Anglo-Scottish classics of David Hume, John Locke and John Stuart Mill, but also in their latter-day Oxford, logical-positive and linguistic successors like Alfred Ayres, J.L. Austen, P.F. Strawson, Gilbert Ryle and the great Austrians Ludwig Wittgenstein and Karl Popper. It was Wittgenstein who squelched much of metaphysics with his immortal epigram, 'That of which we cannot speak we should pass over in silence'! And then there was the appealing modern moral philosophy of Richard Hare, one of whose books I used to impress Gayatri during our courtship in later years.

For obvious reasons, my initial set of friends and companions in Oxford were confined to my college and subject. That changed within a few months. Over time, my friends were spread across several overlapping sets: Some from Keble, some from among south Asians associated with the Oxford Majlis Society (the university was full of societies catering to every interest and persuasion), some from my subject specialization, and some from the opposite gender. Thus, my closest men friends became Chris Verity and Ray Tallis, both studying medicine from Keble, and Robin Christopher, doing PPE. Chris, Ray and I still get together every year for lunch in London, and I (and sometimes Gayatri) have stayed several times in their homes in Grantchester, outside Cambridge, and Manchester, respectively. Chris became a consulting paediatric neurologist at Addenbrooke's Hospital near Cambridge, while Ray became a well-known gerontologist in his day job and has published (so far) about forty books on philosophy and literary criticism, written in the dawn hours when normal humans sleep. Sir Robin became a distinguished member of the British diplomatic service, holding ambassadorships in Ethiopia, Indonesia and Argentina, as well as doing a three-year stint in Delhi as 'first secretary (political)' in the British High Commission in the 1970s, when he became very friendly with my parents.

Perhaps because I had come from an English public school, my early friendships with south Asian men were less close, but included Asad Khan (son of Nawab Ali Yavar Jung, then our Ambassador in Paris), Tariq Hyder (son of Sajjad Hyder, who later was the Pakistani High Commissioner in Delhi), Montek Ahluwalia (a leading figure in the Oxford Union and a year senior to me) and Kumar Advani. Others I knew included Tinoo Puri (later head of McKinsey in India in the 1990s), Ram Chopra, Sudhir Anand (later professor of economics at Oxford) and Prabhat Patnaik (later a well-known Marxist professor of economics at JNU). Some of them became better friends later in life, either during our World Bank years or after Gayatri and I returned to India in 1982.

My English school pedigree did not seem to inhibit my forming friendships among the unusually generous crop of Indian undergraduate girls at Oxford that year; it included Gayatri Dasgupta, Vasundhara Chapotkat, Tulsi Mehta and later, Nalini Jain in Lady Margaret Hall (LMH), and Malavika (aka Bika) Chanda and Lipika Sengupta in St Hugh's College. Actually, during my first two years at Oxford, my closest south Asian female friends were not from India but from Myanmar (Aung San Suu Kyi at St Hugh's) and Sri Lanka (Sunethra Bandaranaike at Somerville), both of whom were in my year and doing PPE. I became close to both Suu and Su, forming deep friendships, which have endured to this day. While not denying traces of romantic interest among us, natural among twenty-year-olds, that was not the core of these friendships, which may be why they have survived over fifty-five years. Romance did become the core of my relationship with Gayatri, but all that happened in the final year and will come later.

Some thirty years later, after Suu Kyi had won a sweeping electoral victory while under house arrest in Myanmar and had been awarded the Nobel Peace Prize, I began to get calls from BBC and other news agencies asking about her political beliefs and preoccupations in her college days. The truth is, she was simply a bright, good-looking, vivacious college girl from a privileged south Asian background, with a good sense of humour, a strong stubborn streak and a deep emotional commitment to a legendary father, who had been assassinated when she was two years old. She was certainly conscious of her good looks as she cycled around Oxford on her trademark Moulton, small-wheeled bicycle. But, at least in her initial years at Oxford, she was quite shy and demure in her interactions with the opposite gender. I may have been her first really close male friend.

Life at Oxford was varied and fulfilling. There were small bouts of academic tension associated with getting weekly essay assignments completed for one's tutors, typically dubbed 'essay crises', but there were no semester or term exams. In fact, the only examinations we faced, other than the final ones at the end of our three years, were the 'Prelims' at the end of the second term in our first year. Luckily, I did well in those, and was awarded a small scholarship of sixty pounds a year. It also meant that as a 'scholar', I had to wear a long gown rather than the short ones worn by non-scholars. Gowns were obligatory at mealtimes in the college dining hall, and when attending tutorials and lectures. How much work one put in for essays and other elements of the curriculum was left to each student. So, very bright students sometimes did badly in the final exams, and vice versa.

There was plenty of opportunity for recreation. In the evenings, we often went for a drink and a game a of darts at the local pubs. Those patronized by us from Keble included the Lamb and Flag round the corner, the Eagle and Child (aka 'Bird and Baby') in St. Giles' and the Royal Oak opposite Somerville. I didn't like beer, so I stuck to cider. During spring and summer, it was a special pleasure to hire punts from the Cherwell Boathouse and go punting with friends on the lovely little Cherwell river, which meandered through the university parks all the way to Magdalen Bridge. Punting did require some practice and skill if one wanted to stay dry and out of the river. There were, of course, all kinds of sports organized by the college and university, and by some clubs. Not being a 'jock', I mostly stayed away from these. I did learn the rudiments of sailing on the Isis, as the Thames is called in Oxford, by the Port Meadow under the auspices of the Sailing Club, taught patiently by fellow student Jill Winter, with whom I had been on a few dates one term. Sometimes, I played squash with Chris. At one stage, I got quite obsessed with playing bridge with some students in Keble, and we used to play from after dinner to dawn! That year, I played bridge for Keble and our team made it to the semi-finals in the inter-collegiate competition.

During the long vacations (fifteen weeks in summer and nearly six each in winter and spring), I usually went home to my parents; though sometimes, I shortened my stay there a bit to spend a few days with college friends in England. Chris, Ray and Robin, and their respective parents, kindly invited me to their homes. That meant interesting trips to Thorner in Yorkshire with Chris, to Liverpool with Ray, and to Cooden (Sussex) with Robin. As they came from different backgrounds, I gained some insights into English society. Mr Verity was the kindly vicar of Thorner village, Mr Tallis was a building contractor and took a slightly dim view of us spoilt college types, while Col. Christopher was warm and bluff, ex-British Army, and had served with Field Marshal Bernard Montgomery in Africa in WWII. I took a particular shine to Chris's warm and welcoming mother, and to Barbara Christopher, Robin's mother, or Aunty B as we called her.

One spring, Chris, Ray and I did a week-long trek in the picturesque Lake District of Wordsworth fame. It was a lot of

fun, but quite tiring at times as we went up and down hills with
scattered snow. There are flattering snapshots of me in my jeans,
anorak and Keble scarf, leaning debonairly against some rocks on
a hilltop, but as Chris is fond of pointing out, these were sham,
as minutes earlier I had been puffing and gasping, 'Chris, I am
exhausted; just can't go on any more!'

Some weekends, I would take the train down to London to
visit the Mintons or Nandita and family, and perhaps see a play
or movie with them. Mike was in the throes of his demanding
medical studies, so I saw much less of him than in my London
year. On one of the return journeys, I got chatting with an elderly
English gentleman, who had retired from being master of an
Oxford college. A few days later, I received an invitation card from
him for a pre-dinner sherry at his house on St. Giles'. I expected
a small gathering and was surprised to find I was the only guest.
A little uneasy, I took my leave after partaking of a glass of sherry
and making polite conversation. As I bade farewell at the door, he
suddenly kissed me on the lips and asked, 'Did you like that?' I
was so nonplussed, I recall replying 'I don't know' and retreating
swiftly in confusion. That was my only, and unsought, homosexual
experience during my three years at Oxford.

In Ottawa, life with Baba and Ma, and friends Krish and Nalini,
depended a lot on the season. In winter, Ottawa had plenty of
snow with temperatures comparable to what we had experienced
in Prague. On one occasion, I remember we made a makeshift
cardboard sledge and the three of us—Krish, Nalini and I—took
turns to slide down a fairly steep slope through the snow near our
home. It was fun until Nalini lost control and hit her head against
the side of a lamp post. We quickly took her back to the house and
applied first aid. Luckily, it was no more than a minor flesh wound.

June 1965 was a was a special time for our family. Dada got
married to Ann Skelley at a registrar's office in London. We were all

present. They had been engaged for quite a while, and 'going out' for even longer. Shortly thereafter, Dada shifted to Birmingham, to work for the General Electric Company in his specialization of turbo generator instrumentation. Over time, and despite some trying circumstances, Dada and Ann built a wonderfully strong and mutually loving family unit with their three children, Lalita, Ranjan and Manjula—or LRM, as we sometimes referred to them. They stayed in England till 1980, before migrating to Ontario, Canada.

Back in Ottawa, Mike visited us from England, and we made a trip to Stratford (also on an Avon) near London, Ontario, which had an impressive, modern theatre given over to Shakespeare productions. The play we saw, I think, was *Henry V.* Robin Christopher also came for a few days. I remember going to a few parties thrown by Nalini's Carleton friends, with the usual drinks and dancing to pop music. That gave me the idea to host such a party (jointly with Nalini) in our spacious entertainment rooms and lawns in Acacia Ave. With Baba and Ma either absent or cloistered in their upstairs suite, the party was far more successful than I had bargained for— in the sense that there was a large number of young gatecrashers, probably having heard about it about it from Nalini's college peers!

August–September 1965 saw the second war between India and Pakistan. There had been skirmishes earlier in the spring, in the Rann of Kutch, followed by sustained efforts at infiltrating sizable irregular forces from Pakistan into Kashmir under Operation Gibraltar. When these were stymied by Indian forces, the Pakistan Army launched a full-scale attack across the ceasefire line in Kashmir in the Chamb sector of Akhnoor. With our supply lines to the Valley under serious threat, Prime Minister Shastri ordered a counter-attack across the international border near Lahore. The three-week war saw substantial loss of life among army and air force personnel on both sides, with multiple air combat episodes between the Indian Gnats and Hawker Hunters and the Pakistani

Sabre jets. The major tank battles at Khemkaran, decisively won by India, were the largest since WWII.

Such wars escalate diplomatic activity worldwide, and the Indian High Commission in Ottawa was no exception. In 1965, another drought year in India, followed by a second monsoon failure in 1966, American President Lyndon Johnson used PL 480 food shipments to bully India on several issues. Thanks in part to Baba's prodigious efforts, Canada came through with sizable shipments of wheat on concessional terms.

In the winter of 1965–66, I became an uncle when Ann gave birth to a baby girl they named Lalita. I remember going up to Birmingham one day to visit the three of them. It's hard to believe that little baby is now a mature lady with a husband of many years and two teenage daughters of her own, and heads a research team in Canada's Parliament Library. Perhaps more importantly, she grew up as a loving daughter to her parents, and as a loving niece to Gayatri and me.

Sometime in that second year, Ray Tallis and I were selected (along with two others) to represent Keble on the well-known ITV quiz show, *University Challenge*, hosted by the debonair and erudite Bamber Gascoigne, who later wrote the very readable and beautifully illustrated *The Great Moghuls*. We went up to Manchester to record the show. I have to confess that I was a complete flop over there, getting the only question I answered wrong. The only minor consolation was that I received a couple of 'fan letters' from unknown girls (one including a photo) commending my appearance and offering to meet on Hampstead Heath or some such place.

As my second year at Oxford drew to its close, I was reminded that for the third and final year, Keble students had to leave college and find university-registered rooms (for rent) in private residences. Suu Kyi helpfully informed me that her close St. Hugh's friend

Ann Pasternak-Slater's mother, Lydia Pasternak-Slater, had a nice house in Park Town (a lovely little double-crescent off the main Banbury Road) with four rooms to rent each year. I promptly informed Chris and Ray, and we rounded up Rick Kean, a Keble engineering student, to call on Lydia and make a bid for those rooms. She kindly assented (with a helpful assist from Ann), and so we set off in June 1966 for our final summer vacation, knowing that we would have a home to return to in our final year. Lydia was the sister of the famous Boris Pasternak, who had won the Nobel Prize for Literature in 1958, mainly for his semi-autographical novel *Dr Zhivago*. Many years earlier, she had wed an English Mr Slater, who had passed on. We also made arrangements to start our rental from September to give ourselves an extra month of self-study before the final year, with its June final exams, began.

By the time I returned to Ottawa, Baba had received posting orders for Brazil (with their foreign ministry and diplomatic missions still in Rio de Janeiro) effective late summer of 1966. So we spent our final few weeks in Ottawa, followed by a farewell week with Ma's cousin and family, Sid(hartha) Bannerji, Ann Bannerji and their children, MaryAnn, Alison and Julian, in their home in Orange, Connecticut (near New Haven), after which I would return to Oxford and my parents would proceed to Rio. I bade farewell to Nalini and her friends, and hoped that we would meet up again.

That last week in Orange was both pleasant and fateful. Sid and Ann were wonderfully warm and hospitable. They had met when they were studying in Cornell University, and Ann had bravely returned to India with Sid, who wanted to set up a small engineering firm in Kolkata producing refrigerating equipment called 'Thanda Kol'. It had been a hard and chequered life for them for twenty years, before they decided to return to the US. One summer evening, as I carried twelve-year-young Julian on my shoulders in their garden, I tripped and fell, breaking the ulna bone in my left arm, which I used to break my fall. After a night of considerable pain, I was sent off to Yale New Haven Hospital for serious medical attention. So I arrived back in Oxford at end-August with my left arm plastered and in a sling.

I settled into my 20 Park Town room at the top of the house, with a little balcony overlooking the back garden. In early September, Oxford was largely devoid of students, except for a few like me who had returned early to prepare for the final year. One day, I dropped in to see Gayatri in her room in the basement of 2, Fyfield Road, next to LMH. And thus began a year-long courtship, which ended with a garnet engagement ring in July 1967. It may have helped that early on, when I looked a little wounded with one arm in a cast, she kindly offered to help cut my nails. The fact that Fyfield Road and LMH were just 250 yards away from Park Town, through a shortcut, may also have also been relevant.

That final year at Oxford was filled with hard academic work, mingled with the joys of courtship in the university's lovely settings, while living with good friends in our Park Town 'digs'. Montek, whom I had got to know a little better, kindly lent me his notes on economics (he had done brilliantly in the final exams the previous year). Lydia provided us with a basic, self-service breakfast, and we had our other meals in college. Gayatri and I got together often, sometimes working together in my room or going out with friends. One evening, Chris, Ray, Gayatri and I took Lydia to see the new hit three-hour epic movie, *Dr Zhivago*, with its all-star cast of Omar Sharif (as Zhivago), Julie Christie (as Lara), Tom Courtenay, Alec Guinness, Ralph Richardson, Geraldine Chaplin, Rod Steiger and Rita Tushingham. It was an all-time great movie. But, at the end of it, when we asked Lydia how she liked it, she shrugged her shoulders and said, 'He was not like that'!

A couple of years later, Lydia gave us a lovely wedding present of a limited-edition lithograph print of Leo Tolstoy writing at his desk, painted by her father, Leonid Pasternak, a leading Russian painter of his time. It hung in our living room in USA and India, though many Indian visitors mistook the old man in the painting for Rabindranath Tagore!

In October 1966, I turned twenty-one. I do not remember any major celebration. I do remember, and still possess, the magnificently generous gift from Chris and Ray of the collected works of Thomas Hardy.

Gayatri's parents were in Bern, Switzerland, with her father posted in the Universal Postal Union, the oldest extant international institution, established by the Treaty of Bern in 1874, and later absorbed into the UN family of institutions. He had come there on deputation from the Indian Postal Service. That is why Gayatri's school and college years in India had been in Chennai (then Madras), Mumbai (then Bombay) and Delhi, where Mr Dasgupta had headed the General Post Office in each of these cities successively. Her sister, Monica, six years younger, had been going to boarding school in Switzerland, but shifted to be a boarder in Headington School in Oxford in 1966 to do her 'A' levels. Gayatri became her 'local guardian' that year. We visited Monica at her school a couple of times, and took her punting and walking in the Port Meadows and University Parks on a couple of Sundays when she was let out. She was a pretty and vivacious sixteen year old. Gayatri claims that she was 'cultivating' me to make a match with her younger sister. If so, she clearly botched up the project!

Most of our mutual friends assumed that with both of us going around a lot together, it meant that matters were getting serious. However, conscious that we were both relatively young (twenty-one and twenty-two), I did not want to 'lock in' either of us by informing my parents prematurely of developments, not even during my first trip to Rio that winter (it was summer over there). Rio turned out to be a stupendously beautiful city, with its lovely clash of mountains and beach-ringed bays all around. There was the storied Pão de Açúcar (Sugarloaf) rock, the great massif of the Corcovado mountain looming over the city, with its huge statue of Christ on top with his arms outstretched, the legendary beaches of Copacabana and Ipanema (remember '*The girl from Ipanema*', sung by Astrud Gilberto?) and so much more.

We lived in a spacious flat just a hundred yards from the Copacabana beach, and could wander there any time, though I don't think Abdul, who was still with us, did much of that! The beach was almost always full of scantily clad young men and women of different nationalities. It was the one place where the subtle colour-coded gradations (with white on top) of Brazilian society were glossed over in the basketball games and other interactions among the glistening bodies on the sand and in the sea.

Back in Oxford, in the winter and spring of that final year, all of us were also grappling with the question of: What happens after Oxford? What does one do? I had realized that politics and philosophy were good subjects to learn and think about, but not great for future careers unless one wanted to teach, which I didn't. That left economics. I decided on pursuing an economics PhD at a top American university. Sometime that year, I had gone down to London to take the mandatory Graduate Record Examinations run by a well-known Princeton-based testing agency, and lucked out to be in the top percentile. Beguiled by an inflated sense of the worth of an Oxford BA (which I had not yet earned!), I applied to only two American PhD programmes, Princeton and Harvard. Princeton declined politely. Harvard offered me a place, but without financial assistance. Baba very kindly agreed to shoulder the daunting costs for the initial years, which, at that time, were $2000 per year for tuition (for the first two years only) and an annual, minimalist living expense estimate of $2000 per year.

Baba and Ma paid a visit to England and Oxford in the spring of 1967. They asked me to invite my close friends to a fancy lunch at a top restaurant. In retrospect, I think my choice of the 'Elizabeth' made an unnecessarily big dent in their limited resources. Anyway, the lucky guests included Gayatri, Suu Kyi, Sunethra (plus boyfriend, Barney), Malavika, Chris, Ray and Robin. I made sure that the seating left my parents guessing about which, if any, female was of special interest!

In the first fortnight of June, we togged up in our dark suits, white shirts, bow ties and gowns, and slouched off, apprehensively, to the examination halls near High Street. One of my early exam papers was statistics, and I told Gayatri I had probably flunked it. She did her best to buoy up my drooping spirits so I could tackle the six or seven papers that lay ahead. As it happened, I managed a first class and Gayatri got a high second in her English literature subject. We found out all this a few weeks later. In the meantime, when everyone's exams were over, we had a boozy evening champagne bash at the LMH boatyard, which included all the Indian LMH and St. Hugh's ladies, Prabhat Patnaik, Sudhir Anand and me. A snapshot remains—minus me, the photographer.

While waiting those few weeks for the results, a small group of us proceeded on a pre-planned three-week holiday to Italy. The group consisted of Gayatri, her LMH friends, Vasundhara and Nalini, and me. The group had to be small as we intended to stretch our limited means by hitchhiking through most of Italy. No car would pick up more than four people. Later, Lipika's feisty younger sister labelled us, inaccurately, as 'Shankar and his harem'! We went from London to Milan, in north Italy, by train.

There, after enjoying the main sights, especially the imposing and distinctive Milan Cathedral, we began our hitchhiking adventures.

Our standard operating procedure, largely designed by me, was to have the ladies dressed in saris at the roadside, with their thumbs out (the universal sign for requesting lifts), and me vaguely hanging around in the background. At the perimeter of the main Italian cities, there would typically be a long line of hitchhikers on the highways hopefully sticking out their thumbs. But there was never any other group with three sari-clad damsels with their pallus wafting in the breeze! It worked. We were able to queue-jump, in a manner of speaking, 90 per cent of the time. When we were not hitch-hiking, the girls wore whatever they wanted—shorts, jeans, and so forth. At each of our stops for the night, we would typically stay in youth hostels (separate dorms for men and women) or in the cheapest 'pension' rooms we could find. Sometimes, we were obliged to sleep all four in a large room. On those occasions, I spent a fair bit of time looking out of the window while the ladies changed into their nightwear in the evening and back into day clothes the next morning!

From Milan, we hitch-hiked due south to Rapallo, a pretty little town on the north-western coast of Italy and swam in the sea with its pebbled beach. Then down the coast to Pisa, with its iconic leaning tower, east to glorious Florence, south to Siena with its lovely campanile, and then the long ride south to Rome.

Of course, we had our little unplanned adventures on the way. Once, a young man in a fancy Lancia picked us up and, on the way to the next destination, stopped at a small lake for a little swim. We joined him happily, but I got a bit nervous when he started devoting special attention to a particular lady in our group. Luckily, nothing untoward happened. Sometimes, as we hitch-hiked, a flashy Italian in an Alfa Romeo sports car would pull over and offer to take two girls from our group. We had to prudently decline. On the whole, we found our ride-givers extremely courteous and generous, sometimes even paying for our sandwiches on the way.

In Rome, we enjoyed the warm hospitality and generosity of Mr and Mrs Sushil Dey. Mr Dey, a former ICS officer, was posted with the World Food Programme, and his wife, Bulbul-di, was a distant cousin of mine and a quasi-niece of Baba's. Apart from lots of good food, we all cherished the leisurely long baths we took to feel really clean after two weeks on the road. We went one evening in Rome to the famous old baths of Caracalla, where a memorable production of Verdi's opera, *Aida*, was being staged open air, with real elephants on stage!

After Rome, followed by a swing through the wondrous Venice, we split up, with Gayatri and me catching a train to Bern to visit her parents. They were very warm and generous to me; Gayatri and I were not yet engaged, though we were considering it by then. I did my bit to impress the family by cooking a dish of 'chicken tarragon', which everyone had to eat and profess to enjoy. Gayatri reminds me that the principal ingredient I used, other than tarragon, was a whole stick of butter! The Dasguptas showed me the sights of Bern, with her mother, an accomplished driver, taking us around. After two or three days, I took a train back to London and Oxford to ascertain my results, and prepare for America. Gayatri followed a little later to learn her results and pack up her belongings to return to her family in Bern. It was sometime during that July that I slipped the garnet engagement ring on her finger.

July–August 1967 was a time for farewells. With their carefree college years at Oxford over, everyone was moving on to the next stage of their lives, more or less purposefully. There were a lot of sad farewells all around. Robin Christopher had got accepted for an MA at the Fletcher School of Law and Diplomacy on the campus of Tufts University in the Boston area. So he and I booked a cabin together on *Queen Elizabeth* I, on one of her last voyages, from Southampton to New York. Chris and Ray were moving on to their respective teaching hospitals for further training, Sunethra was planning to spend more time in England with Barney before returning to Colombo, Suu (like many others) was pondering her next steps at the home of her 'local guardian', Sir Paul Gore-Booth (earlier British High Commissioner in India) and family in London, Malavika and Vasundhara were returning to India, Montek was continuing with his BPhil degree, Kumar Advani was completing his chartered accountancy in London … And so on.

Gayatri and I had to part, but despite the 'trial' of us spending some months apart, we both knew that it really was just a matter of time before we married.

In the second half of August, Robin and I left Oxford for our tryst with *Queen Elizabeth* I at a pier in Southampton.

Oxford was a wonderful place to have gone to college with some very fine human beings. Sometimes, the memory of a place is best conveyed by a random collage of flashbacks:

- Dave Brubeck's '*Take Five*' echoing down staircase 7 of Keble from Chris's record player (he and Ray had facing rooms at the top);
- Teaching Suu Kyi to punt, with modest success;
- A bottle of Mateus rosé wine bursting accidentally to drench Sunethra at a restaurant where Col. Christopher and Aunty B had taken her, Robin and me to dinner;
- Saying the evening's goodbye to Gayatri in the lamplight halfway between Park Town and LMH;
- Climbing, as a prank, the scaffolding (for repairs) around the tower of the Museum of Natural History, opposite Keble, in the moonlight with Chris and Ray;

- Picnicking with Gayatri on the banks of the Cherwell, study books at hand;
- Adrian Darby gently suggesting that I invite him to tea in my rooms along with Suu Kyi;
- Ray holding forth on Proust's *Remembrance of Things Past*, with the improbable painting of a reclining semi-nude behind him … Improbable, because Ray was always the epitome of a young man of 'pure reason';
- Montek's witty epigram about Oxford, 'where you graduate in conversation';
- Robin Christopher zooming around town in his sky-blue Triumph Spitfire;
- Dancing with Gayatri at the Keble ball in the summer of 1967, our last in Oxford.

5

Harvard, Marriage and Pakistan

THE *QE I* OF the Cunard line had clearly seen better days, but was still an impressive ocean liner. It took the vessel only four or five days to cross the Atlantic to New York, carrying Robin, myself our cabin trunks and a few hundred other passengers. We amused ourselves watching movies, swimming, looking at seascapes and eating heartily. We also attempted a game in the ship's squash court, a special challenge in rolling seas. Robin had left behind a close girlfriend and I had temporarily parted from Gayatri. A hit romantic movie of the year was *Two for the Road*, with Albert Finney and Audrey Hepburn, which we watched more than once.

In Harvard, I was billeted in a graduate student dorm for first-year students, Richards Hall. It was a reasonably spacious room, split down the middle by a curtain, with another student on the other side. He was a serious and pleasant Midwesterner, Garry Watzke, but I certainly missed the privacy of my own room in the previous three years in England. Most of the students in the dorms were American, with a sprinkling of other nationalities, including Indian. The latter were mostly scholarship students, doing science (especially computer science) and engineering. In the neighbouring Child Hall were a couple of second-year economics graduate students, V. Sundar Rajan and Satish Singh, whom I befriended.

Another Indian student, who was in his final year completing his doctorate, Suresh Tendulkar, returned to the Delhi School of Economics faculty and went on to become the chairman of the National Statistical Commission and, later, of the Economic Advisory Council to PM Manmohan Singh in 2008. He did me the honour of asking me to look over the introductory chapter of his dissertation for its language and coherence.

Rajan, who became a good friend, was a delightful person who hailed from a village in Tamil Nadu, and had 'made it' on scholarships all the way through to his MStat at the Indian Statistical Institute (ISI) in Kolkata. His entire background was very different from mine (in anglicized elite schools in India and then, in England) and I learnt a great deal from this contrast. Satish was also different, a late-thirties IAS officer, with markedly Jana Sangh views, who had initially come on a Mason Fellowship to do a one-year master's programme in public administration (MPA) and stayed on to do an economics doctorate. Being strict vegetarians, both felt obliged to cook most of their meals on little stoves in their rooms, or otherwise restrict themselves to a diet of soup and grilled cheese sandwiches in the nearby Harkness Commons cafeteria, where most grad students (including me) ate. I also befriended two East Pakistani (later Bangladeshi) economics PhD students, who lived off campus, Abu Abdullah and Mohiuddin Alamgir. Through them I met with Chitrita Banerji from Kolkata, who was starting an MA in English. She still accuses me of self-consciously apprising her of my 'engaged' status in our very first conversation!

Just opposite my Richards Hall dorm was the Harvard Computer Centre, housing large mainframe IBM computers. That's where we went to run all our econometric regressions or to 'invert' our input–output matrices. We had to punch in our data on batches of computer cards, and the particular 'job' was handed over to those manning the centre. The results would come out after several hours on bulky sheets of computer paper for us to pore over. Small errors in punching in the data would lead to gibberish outputs, requiring repetition of the 'job', including re-punching of the data. Today, we probably carry more computing power in each of our smart phones than in the mainframes of those years! I should mention that gender sensitivity was not high in the university at that time. Otherwise, the 'Regression Analysis Programme for Economists' would not have been shortened to RAPE.

In many ways, life as a first-year grad student in Harvard was a sharp and challenging contrast to the pleasant and privileged life I had enjoyed at Oxford. Daily living conditions were more spartan in every respect. Far more importantly, the academic work requirements were much more rigorous and demanding. We had to do four courses each semester, with a final exam at the end of each, as well as term papers and mid-term exams, which were all taken into account for each course's grades. After two years (four semesters) of this, we then had to pass the qualifying 'General Examinations' before embarking on a thesis. If one flunked, one got an MA and said farewell to Harvard. Where Oxford had rewarded 'cleverness', Harvard was focused on encouraging and evaluating hard-learnt knowledge and skills. It required much more sustained application and work, and there was much less time for 'fun'!

The one thing Harvard shared with Oxford was a significant population of elderly and famous professors, who were well past their teaching prime. I had to suffer some of them, including: Wassily Leontief (the father of input–output analysis and a lovely person), with whom I did basic microeconomics; Gottfried Haberler (who still spoke with a thick Austrian accent and was hard of hearing), who taught international trade; and Robert Dorfman (of linear-programming fame), who taught basic macroeconomics without much zest.

Luckily for us, there were good teachers too, including the brilliant expositor Howard Raiffa, who taught statistical theory from a Bayesian viewpoint, Alexander Gerschenkron, who taught economic history, Zvi Griliches for econometrics, Al Musgrave for public finance, and Subramanian Swamy, who taught mathematics for economists as well as econometrics. Gus Papanek and Danny Schydlowsky ran an excellent set of case studies on practical development economics based on the Harvard Development Advisory Service's (precursor to the Harvard Institute for International Development) experience in Pakistan and Latin America. Later, when Martin Feldstein joined the faculty, I relearnt my macroeconomics by auditing his rewarding course on the subject. There were many other 'greats', like Simon Kuznets, Al Hirschman, Harvey Leibenstein and Richard Caves, some of whose lectures I audited selectively. Several of these teachers later won the Nobel Prize in Economics.

Swamy was a recently appointed assistant professor who had completed his PhD in two-and-a-half years under Simon Kuznets. He was also an articulate and persuasive advocate for India's acquisition of deterrent nuclear weapons capability. He was an excellent teacher and generally well regarded in the economics department. After I scored decent grades in my first semester, he lobbied successfully with the department to get my tuition costs waived—that is, to receive a tuition scholarship. That certainly lightened the burden on my parents.

Among the several American students in economics, I got to know well, and maintained close links beyond the Harvard years, were Robert Halvorsen, Mathew Lambrinides (from Greece) and Teresa Terminassian (from Italy) and their respective spouses

Gayatri and I wrote long and frequent letters to each other. Within a couple of months of my arrival in Cambridge, Massachusetts, we had decided to marry and went ahead with planning our lives accordingly. Gayatri firmly attributes this acceleration of intent on my part to the shock of adjusting to the rigours of graduate student life at Harvard. She applied for places and scholarships for graduate studies in English Literature at Harvard and other universities in the Boston area. Harvard did give her a place, but, in the absence of financial support, and given the failing health of her father, she had to decline. Luckily, she got full funding for a two-year MA, beginning September 1968, in Boston College. With that in hand, we and our families planned for a simple registry wedding in Bern in mid-June of 1968, after which Gayatri and I would proceed with my parents for a few weeks in Rio, before returning to Massachusetts.

During the Thanksgiving weekend of 1967, Robin Christopher and I drove in his Triumph to Orange, Connecticut, to spend a very pleasant weekend with the Bannerjis. Later, I returned to spend the relatively short Christmas/New Year break with them once again. They were to become my (and Gayatri's) family anchor in the US for the next four years.

Outside my small world in Harvard, the Vietnam War was raging, with the build-up of US armed forces there approaching half a million. Amongst my American peers, the war was not distant thunder. On the one hand, student protests were mounting daily, though not much on the Harvard campus. More disturbing for those on the campus was the very real prospect of being drafted to serve in 'Nam'. As one of them put it, he was having a hard time applying decision-tree analysis to his life choices when one of the branches led quickly to 'infinite loss'! We foreign students on F-1 and J-1 visas were comfortably cocooned from such grim prospects. Other major socio-political currents were also swirling around the country and its campuses, including the women's liberation movement and the ongoing struggle for racial equality. The latter had achieved major legislative and judicial successes in the mid-sixties on basic civil rights, voting rights and Lyndon Johnson's Great Society programmes. But the road ahead was still long, difficult and strewn with tragedy. Martin Luther King Jr. was shot dead in April 1968 and Senator Bobby Kennedy (by then a presidential contender) in June that year.

Daily life for us single graduate students from overseas was much less varied and enjoyable at Harvard than it had been in Oxford. When there was enough light, we might play some frisbee in the common area between the dorms before dinner. After dinner at Harkness, we often stayed behind in the common rooms to watch some TV before getting back to work. Iconic favourites of that time included *Star Trek* and Johnny Carson's show. I occasionally played squash with a couple of American friends in the courts behind the Law School. On weekends, we might see a movie in the Brattle Theatre or treat ourselves to a good Greek meal at the Acropolis restaurant on Massachusetts Avenue. Basically, the really 'fun' social life was lived by Harvard undergraduates in their well-heeled 'Houses' along Charles river.

I looked forward to a very different existence after June 1968. But first, I had to take care of housing. The main married graduate students' apartments in Harvard were located in a modern complex of three tall, sixteen-storeyed towers, called Peabody Terrace, along the Charles river. It was not easy to get an allocation there. Luckily, my old Oxford tutor Peter Oppenheimer's sister, Ruth (and her husband, Mike Sadler) had a lovely fourteenth-floor apartment they were soon to vacate as they were moving on. So, with their active help, I managed to get it allocated to Gayatri and me from September 1968.

In the second week of June, I was happily reunited with Gayatri in Bern. My parents arrived soon from Rio and I moved in with them at a hotel. Thanks to the service contacts of our fathers, the actual registration before an officer from the Indian Embassy was arranged in the Dasgupta flat in Giacomettistrasse. To add a little bit of ceremony, we went and bought a large, fat red candle on a tasteful candleholder, around which we could do our 'Saptapadi'. My father volunteered to be an amateur 'purohit' (from a Brahmo perspective), and read some appropriate passages. We were extremely fortunate that some of our closest family and friends made the effort to attend the occasion from England. They included Dada, Nandita, Mike Minton and his mother, Gwen. Monica was already there, and one of Gayatri's uncles had come all the way from India. I would meet Gayatri's elder brother (in the IFS, then posted in Mexico) and elder sister (who had just entered the IAS) only several years later. The marriage on 14 June went off smoothly, the key objective in such ceremonies, and was followed by a reception that evening in the Dasgupta home, catered by Movenpick.

A couple of days after the wedding, my parents, Gayatri and I flew to Rio via a stopover in London. During that stopover we made a trip to Rugby to meet with Ann and the three children, with the youngest, Manjula, a baby of four months, and the oldest, Lalita, two and a half. Gayatri well remembers how, when we arrived, a just-woken Lalita sat bolt upright and welcomed her into the family with a chirpy, 'Hello, Kakima'!

Looking back, it must have been big challenge for Gayatri to have left the comfort, love and familiarity of her own family home and adjust to not only a brand-new (and probably immature) husband but also his parents and their expectations, all in a completely new country with its incomprehensible Portuguese. There were also the expectations of Abdul, who took us aside in the kitchen and asked me what/how much did I get, referring, I suppose, to dowry. He was bitterly disappointed to learn that none had been asked for and none given. Given the overall circumstances, Gayatri managed pretty well.

The new environment had its charms though, with the Copacabana beach just around the corner. A couple of family car trips were made, as well as a few of our own in the immediate locality. I especially enjoyed showing Gayatri the great sights of Rio: The Sugar loaf, Corcovado mountain and the lovely beaches that continued south from Copacabana to Ipanema and beyond. The winding road up to the peak of Corcovado was very picturesque, with dense foliage in parts and streams rushing down the mountainside.

Our most ambitious family car trip was a 1200 km drive north-west to Brasilia, the brand-new capital of Brazil, with its amazing new public buildings created by the famous architect Oscar Niemeyer. The journey there and back was also very interesting, with stops in Belo Horizonte and the old mining town of Ouro Preto (Black Gold). I vividly recall the sculptures of the twelve prophets (no, *not* apostles) outside the church of St. Francis of Assisi near Ouro Preto, by the remarkable eighteenth-century sculptor Aleijhadino ('Little Cripple'). He suffered from a degenerative disease which had completely crippled his fingers by the time of these sculptures. So he had to tie a chisel and hammer to his hands to do the sculpting!

In Rio, there were special restaurants, called *churrascarias*, which specialized in barbecued high-quality meat, which was abundant in Brazil. We enjoyed a few good meals at those restaurants. We also picked up a few words of Portuguese, or rather, marvelled at how they mirrored words familiar from India, like *janelas* for windows, *fita* for tapes, *varanda* for veranda and several others. The Portuguese colonizers had brought these words to parts of India. Our most-used phrase remained '*Nao falo portugues*' ('don't speak Portuguese')!

Sometime in August, we flew to Boston to start our first household together. Our one-bedroom flat had a living–dining room, with the kitchen facilities hidden behind a curtain. But the glass wall and balcony at the other end made the place bright and light. The view of the meandering Charles river and of the adjacent Memorial Drive from the fourteenth floor of our tower was quite spectacular, especially at sunset. On the other side, from the bedroom window, we looked down on tennis courts and the road towards Harvard Square. We bought our furniture from the active second-hand market of departing graduate students. We were lucky to get a lot of it from one person at throwaway prices. Some of that furniture still survives in our household, including a large old desk bought separately for $25, on which I wrote my Harvard thesis!

Gayatri registered at Boston College, and began courses, having to commute some distance by subway and then bus, while I had to walk only about 200 yards to my classrooms in or near Harvard Yard.

Within a couple of months, we invested in a small second-hand Fiat (largely financed by a $500 gift from Baba), which gave us invaluable mobility to visit friends around the Cambridge area and make weekend trips quite often. As a couple, our social life improved dramatically compared to my previous year there. Most of our close friends were south Asians, including Rajan, Alamgir, Abu Abdullah, Chitrita (who would soon cross the Indo-Pak frontier matrimonially to wed Abu), Badal and Swapna Mukhopadhay from MIT (later, long-time professors at the Delhi School of Economics and the Institute of Economic Growth, respectively), and in Peabody Terrace itself, Madhav and Sulochana Gadgil, both doing PhDs in science. Madhav later became a leading ecologist in India, winning many awards, and campaigning actively for better policies with regard to ecology and environment. We also socialized with Swamy and his charming Parsi wife, Roxna (who was doing law at Harvard), and with Coomi (now Kapoor), Roxna's sister. Much of this interaction occurred over weekend evening meals, where those participating would bring a dish to an agreed home. Bachelors were typically expected to bring dessert. Swamy, like Satish Singh, held strong Jana Sangh views, which, together with his pro-Bomb views, often invited much debate and discussion with some other Indian graduate students. In small groups, I always found him quite logical and open to genuine debate. At his faculty apartment, he was generally charming and capable of disarming banter. Shouting matches were not his style.

By mid-October, the fall colours were ablaze all over New England and we made car trips to enjoy them. At least one of them, to the White Mountains in New Hampshire, included Isher Judge (later adding Ahluwalia!), who had recently joined the economics PhD programme at MIT.

Gayatri soon got into the rhythm of her course work at Boston College, though she did not enjoy the commutes or the near-daily chore of cooking an evening meal. Unlike other areas of housework, cooking was not a department I became proficient in. Soon after we got to Cambridge, we learnt of Baba's posting to Pakistan as High Commissioner. With retirement less than three years away, this would be his last posting, and a fitting cap to twelve continuous years as head of Indian missions in various countries. Geopolitics would make it a specially challenging assignment.

Our life in Cambridge was full and enjoyable. We worked hard at our respective academic studies, socialized with good friends and made short car trips to neighbouring scenic spots, like

Henry Thoreau's Walden Pond, Cape Cod and Plum Island. Other fun, low-budget activities included: Sitting on the grass by Charles river listening to the Boston 'Pops' (classical) in the summers, driving over to the nearby Howard Johnson's for large pistachio ice-cream cones (only 25 cents each), and occasional splurges at the Chinese Joyce Chen restaurant on Memorial Drive. One evening, we were mesmerized by Ike and Tina Turner belting out their hard rock numbers in the Harvard stadium as the scent of marijuana wafted in the breeze.

We became close to Abu Abdullah and Chitrita over time, and especially after they got married. They were both of a literary bent, and had wide-angle views of life and the world. We would often have meals together and dabble in new things, like attempting to contact the occult through an Ouija board! Other friends with whom we socialized included Teresa Terminassian (from Italy, and later the head of the fiscal affairs department at the IMF) and her Iraqi–Armenian husband, Viguen, (whom she had met on the boat from Europe), Mathew and Margaret Lambrinides, and Bob and Kathy Halvorsen.

Amartya Sen came as a visiting professor from Delhi in 1968-69 and we got to know him, his wife, Nabanita, and their two little daughters. He also guided me in a personalized 'reading course' on Indian economic history. Unsurprisingly, I found Amartya to be a very intelligent and charming person, given to a high degree of precision in his spoken words. Though he was a decade older, it was easy to get along with him. He was amused when I mentioned to him that the first publication of his I ever read, during my Oxford years, was in a well-known philosophical journal, *Mind*, where he explained philosopher Jean-Jacques Rousseau's concept of 'general will' through the logical paradigm of 'a prisoner's dilemma'. At that time, I had no idea he also did economics. We stayed in touch for many years thereafter until his winning the Nobel Prize in Economics in 1998 made him a celebrity for a billion Indians and less easy to get hold of in the normal course of life.

Perhaps surprisingly, Amartya and Swamy got along quite well during that year, with the former, more established, academic recognizing the latter's brilliance. Indeed, Amartya played a large part in persuading Swamy to return to India to teach as a professor in the Delhi School of Economics. However, when Swamy did return the following year and applied for the professorship, which he felt had been pretty much promised to him, the relevant committee did not select him. For the Delhi University to do this to a Harvard doctorate, with five years of teaching experience in the Harvard economics department was, on the face of it, quite unusual and puzzling. It is hard to avoid the inference that Swamy's openly expressed political views played a significant part in the Delhi University's decision. It would not have been surprising given the prevailing leftish politics of both the University and Indira Gandhi's government of that time. Swamy clearly felt betrayed and hard done by. He had to scramble for a job and found one as a professor in the Indian Institute of Technology, Delhi. Later, of course, he became something of 'stormy petrel' in Indian politics, with many ups and downs, including a stint as Commerce Minister in the Chandra Shekar government of 1990–91.

On longer breaks, like Thanksgiving and Christmas, Gayatri and I enjoyed the extraordinary warmth and hospitality of the Bannerji family in Orange, less than a three-hour drive away on the turnpike to New York. Sometime in the summer of 1969, with my 'Generals' safely behind me, they took us with them on a memorable camping trip in Acadia National Park, Maine. Gayatri and I had armed ourselves with a tiny two-person canvas tent for the occasion. As a testament to youthful resilience (and the quality of our waterproof sleeping bags), we slept through a late-night thundershower, even though it partially flooded our tent! The highest point in the park, the top of Cadillac Mountain, is the first place in continental USA to get the sun's rays every morning. It also offered wonderful views over the Acadia peninsula.

On the academic side, after my 'Generals', I began the painful search for a thesis topic. During the summer, I had done some research assistant work for Tom Weisskopf, an assistant professor, who had taught in the Delhi School of Economics for a year, as had Steve Marglin, recently appointed full professor.

As an aside, it was in Delhi in the late 1960s that Steve had won over Frederique, Tom's statuesque and beautiful wife, also an accomplished exponent of Odissi dance. Around the same time, Amartya Sen was winning over Eva, Mrinal Datta-Chaudhuri's Italian spouse. Obviously, the Delhi School of Economics was quite a happening place at the time!

Steve and Tom got me interested in the theory of cost-benefit analysis, and I did write a paper on the subject, which was soon accepted for publication by the Oxford Economic Papers. But I still floundered around for a full-fledged dissertation topic. As my adviser, Steve had taken the view that I was intelligent enough to find my way and should only come back to him when I had made more progress! Meantime, like most other post-Generals grad students, I was a teaching fellow in a couple of classes to make a living.

In this somewhat uncertain and uncomfortable situation, I was also considering a short-term career with the World Bank to gain 'practical experience' in development economics and build up some savings before returning to India. Montek had already joined in 1968, and I knew a couple of other Indians who had also got in through the Bank's 'Young Professional' (YP) programme. Sometime in 1970, I put in an application, and was duly called for interviews and offered a position. At $11,500 a year, it seemed like a king's ransom, especially given that we were then living on a budget of less than $3000 a year. I accepted, but with deferment of entry till October 1971 to allow me a chance to do a thesis. Luckily, I did find a viable topic soon and was into the empirical work by the summer of 1970.

Meanwhile, Gayatri was finishing her MA programme at Boston College in spring 1970, and was looking for a viable PhD programme. Tufts University in nearby Medford came through, asking for only one year of course work requirement (because of her MA) and then the thesis.

In our final year, we used to visit New York City with Rajan as host, after he began teaching at New York University. Rajan was perhaps the simplest and sincerest brainy person I knew. Some of his remarks, full of wisdom and humour, linger:

- 'We used to have ghosts in our village, but after electricity came they went away';
- 'Muslims were just like us, except they wore checked dhotis, while ours were plain';
- After his first IMF mission to Korea: 'Man, in Korea, when they say "hot dogs", they really mean hot dogs!'

He died prematurely of a heart attack in 2010 in Khartoum on a consulting assignment, after retiring from the IMF.

While in Cambridge, we had short visits from my parents and cousins, Nandita and Jayanta-da. Sometime in the fall of 1969, we were visited by Gayatri's father, making a detour on some official trip to Washington. His health was clearly failing, from his kidney ailments, but he remained cheerful and forward-looking. Both her parents visited us one more time, in 1970. Her father was now visibly frail. A few months later, in early December 1970, he passed away in Bern at the tragically young age of fifty-nine. We had made plans to visit my parents in Islamabad over the winter break, which we quickly adjusted. I went on to Islamabad, while Gayatri first flew to Bern to be with her mother and siblings, and then joined us later in Pakistan.

The visit to Islamabad that winter of 1970–71 was fascinating. The political atmosphere was tense, with the December general elections having led to Mujibur Rahman's Awami League sweeping nearly all the seats in the East Bengal Provincial Assembly and winning an absolute majority in the National Assembly. Neither President Yahya Khan nor the dominant party in West Pakistan, the Pakistan People's Party, led by Zulfikar Bhutto, had any intention of handing over power to the Awami League. A deadlock followed, which was to end tragically in March 1971, with the massacres by the Pakistan Army in Dhaka.

In December–January, daily life for Indian High Commission officers was still relatively normal. So we had a very pleasant visit. Our house (the High Commissioner's residence) was situated on the perimeter of Islamabad, just below some hills. From our balcony we could see retired General Ayub Khan taking his evening walk down our road. Our daily life sometimes included evening bridge with mission officers, including Naresh Dayal (who later became our High Commissioner to London) and his charming wife, Romola, and the IPS officer B.L. Joshi (who later became governor of Uttar Pradesh). We had our signature Sunday family picnic outings, invariably followed by a little white Volkswagen with ISI (Pak intelligence) or police operatives, to whom we occasionally sent across some of our parathas. Among our picnic destinations was a fascinating day visit to Takshila.

As for visitors, Abu Abdullah, who was visiting his brother and family in Islamabad, dropped in to see us a couple of times. More improbably, but very pleasantly, Mike Minton stayed a few days with us as part of a longish adventure trip to the subcontinent, having just finished his arduous medical training. It was lovely to see Mike again and good to see how comfortable and affectionate he was with my parents and Gayatri ... and vice versa.

Partly for work and partly for the experience, Baba had arranged to end our Islamabad visit with a 700-km drive to Delhi via Lahore and Ferozepur. So, early one January morning, we drove to Lahore, arriving in time for lunch. It was striking that there were very few women on the streets, and those few were burkha-clad. In the restaurant where we ate lunch, Ma and Gayatri were the only ladies. The contrast with Delhi, which we reached the next evening, was stark. After lunch in Lahore, we found time to visit the great Badshahi mosque built by Aurangzeb, before proceeding to Ferozepur after crossing the border. The next day, we drove to Delhi, stopping for a very pleasant lunch at Panipat (the site of two great battles in Indian history) at the home of Vasundhara, cradling her firstborn, Uday, in her arms, and her husband, Deepak Nath, who ran a family business in textiles. By evening, we were in Delhi—after nine years for me! We spent a few days in Delhi staying at the Ministry of External Affairs hostel. Baba had work, but the rest of us caught up with all the old friends we could find. All too soon it was time to go West again, America for Gayatri and me, and back to Islamabad for my parents.

The next five months till June proved to be a very tense and difficult period for my parents and all the members of Indian missions in Pakistan. The end of January saw the hijack of an Indian Airlines Fokker plane by Kashmiri militants, who diverted the flight to Lahore and torched the plane, after passengers and crew had been deboarded by Pakistani authorities. This led to much bad blood on both sides, with authorities in Islamabad encouraging regular demonstrations against (and some break-ins of) Indian diplomatic offices and residences of diplomatic staff, including the High Commissioner. Tensions waxed and waned, and flared up after the 25 March onslaught by the Pakistan Army on civilians in Dhaka. This prolonged period of daily tension for Indian mission members triggered serious asthma attacks for Ma, followed by the administration of unduly high dosages of steroids. Her health never fully recovered after that.

Back in Massachusetts, I plunged into my thesis work, while Gayatri continued with her first year at Tufts, which she thoroughly enjoyed, making lasting friends, notably Linda Bamber, who later became a leading professor of English in Tufts for many years.

Meanwhile, every year we would have a few young elite civil servants from India and Pakistan—mostly in their mid-thirties— for the one-year Harvard Masters in Public Administration degree under the aegis of the Edward Mason fellowship programme. A few, like Satish Singh, would manage to stay on for a PhD. A previous year's batch had included T.N. Seshan, who became a well-known Election Commissioner of India in later years. In 1970–71, we had a particularly friendly crop from India, including Jyotish Bhattacharya and wife, Ratna (whose family was well-known to Gayatri), and Virendra and Indira Prakash. They were billeted in Peabody Terrace, and became good and lasting friends Similarly, we had got to know a few Pakistani mid-career civil servants (and their wives), doing their PhDs in economics, including Jawaid and Shaida Azfar, Khalid and Shareen Ikram, and Shahid Burki (later Acting Finance Minister of Pakistan for a few months in 1996–97) and Jahanara. On Western university campuses, in those years, it was quite common for Indian and Pakistani students to fraternize. Jawaid and Khalid were senior economists in the Pakistan Planning Commission, while Shahid was a mid-level officer in the powerful Civil Service of Pakistan. Jawaid died of an untimely heart attack a few years later, while the other two ended up in the World Bank. As 1971 unfolded, our friendly relations with them were increasingly tested by the momentous events in the subcontinent.

The Pakistani president, General Yahya Khan, continued to stonewall the convening of the freshly elected National Assembly with its Awami League majority. The political temperature in East Pakistan rose inexorably, with the League and its multitude of followers calling increasingly for autonomy from West Pakistan. The Pakistan government and army remained obdurate, and on 25 March 1971, the army, led by General Tikka Khan, began a programme of systematic massacres in Dhaka to cow the local population into toeing their line, and to eliminate the leadership of the Awami League and the sizeable Hindu minority in Dhaka. The civil war (with only one side armed, initially) had begun. Tikka Khan continued to wage a brutal campaign across East Bengal for the next eight months, leading to over a million civilian casualties among East Bengalis. The geopolitics of Nixon–Kissinger's historic opening up of diplomatic relations with China in 1971 via the good offices of their (and China's) ally, the Pakistan government, ensured that the US administration turned a blind eye (and worse) to the mass atrocities in East Pakistan, despite strong opposition to such policies from the US Congress, the international press, the American Consulate in Dhaka and the weight of opinion in Western democracies.

At a personal level, the massacres of March (and the ensuing months) in East Bengal weighed heavily on us, on our East Pakistani friends like Alamgir and Abdullah, and many knowledgeable faculty and students in Harvard, including my thesis adviser (and friend of Amartya Sen), professor Stephen Marglin. It was he who suggested that Alamgir and I quickly draft a short briefing paper on the economic and political background to the crisis, to which he would add policy recommendations for the US government and then coordinate signatures of a couple of respected development scholars–cum–policy–practitioners at Harvard.

Alamgir and I dropped everything else and worked through the next four days to produce a ten-page briefing paper entitled 'Conflict in East Pakistan: Background and Prospects'. The draft summarized the long history of economic and political discrimination suffered by the more populous East Pakistan at the hands of the Pakistani federal government, heavily dominated, at all levels, by West Pakistani politicians, officials and army brass. It sketched the recent political events, the electorally demonstrated legitimacy of East Bengal's political aspirations and the utterly unjustifiable massacres by the West Pakistan Army. It clearly stated, 'The emergence of an independent Bangladesh appears to be inevitable now. What remains in question is how much blood will flow before it occurs.'

Marglin added a brief final section on the international implications of an independent Bangladesh, which argued that this would be in line with long-run US interests, and ended with a call for cessation of US military and economic aid to the Pakistan government.

Marglin's bigger contribution to the paper was in mobilizing the signatures of respected Harvard faculty members—something that Alamgir and I could never have done on our own. The big win was to get Professor Edward Mason to sign on. Mason, over seventy years old then, was a highly respected figure in both Harvard and US government circles. At Harvard, he was the pillar of development/public administration establishment. A tenured professor since 1936, he had been the dean of the Graduate School of Public Administration (later renamed as the Kennedy School of Government) for eleven years and founder (in 1963) of the Harvard Development Advisory Service (later renamed as the Harvard Institute of International Development). Many of India's best IAS officers have benefitted from the one-year, mid-career Masters in Public Administration Edward S. Mason Programme, which has a long and distinguished track record. Finally, he had a long history of advisory involvement with Pakistan, including in helping to draft their first five-year plan. His credibility in American development policy circles was unmatched.

The other key signatory (other than Marglin himself) was professor Robert Dorfman, who was a coauthor with the famous Paul Samuelson of a well-known graduate textbook on a branch of mathematical economics called linear programming. He too had a long advisory involvement with Pakistan.

The paper was signed by all three Harvard professors on 1 April 1971, and dispatched with a cover letter from Mason to prominent US Senators and Congressmen, and to heads of key US and international development agencies, including McNamara's World Bank and the Asian Development Bank. Some weeks later, as US aid policy to Pakistan and the continuing massacres in East Bengal became important issues in the US Congress, the paper was read into the Congressional record by a sympathetic Congressman. I have been told that amongst those then involved in the cause of an independent Bangladesh, the paper gained considerable currency, if not fame. A year or so after the liberation of Dhaka by the Indian Army and the Mukti Bahini in December 1971, the paper was included in a volume, *Bangladesh Documents*, published by our Ministry of External Affairs. Needless to say, the names of Alamgir and myself do not figure anywhere. And for good reason: Mentioning our names, even as 'research assistants', could have compromised its effectiveness.

Of course, none of this had the slightest impact on the unshakable support of Nixon and Kissinger for the Pakistan military government, especially as they pursued their secret overtures to China through covert channels. Their goals in the subcontinent were thwarted, not by popular opinion or advocacy briefs, but by Indira Gandhi's steely resolve, the rapidly concluded

Indo-Soviet friendship treaty, the tenacity of East Bengalis and the Indian Army's brilliant two-week campaign in December 1971, which ensured the liberation of Bangladesh before the American Seventh Fleet Task Force led by the nuclear carrier USS Enterprise could inflict any damage.

Still, as a young graduate student, it was good to have been in touching distance of the truly epochal events in the Indian subcontinent. Kissinger's 'international basket case' now has an average income 40 per cent higher than Pakistan's and approximately equal to India's.

In June 1971, my father's retirement date came up. With India giving moral and material support to the Bangladeshi freedom movement, relations between the governments of India and Pakistan had plummeted. In those circumstances, there was no point extending his tenure. So he retired formally, and my parents drove home to Delhi in their Mercedes. High Commissioner–level relations between the countries were not renewed for many months. After some days of debriefing in Delhi, Baba and Ma shifted to Ma's flat on Darga Road, Kolkata, to start their retired life. Within months, Baba was appointed vigilance commissioner for West Bengal, a quasi-judicial position to review corruption charges against senior public servants. The following year, he was appointed as central vigilance commissioner (CVC) for the Government of India and served in that capacity for the next five years. During that period, the family was allotted a spacious Lutyens bungalow in Teen Murti Marg, where we visited them from the US several times.

After the initial weeks of the Bangladesh crisis, I resumed serious work on my thesis, conscious that I had to submit it before leaving for Washington DC and the World Bank at the beginning of October. Gayatri helped enormously by typing the entire document on her electric Smith Corona; she was a proficient typist, while I was totally inept. I was able to hand it in by mid-September. Gayatri also had to focus on her second and last semester of her course work at Tufts, and begin to think seriously about her chosen doctoral dissertation topic, 'Forms and Uses of Autobiography'.

As the summer of 1971 drew to a close, we also had to make plans for our life in Washington DC. In late August, Gayatri made a visit to look for an apartment for us. She was able to persuade the personnel department of the Bank to organize a chauffeur-driven car for one day; she drove around the city and inspected several two-bedroom apartments within striking distance of the Bank. She chose one at Park Adams, 2000 Adams Street (off Lee Highway) in Arlington, Virginia, about a mile beyond the rather striking Key Bridge over the Potomac, the river which separated Virginia from DC. The rent was $220 a month. She signed the lease and made a deposit. It was an expertly accomplished mission!

6

World Bank: The First Six Years

ON FRIDAY, 1 OCTOBER 1971, Gayatri and I drove down from the Boston area to Washington DC (about 450 miles), with as much of our belongings as we could stuff into our little Austin America (obtained a year before by swapping our Fiat and some dollars for it), with the rest on the way via a moving company. We drove straight to our unfurnished apartment in Park Adams and unloaded ourselves into our home for the next two years. Over the weekend, in between the chores of settling in, we attended the wedding of Montek and Isher in a judge's chamber. Isher had moved to Washington a couple of years before, joined the IMF and met with Montek. The judge kept mispronouncing the surname as 'Abluwalia', giving birth to the practice, amongst those present, of sometimes referring to the young couple affectionately as 'the Ablus', perhaps unbeknownst to them. On Monday, 4 October, I joined the World Bank as a Young Professional (YP), while Gayatri bore the brunt of the initial settling-in tasks.

At that time, the YP programme required new recruits to serve two or three six-month assignments in different parts of the Bank before taking up his/her initial posting as a regular professional in a particular department or division. Since 1968, when Robert McNamara took over as its president, the institution had been growing fast and already numbered 1500–2000 professionals. So it was very important to have YP assignments compatible with one's skill set, followed by a good placement thereafter. I was lucky to get allotted to the Domestic Finance Division (DFD, later renamed as the Public Economics Division) in one of the two economics departments then extant. It was headed by a charismatic middle-aged Englishman, Stanley Please, who turned out to be the finest mentor I ever had. He valued and nurtured the best in everyone and had a talent for attracting high-quality young economists. He was also a marvellous human being. In those first six months I was there, Montek was promoted to deputy division chief, Martin Wolf (later the globally renowned *Financial Times* columnist and author) joined, as did D.C. Rao (later to head the Bank's first flagship World Development Report in 1978).

Members of the division did two main things: Write analytical papers on resource mobilization, fiscal and monetary issues, and provide 'operational support' on these topics to the regional/area departments (the Bank's engine room) on economic, sectoral and project missions/studies. My first mission, for six weeks, would be to Sudan in November–December as a member of an economic mission. Before I embarked on that trip, I was called to Harvard to defend my thesis. I took Gayatri along. I defended it well enough and earned my Harvard PhD, with the degree certificate issued the following year. After the thesis defence, Steve Marglin, my thesis adviser, took us out to a pleasant lunch in Harvard Square.

On the way to Khartoum, I stopped over for two days in London, staying at the Cavendish Hotel, off Piccadilly, near Fortnum and Mason. It was to be my preferred stopover 'home' (at the Bank's expense) in London for the next eleven years. I used the time to renew contacts with my old English friends, including Mike. Then, it was off to Khartoum on a BA flight, flying first class (Bank entitlement then); I was easily the youngest passenger in that section. At a brief halt at the airport in Rome, I met Gayatri's brother, Shekhar, and his wife, Devika (aka Twinky), who had come to see me, for the first time. As the plane flew south over Egypt and I looked down from the window, I could see the thin black line of the Nile with narrow strips of green on either side, and the desert stretching endlessly beyond. That one look brought home the critical importance of the Nile for the populations and economies of Egypt and Sudan.

Bank missions were very different then compared with what they became in later decades: They were long, often of four to six weeks' duration; at one's destination, one was completely cut off from home except via exorbitantly priced long-distance calls, which one almost never made; and one's tools of the trade were a pen, notebook, hand-held calculator, briefcase and a little bag of Bank-issued medication, including anti-malaria and sleeping pills. Laptops, tablets and mobiles were in the unimagined future, as were concerns about the side-effects of various pills. Other mission members were one's main social group and, as a young staffer, one had no choice over those. Most of one's working day was spent in meetings with officials of the government or of parastatal entities. We often wasted their time unduly. Off-duty time was spent mostly on meals with mission members and, occasionally, with the local staff of UN-family agencies, and some sightseeing. I recall singing a couple of Bangla songs 'for my supper' one evening at a Bengali UN staffer's home! On return to headquarters, you had to write a report on your area of responsibility and give it to the mission chief for integration into the overall mission report.

What made these missions interesting were the country/city one was visiting (often for the first time), the preoccupations and concerns of the local officials and analysts, and, of course, the new cultures one encountered. Sometimes, one got to know and learn from one's mission colleagues in a way one may never have back in Washington. What I recall from my Sudan mission were: The magnificent confluence (Mogran) of the White and Blue Niles; the ubiquitous *phool*, or peanuts, which featured in every meal; the open-air cinemas; the rail journey to Atbara, north-east towards Port Sudan on the Red Sea; and the overnight trip to the amazing colonial-era Gezira irrigation scheme (one of the largest in the world), with cotton as the main crop, where Stanley Please joined on a passing visit.

Back in South Asia, the Indian Army was closing in on Dhaka towards the end of the two-week December 1971 Indo-Pakistan war over Bangladesh. Stanley commented: 'India and Pakistan need another war like I need a hole in my head.' I kept my counsel. When news came of the liberation of Dhaka by the Indian Army and the Bangladeshi Mukti Bahini, I was elated.

It was good to be home after such a long trip away, especially as Gayatri's driving skills were still a little rudimentary. Indeed, we had arranged for Rajan to come down from New York and 'babysit' her for some of that time. Shortly thereafter, Gayatri's mother (widowed a year ago) and her aunt came over for a few months, renting a separate apartment in the same building. After I bought a new Volvo, my mother-in-law took to driving around in our little Austin quite confidently. I remember Gayatri's aunt (who had never been outside of Kolkata before) asking with a puzzled look out of the window: 'Where are all the people?'! She was also dazzled by the cornucopia of goods in the supermarkets and asked in wonder, 'You mean you can buy as much milk as you want any time?' Milk was then rationed in Kolkata. Monica also came and stayed with us for some time while her mother was there.

A new home in a new city meant making new friends. A few we had known before. For example, we spent more time with Montek and Isher, and Teresa (who had joined the IMF) and Viguen. Some of my new colleagues at the Bank soon became good friends, including Martin and Alison Wolf, DC and Gita Rao, Armeane and Mary Choksi, and Ram and Marie Chopra. Amongst the young IMF staff (and their spouses), we soon befriended Anupam and Ranu Basu, Gopal and Radhika Yadav, and Dhruba and Roberta Gupta. Over weekends, we would typically dine with one or more of these friends, sometimes explore Washington's magnificent museum system, or go for a picnic on the Skyline Drive in the Shenandoah Hills. We also came to know some of the India-based staff in these multilateral institutions, like the Indian executive director in the Bank, Dr Samar Sen (whose two boys, Abhijit and Pronab, also grew up to be prominent economists in India) and his technical assistant, Arvind Pande (many years later, he became the chairman and managing director of the Steel Authority of India), and his wife, Mrinal (aka Minu, later a well-known editor, writer and journalist in India). The last couple lived close to us, and the first time we dropped in to see them, their baby Rohini was bright-eyed in the crib. She has now been a professor of economics at Harvard and Yale for many years!

Each New Year's Eve, the Bank and the Fund organized a joint dinner-dance party for their staff. We went regularly in the early years if we were in town and threw ourselves around with energy, if not grace. One of those years, Gayatri won a prize for her dancing—a beautifully wrapped but modest Sharp calculator!

After my first six months at the Bank, I did my second stint of YP rotation with the East Africa area/programme department.

Soon, in spring 1972, I had to go on my second Bank mission, to Zambia. Once again it involved stopovers in London, allowing me to catch up with Mike, and Dada and family. They had moved down from Newcastle upon Tyne in the north to Barlestone in Leicestershire. My visits with them, usually at least once a year, were typically short but sweet. Each time, the three children were a little older and Gayatri guided me on what gifts would be appropriate.

The mission to Lusaka was a little shorter—four weeks. The highlights included the incredible Victoria Falls in Livingstone and going 4000 feet down a mineshaft in the Mufulira copper mine, which produced 4 per cent of the world's copper. The metal then accounted for over 90 per cent of Zambia's exports. At a sumptuous dinner with the mine management, I noted our hosts were all white, while the actual miners had been all black. I also met up with Bob Liebenthal and his Zambian wife, Ompie, in Lusaka. Bob was working at the Bank of Zambia. He had been Montek's college mate at Magdalen College in Oxford and in the subsequent BPhil programme. We soon became friends, a friendship that has lasted many years. In 2011, on a conference trip to South Africa, Gayatri and I made a detour to meet up with them in Livingstone (they had retired to Lusaka after a long World Bank career).

An unusual highlight of my visit to Lusaka was being in the same lift in the Intercontinental Hotel (where we were staying) as two tall, handsome men: Sidney Poitier and Harry Belafonte! They were there to promote their new maverick 'western' film, *Buck and the Preacher*, set in post-Civil War southern United States. I saw it in Lusaka amidst the roaring applause from the local audience as our two heroes fought and beat the redneck opposition. Another little anecdote: Our mission, led by an avuncular Dutchman, Willem Maane, included an elderly Englishman and a young German. It transpired that during WWII, the latter was often cowering as a small child in the rubble of Berlin, while the former was piloting British bombers above!

Sometime in 1972, Jayati Mitra and Gautam Datta (he of the Western Court in 1949; see chapter 1) rented an apartment in Park Adams, having joined the World Bank from Columbia University, where they were both enrolled in the PhD programme. Although they were known to my parents (through the ICS brotherhood), it was only in Park Adams that our friendship really bloomed, and has continued to this day. They became Datta-Mitras after marriage.

In the autumn of 1972, after finishing my two YP rotations, I joined back in the DFD as a full-fledged staff member. Stanley was soon promoted as chief economist for East Africa. His successor, Oktay Yenal from Turkey, was also a fine person. Soon after I joined, I was asked to go on a major economic mission, which was tasked with writing a new breed of 'Basic Economic Reports' on Yugoslavia. The mission was led by the excellent Vinod Dubey, a former professor at Allahabad University, and had another seven or eight of us from different disciplines. It was to be an intellectually challenging exercise, given the country's transition to a quasi-market economy with the goal of worker-managed firms, against a political backdrop of strong autonomy-seeking forces in the various major provinces/nationalities: Serbia, Croatia, Bosnia, Macedonia, Montenegro and Slovenia, among them. We arranged for Gayatri to take a cheap flight to Frankfurt and thence the Orient Express train to Belgrade, so we could spend much of the mission time together. It was a wonderful experience to travel around all the provincial capitals (Belgrade, Zagreb, Ljubljana, Sarajevo, Skopje, and so on), enjoying the enormous variety of sights, cuisines and cultures. The Balkan tragedies of the 1990s were still twenty years away.

At one point, I asked our helpful translator-cum-liaison officer about the restaurant chain called PECTOPAH, which seemed to be everywhere. She giggled and informed us that in the Cyrillic script that simply meant 'RESTORAN' in the Latin script! In Belgrade we stayed at the Metropole Hotel, with its marvellous palachinka crepes for dessert. It was rumoured that its top floor was devoted to a 'worker-managed enterprise' of the world's oldest profession. One of our bachelor mission members confirmed that! I also had the chance to attend a Dizzy Gillespie jazz event in Belgrade one evening.

In Ljubljana, the capital of the richest province, Slovenia, we made contact with a young economist, Peter Miovic, in its premier research institute. Peter had been Gayatri's classmate in Cathedral School in Mumbai in 1959, when his father was working as an engineer in India for a while (this was not unusual then, given the close bonds between Nehru and Marshal Tito). Around 1980, he joined the World Bank, where, many years later, he met and married Monica. He has been my brother-in-law for at least fifteen years now!

This may strain credulity, but after all that travelling and exploring, we did write a pretty good report, which was published by the Johns Hopkins Press after approval from Marshal Tito's government. I was responsible for the chapter on monetary and fiscal issues.

In January–February of 1973, we took our first home leave. This was a valuable benefit given by the Bank to its regular non-US employees. It allowed us to travel business class to India once every two years, including two nights of paid stopovers each way. We made that first home leave into a round-the-world trip, first stopping in England to meet with Dada and family, and Mike and his new bride, Liz, then a couple of nights in Rome, followed by a few days in Egypt. Aside from the usual sights of Cairo (including the pyramids of Giza, the Sphinx and the National Museum), we did a detour by air to the old capital, Luxor, to see the tombs in the Valley of the Kings (and Queens), and the great temples of Hatshepsut and Karnak. I still vividly recall the utterly gripping sound and light show one evening at Karnak, with recorded voice commentary by Richard Burton.

In India, we stayed a while with Jayanta-da and family in Mumbai (seeing some hit movies like *Koshish* and *Amar Akbar Anthony* and having bhel on Juhu beach), and spent a couple of days with Nandita and her newly-wed IAS husband Smarajit (aka Sanu) Ray in Sangareddy, Andhra, before joining my parents in Delhi to spend the bulk of our leave with them and catch up with some old friends, including some from Oxford. We, including my parents, then proceeded together to Calcutta, where we split our time between Darga Road and Swinhoe Street, where Gayatri's Ma had her newly built house. We also made a short trip to Cooch Behar to meet with Gayatri's elder sister, Krishna (aka Kajal), then sub-divisional magistrate (SDM) there, and her husband, Nirmal Jhala, SDM in neighbouring Jalpaiguri. I recall how the Dakota flight from Kolkata almost landed at the gate to Kajal's house!

Then it was time to return to the US, but we did stop in Japan to see beautiful Kyoto, before proceeding to Honolulu in Hawaii, and then Seattle to go snowshoeing in the hills with Bob and Kathy Halvorsen (Bob had joined the University of Washington there), before going home to Virginia. Where did we get the energy for all this, I now wonder!

Back in the Washington area, Richard Nixon had begun his second term as president, with Henry Kissinger as secretary of state. The Paris Peace Accords between the US and North Vietnam had been signed after the brutal bombing of Hanoi and Haiphong by American B-52s over Christmas 1972 (though peace only came two years later, when North Vietnamese tanks rolled into the presidential palace in Saigon in spring 1975). The Watergate break-in at the Democratic headquarters had happened, and the unravelling of the Nixon presidency had begun.

In the spring and autumn of 1973, I was roped in for 'operational support' to a Basic Economic Report exercise for the Commonwealth Caribbean nations. It involved two separate trips to the Caribbean countries, both of which were dismissed by envious colleagues as 'five-star tourism'. They were not far wrong! The countries consisted of the 'big four' of Guyana (the only non-island), Trinidad and Tobago, Jamaica and Barbados, and several little, but gorgeous, ones like St Lucia and Antigua (of cricketer Vivian Richards fame). I had the indubitable pleasure of visiting all of these six nations for 'work'. Guyana and Trinidad had very sizeable communities of Indian-origin people, which made them particularly interesting for me. The relationship between blacks and browns was somewhat toxic in Guyana, which had a slim, but disputed Indian-origin majority; however, the political and police powers were held by blacks. My official Indian-origin counterpart had had his skull cracked open in racial riots a couple of years previously!

On one of these trips, our team, led by the jovial Sidney Chernick, met with Sir W. Arthur Lewis (from St Lucia), whose famous 1954 paper, 'Economic Development with Unlimited Supplies of Labour', and other works won him the 1979 Nobel Prize for Economics. I still remember him saying, on the subject of political constraints to good economic policies, 'There is no law which guarantees that these islands will prosper if they cannot overcome political constraints and follow the right economic polices', or words to this effect. I recall that remark whenever someone says solemnly that one or other sensible economic policy cannot be implemented somewhere because of political obstacles. There is no law which says any nation will prosper ... if it cannot implement good economic policies, for whatever reason. In my view, China's miracle economic progress over the last forty years can be mostly explained by its sustained adherence to the Lewis model of development. Correspondingly, India's relative poverty was largely due to our failure to make better use of our most abundant resource, unskilled labour.

During our two years at Park Adams, Gayatri was trying to work on her dissertation, but was often distracted by household chores, visiting family and friends, and our active social life. She was also chafing at her new primary identity as housewife. She applied to a couple of local universities for teaching positions and was called for day-long interviews by the English department of George Mason University (GMU). They were so impressed by her composure and confidence, especially when she sought time out for a thirty-minute nap after lunch, that they readily offered her a position as assistant professor. She promptly accepted and thoroughly enjoyed that role for the next nine years (beginning in fall 1973), teaching a range of courses, including Indian literature, especially the Mahabharata in translation, which students loved. Thus, she was far more engaged with real American life through her daily contact with colleagues and students than I ever was as a World Bank employee.

Since GMU was in Fairfax, Virginia, some 20-plus miles from the World Bank, we had to move house for her to be nearer her place of work. We chose and bought, with a mortgage loan from the Bank–Fund Credit Union, a small townhouse in a new development called Pinecrest Heights in Annandale, midway between our two places of work. Importantly, given her limited driving skills, her journey to GMU entailed a straight drive for 10 miles and then one left turn in Fairfax. Despite this, she had a couple of minor road accidents during those years, including one with a stationary school bus! So, from September 1973 to

June 1982 (and again, from December 1990 to March 1993) 4526, Airlie Way, Annandale, Virginia, was our home.

With our home in Virginia, we spent more time with our 'Virginian' friends, Anupam–Ranu, Gopal–Radhika and Dhruba–Roberta. Anupam and Ranu had met in Presidency College, Calcutta, and gone on to do their doctorates in Stanford and London, respectively. Gopal (from Allahabad) and Radhika (from Pune) had met during their respective graduate studies in Canada, while Dhruba (from Delhi) and Roberta (from Wales) had met and married in England. At some point during those early years, one of us coined the label 'hard core' to refer to this group. Over the next decade and much beyond, we shared many joys and some sorrows together. We have remained in fairly close touch for the last forty years, even after Gayatri and I moved back to India in 1982.

One of the best compliments I ever received from a young lady was in the late 1970s, from little three-year-old Alo, Anupam and Ranu's daughter. We had all tucked into the special fruit tarts and cappuccino in the La Ruche café in tony Georgetown, and had got up to disperse to our respective homes. In those days, I was a fairly fun-seeking youngster. So Alo put her little hand in mine and firmly squeaked, 'I am going with him!'

During this period, Sid and Ann Bannerji would sometimes drive in from Orange to visit us as a southern base for their marketing of Indian handicrafts, under a new venture, 'International Rovers', that Sid had started. It was our chance to reciprocate, in very small measure, the boundless hospitality and affection they and their three children had showered on us and our friends during our student years in Massachusetts.

Sometime in the early 1970s, Mrinal Datta-Chaudhuri, a well-known professor at Delhi School of Economics, whom I had met before in Delhi, came to the Bank as a consultant for a few months. At a lunch at our house, he met with Monica, who was visiting. A couple of years later, when she was doing the field work for her social anthropology doctorate from LSE, they met again in Delhi and became close, finally getting married in 1975.

In the latter half of 1974, Stanley Please, by then director of the East Africa programme department, arranged for me to move to his front office, with an initial brief of focusing on Tanzania. The charismatic Julius Nyerere was its long-time president and a darling of the Scandinavian aid community, though his experiments with the 'ujamaa' brand of socialistic rural development was beginning to run into economic performance issues, especially after the oil price shock of 1973–74. My senior colleague Steve O'Brien and I (and research assistant Sally Chan) flew to Dar es Salaam to lay the groundwork for a World Bank/IDA (International Development Association) programme credit to help the country cope with surging oil prices. We had useful meetings with our counterparts in various ministries and the central bank, and I began to know and like the place. Most of my next three years of economic work would be on Tanzania, culminating in an eight-volume Basic Economic Report exercise I led in 1976–77.

It was on that initial mission that we met Gene and Kathryn Tidrick. Gene was working in the planning department as part of a Harvard-funded technical assistance programme, and Kathy was writing her first book, *Heart Beguiling Araby*. They were to move to the World Bank in Washington DC a year or so later, and become good and lasting friends with Gayatri and me. We also paid a visit to the University of Dar es Salaam, and met with the Ugandan-born professor Mehmood Mamdani, whom Gayatri and I knew from Fletcher and Harvard. Some years later, he was to marry the well-known film director Mira Nair. During that visit, I had my first exposure to an East African game park, Mikumi, to which Steve, Sally and I drove one weekend, and had some adventures, including having our self-driven car stuck in a gully as the sun set, in an area frequented by elephants and lions. We got out before they got us!

Later that year, my parents came to spend a few weeks with us in Annandale. It was good to have them with us and show them the sights around town, and introduce them to our friends. At the same time, as was often the case with visiting parents in American suburbs, our full-time jobs meant they were often confined to our small house with plenty of time on their hands. One day, when returning from a walk in the nearby wood, Ma tripped and fell. She had had a problem in one leg resulting from a whiplash injury in a car crash in Canada ten years back, but after this fall she had to always use a stick or a crutch.

That autumn, cousin Atashi, who had settled in Minneapolis as a trained social worker joined us, along with her friend Bithi, for an enjoyable ten-day car trip through the Carolinas and Georgia to Florida in our red Dodge Dart ('Big Red', as we called it, had replaced our 'little red' Austin). The only time I had a faint idea of what it was like to be black in America was when, with sirens wailing, I was hauled up for speeding by a heavily armed cop in his black-and-white police cruiser for speeding outside Savannah, Georgia. My apprehensions drained away when he returned my driving licence with a verbal warning. We enjoyed picking bagfuls of melons and grapefruit in the Florida orchards, doing the popular rides in Disney World, Orlando, picking seashells in Sanibel Island and driving on the beach in Daytona.

Back in Annandale, Gayatri was thoroughly enjoying her teaching at GMU alongside good, interesting colleagues and with genuinely interested students, including older ones returning for a degree. Quite a few were Vietnam veterans, especially as the US army was being downsized as the war drew to a close. One day, she was startled to see a two-star general in full-service uniform in the front row of her class! He was dressed for an official meeting after the lecture. A growing number of her students were Vietnamese immigrants, sometimes starting courses with broken English and ending them with straight A grades, driven by the necessity to succeed and survive. One, a 'boat people' refugee with no English training, went on to earn a Harvard doctorate in the subject.

Early in 1975, I was seconded to the International Labour Office (ILO) for a few weeks to be a member of their special employment mission to Sudan. Since the early 1970s, the ILO had been producing a series of trademark red-cover employment reports/books on countries, especially in East Africa. This fifteen-person mission was led by Just Faaland, head of the Christian Michelsen Institute in Bergen, Norway, and included some interesting members, such as Ashok Mitra, former chief economic adviser in India, who later became finance minister of West Bengal, Marg Blaug, the well-known economic historian from London, and Gunnar Haaland, a Swedish social anthropologist. I enjoyed returning to Sudan for three weeks to work alongside this eclectic group of international development experts. I particularly remember the long evening walks along the Nile with Ashok Mitra, listening to his views on the political economy of India. My initial contribution was well appreciated, and I was invited to join a core group of six in Geneva for two weeks to draft the main report. It was certainly very pleasant to spend the days writing chapters of the book in the ILO's comfortable hilltop offices and spend the evenings partaking of excellent Swiss cuisine and wine at restaurants on the shores of Lake Geneva. On the weekend, our ILO colleagues took us for lovely drives in the surrounding Alpine countryside. The book, *Growth, Employment and Equity: a Comprehensive Strategy for Sudan*, was published in 1976, with the traditional red covers of the series.

I was enjoying my work on Tanzania alongside a committed and talented group of Bank colleagues, including (aside from Stanley and Steve) Ping Loh (from Taiwan), Richard Stern (older brother to economist—and later Lord—Nicholas Stern), Kingsley Amoako (from Ghana, later executive secretary of the UN Economic Commission for Africa) and Jim Adams. My trips/missions to Dar continued, adding to our collection of striking Makonde wood carvings, which also made for great gifts to friends and family. The Makonde were a tribe that had originated in Mozambique, and gradually migrated northwards to Tanzania as civil war afflicted their nation. Some of Picasso's paintings were inspired by such African carvings.

In the spring of 1975, I lead my first small mission to Tanzania to assess the fiscal implications of the government's recently announced goal of universal primary education. One of my mission members was Suman Bery (later director general of the NCAER in India), who was now a staff member in my old domestic finance division. Rakesh Mohan (later deputy governor of the RBI) had also joined a division on urban economics, and Surjit Bhalla (later, our executive director at the IMF) was not far behind. We used to call them the 'young bachelors'.

That summer, Steve and I went to Dar to follow up on the programme credit negotiated earlier. By then, I had earned enough 'points' (nights away from home on duty) to qualify for a Bank-paid trip for Gayatri. She had been working very hard and had just submitted her doctoral thesis on 'Forms of Autobiography' to Tufts University. So, she joined me in Dar in the final days of our mission. As usual, we stayed in the iconic, if slowly decaying, Kilimanjaro Hotel, sometimes dining in the Italian restaurant at the Agip petrol station. During Gayatri's short stay in Dar, we also visited the beautiful Bahari Beach Resort on the Indian Ocean a few kilometres outside Dar. Then it was off by air to Arusha, near the foothills of the towering, but extinct, Kilimanjaro volcano, the highest mountain in Africa.

As a sociological aside, Gayatri's flight into Dar from London on BA proceeded to Johannesburg. The flight crew in first class included a young white South African hostess, who avoided serving Gayatri her meals. When chastised by the cabin steward, she broke down and confessed that she simply could not bring herself to serve a 'coloured' person! Such were the times.

After a tour of the nearby Arusha National Park, we were off on our big adventure, a five-day pre-arranged tour of the famous Lake Manyara and Ngorongoro National Parks in our rented personal VW van with driver. The road to Manyara took us up to the lip of the Great Rift Valley, with its lovely views. We spent a couple of nights in a lodge there, overlooking Lake Manyara, and spent an entire day being driven around the Park, seeing herds of elephants and other animals close up. Though we saw lions, they were not up on trees, which sometimes they are in Manyara.

Then it was on to the great crater of Ngorongoro mountain, with its massive salt flats and extensive savannah grasslands, all in the enormous crater floor. The large variety of wildlife, including elephants, lions, rhinos, zebras, gnus, gazelles, warthogs, hyenas and flamingos, dwelt in unusual proximity to each other (except when the lions got hungry!) on the crater floor, and preferred not to venture up and outside the crater walls that surrounded them. Our lodge was on the lip of the crater, and each day we would go down to the crater floor in a Land Rover with a driver-guide, who would bring us close to different groups of large animals. The sights and sounds we saw were truly unforgettable. Ngorongoro is in the south-east segment of the huge Serengeti plain. Not far away is the Olduvai Gorge, where some of earliest remains of Homo Sapiens were excavated by the famous Leakey family many years ago.

Driving to and from these great parks was a pleasure in itself, going through small villages (where Gayatri bought her colourful *kitenge* skirts), with occasional sightings of Masai herders, and sudden glimpses of ostriches and giraffes ambling near the road. Everyone's 'bucket list' should include a journey to the East African game parks!

Back in the Washington area, our life followed its now settled rhythm. After the 1974 oil price hike by petroleum exporting countries, my commutes to and from the Bank were typically in a car pool, which included Gopal, Dhruba, Anupam and, sometimes, Arun Shourie. The chatter was usually amicable and only occasionally heated. Arun was a very serious and thoughtful person, who was clearly very emotionally invested in the economic, social and political developments in India. He returned to the country after another couple of years to a remarkable career in journalism, book writing and politics, including as a very successful minister for disinvestment in Atal Bihari Vajpayee's government. Aside from his seriousness of purpose, he was endowed with a rapier-sharp wit with which he could amuse companions as well as write sharp and engaging articles and books.

As time passed, we made more use of Washington's considerable artistic and cultural offerings, seeing shows in the Kennedy Centre the Arena Theatre by the Potomac, and the Wolf Trap National Park for the Performing Arts. We made quite a few little trips, sometimes with friends, to nearby tourist spots such as Williamsburg and Harper's Ferry. We also went up to Orange, Connecticut, to attend the wedding of Mary Ann Bannerji (eldest daughter of Sid and Ann) and Jonathan, early one morning by a little lake near their home.

That July, I gave Gayatri a surprise birthday gift of a second-hand upright piano. Shortly thereafter, we both started taking weekly lessons from Fran Hollenbeck. We made some progress over the next year or so, before our discipline eroded. At least, it reduced my complete illiteracy when confronted by sheet music. I also recall our taking sessions on transcendental meditation (TM) from a young American physicist. Gayatri took to it and learnt the technique, benefiting significantly throughout her life. I did not imbibe its lasting benefits.

In the winter of that year, we took our second home leave. Aside from the usual time spent in England with Dada and family, and Mike and Liz, we also had the special pleasure of seeing little Ollie Minton. We went on to spend a few days in Greece, the cradle of Western civilization. Mathew Lambrinides, my fellow graduate student from Harvard, kindly showed us around Athens and drove us down to Sounion and its Temple of Poseidon before he put us on a tour bus to see the other usual places and sites. On our return to Athens, he gave us a special treat: An open-air concert in the national stadium by Michail Theodorakis, the great Greek composer and lyricist, who had written the music for *Zorba the Greek* and *Z*. It was a spellbinding performance, and especially moving since Greece had emerged only the previous year from seven years of harsh authoritarian rule by the junta of 'the Colonels'.

We arrived in Delhi only a few months into the Emergency. The atmosphere was palpably different, even though we were mostly cocooned in 4, Teen Murti Marg with my parents or in friends' homes. When we met our friends, there was a sense of not speaking as freely as we had always earlier. We also went to Kolkata to be with our relatives. This time, it was a special treat for Gayatri as all three of her siblings were there at the same time. So were four 'littluns' (two of Shekhar's, and two of Kajal's). It was a real Dasgupta clan get-together, with my mother-in-law presiding benignly.

On our return trip, we first went south to Colombo to be hosted in style by our old friend Sunethra Bandaranaike and her then husband, Kumar Rupasinghe, in their spacious home in Guildford Crescent. It was wonderful to see Su again, several years after bidding her farewell in Oxford. She was very hospitable and kind, and took us down to the beaches near Bentota, then much less developed as a tourist hotspot, fed us hoppers and other Sri Lankan delicacies, and then packed us off with her charming cousin, Skanda de Saram, for a long day trip to Kandy, Dambulla and the magnificent Sigiriya Rock. Now, traffic would make it impossible to do all three in a single dday! We could not have asked for a better introduction to her beautiful country, which we have since visited many times.

Then onwards to Iran, where we stopped for a day in busy, congested Tehran, and two glorious ones in Isfahan, the jewel in the crown of the Safavid dynasty, which had ruled Iran for over 250 years, overlapping mostly with our Mughal period. The lovely palaces, squares, mosques and bridges of the town are unforgettable, as is the brilliant blue tile work, which pervades the structures of that period. It is said that there was a significant two-way interchange between master craftsmen in Mughal and Safavid times.

Back in Washington, Stanley asked me to put together a team, and lead the Basic Economic Report exercise on Tanzania. Supported by him and Steve, I was able to gather together an outstanding group of economists including: Gene Tidrick (by then country economist on Tanzania) on industry and trade policy, Inder Jit Singh on the logic of semi-collective peasant agriculture, Suman Bery on fiscal issues, Anders Fosse (consultant) on foreign aid strategy, Steve on agriculture, Jan Gunning on macro-analytics and Paul Collier (consultant) on labour markets and poverty. Paul was a recently appointed young Oxford don, whom Martin Wolf had recommended highly; he went on to garner significant plaudits and awards in development economics, and gained a knighthood. We went on a preliminary visit in the spring of 1976, followed by the main four-week mission in the summer. It was both a challenging and fulfilling exercise, perhaps my best effort during my Bank years. On mission, I started a practice of pre-dinner sessions, where a designated person would present ideas and preliminary findings almost every other evening. It seemed to work, both for bonding and as a genuine ideas exchange. We also had quite a lot of fun, seeing amongst other things the Bollywood hit movie *Sholay* in downtown Dar!

Our labours led to an eight-volume report (I wrote the integrating main volume) the following summer, which was widely appreciated by those in the Bank who read or peer-reviewed it. But when Stanley and I went to Dar to discuss the penultimate 'green cover' version with the Tanzanian ministers and officials, it had a mixed reception, perhaps because it was too critical of the government's economic policies. Nyerere's administration refused permission to publish the volume. But after many years, and with the advent of digital technology and new Bank transparency rules, the entire report can be found on the Bank's website! (Just google: world bank Tanzania basic economic report 1977.)

7

World Bank: The Next Five Years

IN THE SUMMER OF 1977, with the Tanzania economic report essentially completed, Stanley asked me to conduct a similar exercise for Kenya. I initiated some work, including arranging for Paul Collier, Jan Gunning and Deepak Lal (then professor at University College, London) to do an assessment of labour market and income distribution issues. Fate intervened suddenly to end my association with East Africa.

In 1968, Robert McNamara had been eased out from being Defense Secretary of US by President Johnson because of his rising scepticism about the ends and means of the Vietnam War, and was made president of the World Bank. Two years later, he had inducted Hollis Chenery from Harvard to upgrade the Bank's economic and sector work, and oversee a serious research programme on economic development aimed at generating best-practice answers on how to accelerate broad-based economic development and poverty alleviation. The development policy staff (DPS), with its three main departments, had been established through reorganization in 1972. DFD/Public Economics was one division in the development economics department. By 1977, McNamara felt that enough time had passed on research and analysis to now pull together and disseminate the 'lessons' of development in a slim annual flagship document to be called the 'World Development Report' (WDR). He asked Ernie Stern, vice president for South Asia and earlier Hollis's deputy in the DPS, to oversee the exercise for the first report. Ernie selected D.C. Rao (also a 'graduate' of DFD) to head up a small 'Core Team', picked from anywhere in the Bank, to put together the first WDR, for 1978.

That first core team included Montek Ahluwalia, Martin Wolf, Ross Gilmartin, I.J. Singh, David Green and me. So I was summarily hijacked from the East Africa programmes department and tasked to write the key background paper on development in sub-Saharan Africa. I took this seriously, and, in the course of the next five months of extensive reading and writing, produced a paper entitled 'Perspectives and Problems of Development in Sub-Saharan Africa' (later published as a Bank Staff Working Paper and then as an article in the journal, *World Development*). That seemed to satisfy DC and Ernie, and allowed Gayatri and me to proceed with our plans for our third home leave in the winter of 1977–78, with me having promised to draft the corresponding, condensed chapter for the actual WDR on return.

As usual, we stopped over in London to visit with Dada and family, now back in Rugby, though still with GEC, and Mike and Liz. We also spent time with Gayatri's brother, Shekhar, and family, who were then posted in London in the Indian High Commission. Indeed, during those years I would always visit them on my London stopovers and usually have a joint tuck-in at Lee Ho Fuk restaurant in Chinatown, near Soho. We also made a side-trip to

Oxford to look up Suu Kyi and her family, including her husband, Michael Aris, a Tibetologist, and their two small boys, the youngest only a few months old. They lived in Park Town, just across from where I had roomed in my final year in Oxford. We were struck not just by her domesticity but the almost fierce perfectionism she brought to all the little tasks of raising small children and doing housework. It would be a far cry from her life after 1988, when, on a visit to her ailing mother in Rangoon, she would be swept up in the vortex of turbulent Burmese politics.

Then we proceeded to India, but this time, our first stop was to Kolkata, not Delhi. Baba had finished his CVC-ship in 1977, accelerated by some differences with Sanjay Gandhi (the extra-constitutional power in the land), and so my parents had reverted to Ma's little flat on Darga Road, Kolkata. It was a stark contrast to the lavish ambassadorial mansions and spacious Lutyens bungalows of their earlier life. Gayatri and I tried to brighten up the place with some new furniture and fittings, but some basic limitations of size and location could not be overcome.

We went on a trip to Odisha (then Orissa) with them, staying at the well-known Railway hotel, built when it was known in the region as the Bengal Nagpur Railway, on the beach in Puri, and visiting the Jagannath temple, going on to Bhubaneswar, and its Lingaraj and Raja Rani temples, then proceeding, through colourful Pipili, to the magnificent Sun Temple of Konark on the Bay of Bengal. In both Puri and Bhubaneswar, our stays were enriched by the company of Jyotish and Ratna Bhattacharya, friends from Peabody Terrace. Jyotish was now a secretary to the Odisha government.

After spending a couple of weeks back in Kolkata with my parents, and Gayatri's Ma and family, we proceeded on a long-intended tour of south India. We first went to see Nandita and Sanu in Hyderabad and Warangal, where Sanu was district magistrate.

After that we went to Bengaluru (then Bangalore), at the time a leafy retirement city with a pleasant climate, staying briefly with Madhav and Sulu Gadgil, who had been neighbours in Harvard's Peabody Terrace, now on the faculty of the prestigious Indian Institute of Science. Another scientist colleague from Harvard, Giri Prabhu, and his wife drove us to Mysore to see the sights both on the way and in the city. Somewhere in that itinerary we rented a car (with a driver) to visit the famous old temples of Halebid and Belur in Karnataka, built by the Hoysala kings of the twelfth century, before proceeding further south to Chennai (then Madras) and the beautiful windswept temple complex by the sea at Mahabalipuram. Then it was onwards for a couple of days on the unspoilt beach at Kovalam, followed by visits to Thiruvananthapuram (then Trivandrum) and Kanyakumari at the southern-most tip of India.

Back in Washington by end-January, I delivered on my promise to DC to draft a chapter for the WDR based on my earlier background paper. The first two WDRs, rightly or wrongly, were broad-spectrum documents, not focusing on a particular sector or theme. By May or so, the work was mostly done on WDR 1978, and I was wondering about returning to the East Africa programmes. But then, lightning struck again. At a pleasant celebratory party given by Ernie on the just-completed exercise, he announced to us that I had been anointed core team leader for the next WDR, for 1979. The glass of wine in my hand turned sour!

By then, Ernie had become senior vice president for all operations at the Bank (effectively, McNamara's deputy), and so the management-level oversight role for WDR was shifted to Atilla Karosmanoğlu, Hollis's deputy in the DPS. He was a very nice, wise person, who had once held a ministerial position in the Turkish government. But he lacked Ernie's clout in the organization. So I made sure to keep Ernie in the picture on any large issues during the course of the year, sometimes over lunch.

My first task was to create an office and a budget for the WDR unit. DC and Ernie had managed to beg, borrow and bully the necessary resources. Having done that, I persuaded my efficient, cheerful and loyal secretary from the East Africa programmes, Rhoda Blade, to join me in the venture and boss over the other secretaries in the unit. The most important task, I knew, was to indicate how WDR 1979 would be different from its predecessor, and to staff up the core team accordingly. I managed to get approval from Ernie, Hollis and Atilla (and through them McNamara's) for the new WDR to be still broad-spectrum, but with focus on 'structural change and development policy'. Accordingly, I picked Armeane Choksi for industrialization, Johannes Linn for urbanization and Lyn Squire for structural change in labour markets. Their subsequent stellar careers (two became vice presidents)vindicate those choices. I persuaded Don Keesing to join us on international trade issues, bolstered by Martin Wolf, now as a consultant, since he had left the Bank to go on leave to University College in London, followed by Nuffield College in Oxford. Ram Chopra would anchor the work on energy and Joel Bergsman would be our expert on Latin America.

McNamara followed a practice of holding monthly meetings on WDR, with Hollis, Ernie, Atilla and myself, and one or two other vice presidents. This was the first (and last) time I was regularly in small group meetings with him in our ten years of overlap in the Bank. I found him very focused and interested, and nearly as domineering as I had feared. The monthly meetings gave me a sense of mandate and empowerment in mobilizing the necessary resources across the institution, especially in terms of background papers to be done by staff outside the core team. Getting outlines and hard delivery dates agreed to by all paper writers (in and outside the core team) was time consuming but essential for the success of the enterprise. I was quite happy to cajole and flatter (and, very occasionally, bully) the contributors.

My only real break in those initial three months was a week in July, when Dada, Ann and their three children (Lalita, Ranjan and Manjula = LRM) came to visit us for a week from England. We had a good time with them, showing them around Washington, Skyline Drive, Toys 'R' Us (where Gayatri gave LRM modest allowances for spending) and *Star Wars* at a drive-in cinema. Today, our nieces recall the toy shop, *Star Wars* and McDonald's as the top hits of their trip. So much for Washington's great museum chain, except that Manjula still remembers the 'ice-cold Coke at the Smithsonian'!

Once the core team members were well in harness, and all background papers had been identified and allotted, I felt Gayatri and I could take off for a fortnight's vacation in September. We decided on a 'fly-drive' tour of south-west USA. It turned out to be our best holiday in America. The vastness and natural beauty of the region is breathtaking. We flew to Denver at the foot of the Rockies and picked up our rental car, a sporty maroon Chevy Corvette with plenty of horse-power under the hood. We proceeded up into the Rockies, through Colorado Springs to the Black Canyon of the Gunnison National Park and on to the high Sierra plateau, driving at speed through vast, unpopulated territories to the Mesa Verde National Park with its fascinating Puebloan archaeological sites. The American Indians living there dismissed our claim to be Indians with a hearty laugh! Then a long fast drive to the Grand Canyon in Arizona with its extraordinary 5000-foot-deep gorge cut out of the mountains by the Colorado River over millions of years. After three National Parks, we accepted the call of 'sin city' and drove over the famous Boulder Dam to the night life in Las Vegas in Nevada for a couple of great shows and some losing fights with 'one-armed bandits' (slot machines), which impassively swallowed our money. Each morning's newspaper, slipped under the door of our hotel room, essentially comprised lots of advertisements for disease-free purveyors of fleshy pleasures!

From Vegas, we drove across the sun-baked Mojave Desert to thriving Los Angeles with a visit to Universal Studios, where Bruce, the shark from *Jaws*, reared up scarily to threaten our little 'boat' of tourists as it took us through many iconic film sets from Hollywood's rich history. From Los Angeles, we drove north up the famous and very scenic Pacific coastal highway to San Francisco, pausing at various sites along the way. We took in some of Frisco's famous sights, like the Golden Gate Bridge and the 'crookedest street in the world' (both of which feature in many movies), before driving further north to the spectacular Yosemite National Park. With its towering forests of redwood trees, great snow-capped mountains, limpid lakes and the famous Half Dome, it has to be among the most beautiful of America's national parks. Back in Frisco, we turned in our rental car and flew back to Washington, amply refreshed by America's natural wonders to renew engagement with WDR 1979.

Soon, early drafts of background papers began to come in, and the whole process of iterations with authors and integration of principal insights and 'lessons' into early draft chapters took up our time in the core team. Happily, the quality of most of the background papers was very good. Four, including one by Johannes and one by Lyn, subsequently became books. Many of the others later morphed into Staff Working Papers or journal articles. The team members delivered in full measure, and drafting of the report went reasonably smoothly. In the final stages in March–April, I took over the whole document to put it in my style of writing and clean out the bugs. The latter was real drudgery for me, Rachel Weaving (who had helped edit the first WDR too) and the secretarial staff in those last years before word-processing programmes became ubiquitous. By May 1979, we had a decent-enough draft to circulate around the Bank and get comments. By June, we had presented it to the Bank's board of executive directors and got their go-ahead. I could finally relax. After that it was the headache of Oxford University Press to get printed versions finalized. In July, Gayatri and I went off to Bermuda for a week's vacation.

As WDR 1979 ended, I was promoted and appointed as Research Adviser (RA) to the Bank. The position was in Hollis's office and the basic job was to supervise/manage the process of review, selection, monitoring and evaluation of research projects that drew on the Bank's fund for 'external research', then amounting to about $3 million a year. The bulk of the research was done by the Bank's researchers in the DPS departments, with our research budget funds being used to finance consultants, surveys, travel and conferences. The RA and the secretary to the research committee managed the process, with all new proposals being formally reviewed/approved in quarterly meetings of the research committee of twelve to fifteen senior staff from all over the Bank, chaired by Hollis.

The burden of day-to-day administration was borne largely by the secretary to the committee, who had to be very good. I managed to persuade Gobind Nankani, a Ghanaian of Indian origin and another 'graduate' of DFD, to join me in that role. He had, at my request, done an excellent background paper for our WDR. He proved to be a very good choice. Later, he rose to be vice president of the Africa region. Unfortunately, a few years after retirement, he died prematurely in a London hospital.

My immediate predecessor in the RA's position had been Professor Bela Balassa, as a part-time consultant from Johns

Hopkins University, and before him, Professor Ian Little from Oxford had done it for a year. My successor in 1982 was Deepak Lal. Frankly, I did not take to the job like a duck to water. From my perspective, it entailed too many bureaucratic headaches and occasional skirmishes with opinionated department heads and division chiefs in DPS, without the satisfactions of the country economic work in motivated teams that I had enjoyed in East Africa. Hollis was a somewhat shy and stiff supervisor, with whom I never developed an easy relationship.

It did not help matters that I was never wholly convinced about the net value added by the Bank's large research programme, amounting to about $15 million a year, including both internal research staff time and the 'external research budget'. Looking back, I think the greater value of this large research establishment was less the research actually produced, considerable though it was, and more the quality of Bank staff participating in the operational work, through both 'operational support' and the provision of well-trained economists for the Bank's management cadres.

The good side of the assignment was that it left me with ample time to do other things. One of the pleasanter of these was a ten-day visit to Indonesia sometime in 1980 to join Armeane Choksi's industry sector mission as a fifth-wheel adviser. It gave me an opportunity to visit the famous Borobudur and Prambanan temple in Yogyakarta and join the mid-mission review in Bali. Indonesia had a 99 per cent Muslim population. The character of Islam there at that time was quite soft and syncretic, with various Hindu themes and traditions woven into the culture, including in the names of people and places. I still recall that as we entered Prambanan, our guide, a young Javanese lady, very naturally and easily did a namaste. Now, forty years later, I understand that Islamic fundamentalism has become quite common in the country. Bali was as beautiful, as expected, and I remember a day trip with

Armeane up to Ubud, the artist settlement in the hills, where I
bought a couple of paintings. In bustling, spread-out Jakarta, it was
good to see former East Africa colleagues such as Ping Loh, then
deputy head of the large resident mission.

In the winter of 1979–80, when Gayatri and I went on our
fourth home leave, it had become clear that my father's health
was deteriorating and that he was not really happy in Kolkata.
My mother's asthma was also bothering her. Gayatri's Ma was
fortunately in good health, surrounded by Kajal and her family. We
began to think seriously of our old intention of working in the
Bank for a few years, saving some money and returning to India
to 'serve the country', and provide moral and material support to
our ageing parents. Such thinking may also have been influenced
by D.C. Rao's going to the Reserve Bank of India in Mumbai
for two years as an adviser in 1978 on leave from the Bank, and
Montek following the next year as economic adviser in the finance
ministry in Delhi.

Health had become an issue in our immediate family too.
Gayatri had picked up amoebic dysentery during her trip to
Tanzania in 1975. It had been diagnosed much later and treated by
strong and inappropriate drugs prescribed by a doctor in Kolkata
on our home leave. The result was an unfortunate combination
of a chronic ailment with side effects of the drug. On our return
trip to Washington, when we were visiting Dada and family in
Rugby, she developed a high fever and had to stay behind for a few
extra days to recover. She still recalls gratefully the love and tender
care administered by Ann and LRM, which helped her recover
soon. During that summer of 1980, feeling the need for a longish
period of full rest, Gayatri went to her Ma's home in Kolkata for
nearly two months, and recouped her strength and energy. As 1980
unfolded, my genetic trait for asthma conspired with Washington's
allergy-inducing environment to trigger bronchial asthma issues

for me. These would trouble me for the next twenty years, sometimes seriously.

On the brighter side, Mike, Liz and their two little children, Ollie and Katie, came to stay with us in the late summer of 1980 to spend some very enjoyable days together, going around Washington and the Shenandoah Hills. I still remember four-year-old Katie on a picnic there, returning from a leak behind a bush, cheerfully twirling her panties!

An interesting second cousin came from India in 1980 and rented a house in our locality. This was Babi Dey, middle son of Bulbul-di (see chapter 4), who had been an exceptional test pilot for the Indian Air Force and had got posted as air attaché in the Indian embassy. We knew about him and his family, but had never met them. It was time to rectify that lacuna. He and wife, Asha, turned out to be warm and friendly, and their very pleasant and earnest young son, Nikhil, enrolled in GMU. He started to ride in to the university regularly with Gayatri. Later, he became a committed and well-known social activist in India, working closely with the famous Aruna Roy in their organizations. Many years later, when Gayatri quizzed him about some of the difficult and dangerous situations he had faced as an activist, he confessed wryly that it was while being driven by Gayatri that he had experienced the scariest moments of his life! This was also the time I got to know Y. Venugopal Reddy, who later became one of the best governors of the Reserve Bank of India. He had just come to the Bank as adviser to the Indian executive director. As our thoughts turned to working in India, I often sought practical advice from Venu.

On the work side, Gobind and I wanted to encourage more economics research by the Bank on African countries. During the course of the year, I met up again with Paul Collier to get his ideas, and we began to develop a research project on the impact of the coffee boom on East African countries, how the windfall had been used differently across those countries and what policy lessons could be inferred. We roped in his Oxford colleague David Bevan and, of course, Jan Gunning. I remember several pleasant days in Paul's rented cottage outside Geneva, where the four of us gathered to write the proposal. We got approval for the project from the research committee in 1981, with me anchoring and supervising the project in the Bank, and the others doing most of the survey and empirical work.

During 1979 and 1980, I also undertook some 'WDR dissemination' travel to various places, including Belgrade, Dhaka, Tokyo and Delhi. The last included a visit home to Kolkata and a trip with my parents to Shantiniketan, where Rabindranath Tagore founded his Visva-Bharati University in 1921. What remains indelible in my mind are the striking open-air sculptures by Ramkinkar Baij scattered across the campus. The return to Dhaka after my early school days there was also interesting. From a small town it had now morphed into a teeming city. There was also a significant personal dimension, of meeting up with Abu and Chitrita after nine years, and also with Gopal and Radhika (Gopal was posted there in the IMF office). Sadly, the former couple informed me of their impending split.

As 1981 unfolded, Gayatri and I increasingly mulled over the India-return issue. Aside from supporting our ageing parents and the noble sentiment of service to one's home country, there was a sense that we wanted change a change from our now decade-long experience of 'world-banking' and university teaching. Put simply, we wanted to experiment with living and working as adults in India—something neither of us had yet done. Of course, we worried about the possibility of failure and 'what if it doesn't work out?' However, this is where the Bank's flexible approach to granting leave without pay (LWOP) provided much comfort and insurance. One could come back to the organization at the same grade and salary as one left it. The only 'cost' was losing one's preferred position in the promotions rat race.

I did not want to go straight into a government position; lateral entry was not at all easy, and also, I didn't want to take a senior position with limited knowledge of the complex Indian economy. Fortunately, I had had several discussions with Raja Chelliah, a respected fiscal expert who, until recently, had headed IMF's Tax Policy division. He had returned to India and established, with government backing and support, the new National Institute of Public Finance and Policy (NIPFP). Before leaving, he had in effect given me a carte blanche to join him any time as a senior fellow (a post later designated as professor). In 1981, I wrote to Raja that I was available to join him mid-1982. He promptly reverted with a formal offer, which became part of my written request to the Bank to grant me two and a half years of LWOP, preceded by six months of paid leave in Washington, when I could take econometric/statistical courses in George Washington University to brush up my research skills. The Bank generously agreed. So I ceased being RA at the end of 1981, and started organizing our affairs for at least thirty months of absence from the DC area from July 1982.

As NIPFP did not provide housing, our first priority was to rent a decent flat. We lucked out when Ajit Mozoomdar, former expenditure secretary in the Indian government and recently appointed director of the Bank's Economic Development Institute, kindly offered to rent us his flat in Feroz Shah Road in a central area of Delhi, at an affordable, sub-market rate. The great side benefit was that it came with an extant phone connection, something we could never have got in a couple of years (or even five) since we were not government employees.

My parents and Gayatri's Ma were very happy to learn of our plans, and looked forward to our return to India. Tragically, that was to happen sooner and for the wrong reason. Baba's health took a sudden turn for the worse and he passed away on 17 April 1982, a fortnight short of his seventieth birthday. I promptly took a flight home to Kolkata to be with Ma for some days and help with all the paraphernalia of wills, bank accounts, etc. Dada did the same from St. Catharine's, Ontario, where he and his family had migrated to the previous year.

Baba and I had been close until I went to college in Oxford, after which the consequences of too many years away from home and the natural 'individuation' that occurs in a young adult gradually reduced the closeness of our relationship. It was only later that I fully appreciated the very sizeable sacrifice of my parents of their own economic security, entailed by the substantial expenses of my education in Oxford and Harvard. Even more important was the intangible gift of cultural roots in India, which lead us back to our home country after many years abroad.

Back in Virginia, May and June passed swiftly as we made arrangements for renting our house, and sorted our belongings, placing most of them in storage (expecting to return in two years) and taking only 2500 lbs (the Bank's permissible weight allowance) with us. By early July, we had left behind our eleven years of life as young professionals in the Washington area.

Looking back on those years, as well as the previous four in Boston as students, I must say that living in these east coast cities of America was a very pleasant and positive experience. The America of that time was a remarkably open and forward-looking society, easily accepting foreigners. In America, unlike in my eight years in England in the 1960s, I was very rarely conscious of the colour of my skin or made to feel unwelcome in the daily interactions at office, public transport, supermarkets and other retail establishments. Of course, my office was at an international organization, but Gayatri's was at a state university, overwhelmingly staffed by native-born Americans. Her experience was perhaps more authentic and at least as positive. Americans generally dealt with you as an individual and not as a representative of a particular community. Northern Virginia in those years was host to a growing number of immigrants from south-east Asia and Latin America. It may not have been the proverbial 'melting pot', but tolerance and positivity seemed to be the dominant experience, even if not universally so. I am told that some of this changed for the worse after the traumatic experience of 9/11 in September 2001 and even more so during the recent Trump years of heightened racial polarization.

8

Back to Delhi after Twenty-three Years Abroad

WHEN OUR FLIGHT TOUCHED down in Delhi in early July, after stopping over in Singapore with Shekhar and Twinky for some days (he was our High Commissioner there), I was returning after twenty-three years abroad and Gayatri after nineteen. We spent a few days with Monica and Mrinal in their home in Alipur Road near Delhi University, and then moved to the India International Centre (IIC), where I had booked a one-bedroom flat (they had a couple of these then) for three months to allow time for our shipment to arrive from Washington before we moved into the unfurnished Mozoomdar flat. It helped that Pabi's father was the honorary treasurer of the IIC in those years.

The IIC was, and is, a marvellous institution, essentially a club for non-sporty, 'intellectual' types, abutting the beautiful Lodi Gardens. By far my best investment decision in life had been to become a life member by paying Rs 2500 in 1975 on Baba's sound advice. We set up our temporary household there, with amusing missteps like trying to buy milk at the big shop, Sovereign Dairy, in nearby Khan Market. We didn't know milk could only be bought at the ubiquitous booths of the Mother Dairy chain. Of course, since the IIC had a dining room and a lounge café, we could always keep ourselves well nourished.

After a couple of days, I reported for duty at the NIPFP's new building in the institutional area near Qutb Hotel, about 12 kms from the IIC. The new three-storeyed building looked fine and airy, except that the offices (other than the director's) only had fans and coolers, no air-conditioning at the time. This was quite challenging in the monsoon months of June–September. Raja Chelliah was temporarily on deputation to the Economic Administrative Reforms Commission (EARC) being headed by redoubtable L.K. Jha, who had, in his illustrious career, held all the top economic administrative posts (including governorship of the Reserve Bank) and had been ambassador to USA as well and, most recently, governor of Jammu and Kashmir. He was one of the early pre-eminent economic reformers of the country.

So, I was welcomed to the NIPFP by the acting director, Dr Amaresh Bagchi, on deputation from the Ministry of Finance (MoF). Over time, I came to know him well as a good, warm, trustworthy friend, though he was fifteen years my senior. He had been an income tax officer in his youth before earning his PhD in economics and becoming a rare fiscal policy expert in the MoF. On my first day in the NIPFP, Amaresh-da settled me down and confirmed that I was to head a study, recently commissioned by the MoF, on the dimensions of India's 'black money' problem. That was going to be my central academic preoccupation for the next thirty months.

Delhi of 1982 was very different from now, or even from 1995. The liberalization of the early 1990s had not yet occurred. The urban landscape was fairly austere. There were only three brands of cars on the road, and not many of them: The Fiat Padmini (1100), the Ambassador (basically a 1960s Morris Oxford) favoured by government and public enterprises, and a few Triumph Heralds. Thus, Manmohan Singh's personal car, just before he left for Mumbai later that year to be governor, RBI, was a Padmini. A few months later, I bought it from him, rather injudiciously, as it gave me quite a lot of trouble. The few imported cars on the road either belonged to embassies, international organizations or some rich businessmen, who may have bought them from the first two categories. Colour TV transmission had started recently, with costly local sets assembled behind steep import barriers.

Affordable restaurants were few, either kabab joints or 'Indian Chinese' outlets. If you had money, you could splurge at the Taj, Oberoi, the governmental Asoka or a few new five-star hotels that had come up to cater to the Asiad Games of the time. Telephone connections were very hard to get for individuals, unless they were employed by the public sector or large companies. Khan Market was a genteel place with long-established shops selling fairly essential products. Throughout the 1980s and most of the 1990s, whenever someone travelled abroad on work or business, he or she was usually burdened by family and close friends with lists for fairly simple 'imported goodies', such as Gillette razor blades, good-quality ballpoint pens, cosmetics and various edibles. In my case, my weakness was for Kellogg's cornflakes, which were cheap but bulky!

Another striking characteristic of Delhi in the early 1980s was that publicly provided goods and services in short supply were difficult to get hold of legally without 'connections'. Thus, when we moved to the Feroz Shah road flat, we immediately needed a cooking gas cylinder and an assured supply of refills. That could either be bought on the black market or obtained through connections. Luckily, my cousin's husband, Sanu Ray, was then special assistant to the petroleum minister, and a suitably pathetic letter to him did the needful. On the other hand, when I tried to get a ration card, mainly for identity purposes, and filled in various forms in triplicate, I got nowhere. It was a striking reminder of a very desirable aspect of a well-functioning market economy: Anonymity in routine transactions. You just paid your money and got your good or service without having to know and request anyone.

We faced one other novel and unusual challenge: How to employ and manage domestic servants. In the fourteen years of our married life in the US before returning to India, we had never even thought of employing servants in our households in Massachusetts, or the Washington area. We were used to sharing all the necessary housework amongst ourselves. Broadly, I did the laundry, dishwashing and house cleaning, while Gayatri did the cooking and gardening. We generally did the grocery shopping together. Given the facilities in Delhi and the nature of the work involved, we clearly needed to have domestic staff. So, gradually, we got ourselves a cook, a maid and a driver. But how to manage them in the appropriately semi-feudal manner, of which we had no first-hand experience? It proved to be quite a challenge as we strove to strike the right balance between being too democratic and too authoritarian. We never quite mastered the skills required. I suspect that we probably erred on the side of being too democratic in manner and generous as paymasters, since our current staff have remained with us for at least fifteen years, and one of them for twenty-five.

For fresh returnees like us, the biggest benefit of being back in India was the easy connectivity to relatives and friends, some from our old school and college (for Gayatri) years in Delhi, and some from our time in Oxford, Harvard and Washington. The last category included Montek and Isher, Malavika, Vasundhara and Nalini (and their respective spouses), Arvind and Minu Pande, and Swamy and Roxna. It was not always easy to get in touch with old friends. For example, I was able to find an office number for my old St. Columba's school buddy, Ravi Bhoothalingam, but it took forever to get past his secretary. He was then head of the personnel department of the multinational ITC, and protestations of 'I am an old childhood friend' cut no ice with his gatekeeper secretary! Of course, with time, we also made new friends among neighbours and work colleagues, and found long-lost cousins, especially after joining government in early 1985. Amongst close relatives, there was Monica and Mrinal, and, on posting from their 'home states', Kajal and Nirmal, and Nandita and Sanu.

At NIPFP, I gradually acclimatized to my new, more spartan work environment and got used to taking a chartered bus to commute to my office. It was a sharp contrast to driving in a comfortable Toyota Corona to my spacious, centrally climate-controlled office in the Bank. Matters improved when I bought Manmohan Singh's Padmini and drove myself to work. But after a dozen years of good lunches in dining rooms and restaurants, I never fully adjusted to the routine of bringing packed 'tiffins' from home or risking the fairly basic, fly-infested cafeteria at NIPFP.

At work, I immersed myself in the subject of 'black money', 'unaccounted economy', 'underground economy', tax evasion, and so forth. I recall putting together a useful survey paper on the extant literature, which was published in 1983 in the *Economic and Political Weekly*, the leading Indian journal for research on economics and other social sciences. Conceptual distinctions between stocks and flows on the one hand, and between tax-evaded income and underestimated national income arising from illicit behaviour to evade taxes and controls on the other were crucial. My objective was to clear up the conceptual jungle and then proceed to pick the concept that allowed for a reasonably credible method of estimation. Bearing in mind that the study had been commissioned by the Central Board of Direct Taxes, I focused mainly on the concept of tax-evaded income. Two members of my team were particularly helpful. One was Dr Arun Kumar, a former physics student, with whom I had many discussions to clarify my thoughts, though his contribution to the final written report was minimal. The other was Dr A.V.L. Narayana, whose hard work and competence in processing household income distribution survey data was absolutely central to the empirical part of the exercise. We also did some sector-level analyses, reviewed earlier policy initiatives and came up with a comprehensive set of recommendations. Though simple to summarize, it all took over two years. Those years also provided me an opportunity to read widely, and sometimes deeply, on the Indian economy.

Soon after settling down in Delhi, we visited Kolkata to spend some time with my mother, and tie up various financial and legal matters, which typically follow after the death of a parent. We also spent our free time reconnecting with our old friends in Delhi and catching up with their lives over the many years we had been away. We began to make forays out of Delhi too. For example, in that first winter, we made a very pleasant trip to the underrated Bharatpur bird sanctuary with Bika and her two children, and Nalini. Its beautiful 3000 hectares of wetlands attracted a great variety of colourful migratory birds in the winter months. For Gayatri, having both her sisters in the same city was of great comfort. And I got to know them and their respective spouses much better. A happy coincidence was that Sanu Ray, cousin Nandita's husband, was an IAS batchmate of Kajal and her husband, Nirmal Jhala.

Our Feroz Shah Road home was walking distance to various theatre and concert venues, such as the Shri Ram Centre for the

Arts, Kamani Auditorium and Rabindra Sadan, and we made full use of this proximity. A particularly memorable concert we went to in the nearby Modern School auditorium was one with Ravi Shankar, Ali Akbar Khan, Alla Rakha and his young son, Zakir Hussain. I recall Ali Akbar Khan making some reference to Zakir's '*nanhe munne*' fingers!

There were other things also going on in our lives. In Delhi we were pursuing options for adopting a child. Our initial foray with a well-known Delhi-based agency foundered when the concerned social worker asked for large 'side payments' to approve our suitability as parents. Shortly thereafter, we met up with Dipika Maharajsingh (elder daughter of L.K. Jha, aka Pikoo) and learned that she was the coordinator of a Pune-based social welfare agency for children. When she heard of our interest, she got us to make a trip to Pune in March 1983 to meet with some of the babies in her agency. It turned out to be an excellent organization—efficient, humane and empathetic. We were deeply grateful to Pikoo for all that she did. Three days later, we flew back to Delhi with ten-month-old Maya Prajakta Acharya (aka Ta) in our arms, with Pikoo very kindly following up with the necessary paperwork later. In a wonderful gesture, we were welcomed at the airport by Isher Ahluwalia and Rakesh Mohan, who had recently come on LWOP to the Planning Commission. What's more, Isher had very thoughtfully arranged to send a crib, successively used by her two boys, to our home to be ready for Ta. She had even personally supervised the making of a new mattress at short order. We were overwhelmed.

A baby in the home certainly changes the daily routine, as every parent (especially the mother) knows. Along with the baby came an 'ayah' and many other accessories. Happily, not just our friends, but all the residents of Diwan Shree Apartments, 30, Feroz Shah Road too gave Ta a warm welcome whenever we took her down to the lawns downstairs to play. Soon, my mother came to stay with us for some months. She had been somewhat opposed to an adoption out of family, not a common practice in India then. But within weeks, she and Ta had bonded irrevocably. A couple of years later, she told Gayatri that she felt more affection for her new little granddaughter than she ever had for her own children! Our successful adoption of Ta set an example for several of our friends in India and the UK.

Shortly after Ta arrived, Monica had her first child, Timir. Ta's little brother, Nikhil (aka Nixi), showed up (aged six months) at the beginning of 1985, and Monica's second boy, Mihir, arrived in May 1986. These four cousins grew up together in their early years and were thick as thieves. Their other three boy cousins in Delhi (children of Kajal and Nirmal) were a little older, but extremely affectionate to the 'littluns'. With so many small cousins, family trips soon proliferated. I remember well our trips to Agra (and the Taj Mahal) and Kulu/Manali, along with Kajal, Nirmal and their three boys, with Ta ensconced in a child-carrier on my back as we wandered around in these destinations. Our five-day trip to Manali one summer was particularly enjoyable; we stayed in the Hamta Birchview cottages of Himachal Pradesh Tourism. The three Jhala boys enjoyed exploring the forested hillsides, the banks of the Beas river and the Hadimba Devi temple with me. That, incidentally, is only temple to Hadimba as a goddess; elsewhere she is depicted as a demon. At one point, we had to cross the rushing Beas on a somewhat rickety rope-and-wood-plank bridge, which the boys immediately dubbed the 'rickety-rackety bridge'. Mentions of that still brings smiles to these very brainy forty-plus computer professionals in the Silicon Valley today. When Nirmal went to the market to fetch our daily grocery requirements, he always remembered the 'little monster who eats three boiled eggs at a go' (Ta)!

In Delhi, many of our weekends and festival holidays, especially Diwali, were spent in Mrinal and Monica's Alipur Road house, where the whole tribe, or some subset, would gather to have a good time, with some of the adults often playing bridge. That's where I got to know some well-known economists, like P.N. Dhar, Dharma Kumar and Khaliq Naqvi. Sometime in 1984, we had a very nice visit to the spacious home of Pabi and her husband, Avinash Wadhawan, who was then chairman and managing director of Hindustan Zinc Ltd, a government company, in Udaipur. They looked after us with great warmth and affection, with Avinash carrying little Ta on his shoulder for morning walks. They took us around the Udaipur palaces and museums, the Hindustan Zinc mines, and the gorgeous marble Jain temple at Ranakpur 50 kms away.

During my thirty months with the NIPFP, Amaresh-da introduced me to some of the older, well-known Indian academic economists like Mihir Rakshit, Idrak Bhatty and Iqbal Gulati. Through Montek and Isher, we met government economists like Arjun Sengupta, Vijay Kelkar and Nitin Desai. Arjun, who was then economic adviser to PM Indira Gandhi, used to have an informal monthly lunch at his office in South Block for some government and academic economists, to which I was kindly invited on some occasions. I recall walking out from one of these with Montek one day and him saying, about the list of attendees: 'Pretty impressive bunch, don't you think?' My response was, 'Is that all we have for this nation of 800 million?' He laughed.

My project at NIPFP was proceeding reasonably well. Dr A.V.L. Narayana's painstaking work on household income distribution data was proving invaluable as we steered our analysis towards the first serious quantitative analysis of black income in India. I did the bulk of the report-writing in the relative comfort of the air-conditioned IIC library. But as 1984 unfolded, I became increasingly sure that conducting solitary research was not my preferred vocation. My comparative advantage and preference lay closer to policy work. The choice was between being a government economist or going back to the Bank. No attractive opening for joining laterally as one of the handful of economic advisers in the economic ministries was in sight.

So, around the middle of 1984, I indicated to the Bank that I would be returning at the end of the year, the end date of my LWOP. Accordingly, I was called to Washington for interviews for a couple of possible positions in early October. On the way, I stopped over in England to meet with Mike and Liz, and drove up to Oxford with Mike for his interview for a medical consultancy position in an Oxford hospital. That job didn't fructify, but one did a few years later, taking them to Oxford for the next thirty years. While he had his interview, I spent time with Suu Kyi. Little did we know that in less than four years, her relatively humdrum life as an Oxford don's wife would be utterly transformed forever. In Washington, my interviews led to a firm offer as chief of a division on agricultural economic policy in the vice presidency headed by Shahid Hussain, who had been vice president of the East Africa region a decade earlier.

When I returned to Delhi, we began, sadly, our preparations for our return to the Washington area. But before October ended, India was convulsed by tragic events which were to change the trajectory of our lives.

On the morning of 31 October, Prime Minister Indira Gandhi was gunned down by two of her Sikh bodyguards. As news spread, some of the populace turned on the Sikhs in Delhi, killing thousands before order was fully restored several days later. Although her son Rajiv was sworn in as PM before the day ended, the avoidable and inexcusable delay in calling in troops to quell the massacres and riots was rightly laid at the door of the Congress party leadership.

From the roof of our Diwan Shree Apartments tower, we could see the smoke rising in several directions, especially in East Delhi. As it happened, I was suffering from a severe bout of asthma and could not venture out on the streets to see more for myself. Gayatri soon got involved in some NGO relief efforts being organized by her old Miranda College classmate Jaya Jaitley.

As Rajiv Gandhi settled in, he restaffed the Prime Minister's Office (PMO). Soon, Montek was shifted from his post as one of two economic advisers (EAs) then serving under Chief Economic Adviser (CEA) Bimal Jalan, to the PMO as EA with rank of additional secretary. That created a vacancy in the MoF. I was sounded about joining on an ad hoc basis. Under the rules then prevailing, such appointments could be made for a year in positions like this one under the purview of the Union Public Service Commission (UPSC), before the end of which the full UPSC process for advertisement/selection/recruitment would have to be done. I agreed to come on board by early February, on the condition that the government would get my LWOP status with the Bank extended by two years. I did not want to resign my permanent position in the Bank for a one-year assignment. So Bimal talked and wrote to Ernie Stern, and got it sorted out accordingly.

Our lease in Diwan Shree was also running out and we had little chance of getting acceptable government housing in an ad-hoc appointment. So, we looked for alternatives and struck lucky. The upstairs flat of Rabi Dutt's Kautilya Marg house was being vacated by the previous tenant, Ashok Mitra, our friend Jayati's father. A retired ICS officer, he was credited with the transformation of the Indian census into a modern database during his tenure as registrar-general and census commissioner of India. After retirement from government service, he was professor of population studies in JNU.

Rabi kaka was happy to have us and we were happy to go there, which we did early in 1985 with two little kids, one a six-month baby. That became our home for the next six years.

Our report, entitled 'Aspects of the Black Economy in India', was duly submitted to the government in early 1985 and made public shortly thereafter. It made quite a media splash and drew some attention from V.P. Singh, the new finance minister in the Rajiv Gandhi government. The newspaper commentary focused on the estimates of tax-evaded income, which ranged widely depending on alternative sets of underlying assumptions deployed. For 1980–81, tax-evaded income was estimated to be between 70 per cent and 140 per cent of income actually assessed to tax. A broader and more speculative estimate assessed unmeasured 'black income' to be about 18 per cent to 21 per cent of GDP in 1983–84.

The report also went into the causes and consequences of black-income generation and devoted a full chapter to policies for scaling down black income. Interestingly, based on a review of past experience in India and abroad, it was sceptical about the efficacy of demonetization and voluntary disclosure schemes to deal with the problem. Among the policies we recommended were: Reduction of the prevailing high direct tax rates on income and wealth; massive simplification and rationalization of tax structures for excise and customs; a systematic shift away from direct controls on prices and quantities, and towards greater freedom of the market system and prices; and a serious move towards state funding of the basic election expenses of competing parties in central and state elections. Later, in 1986, the report was published as a book by NIPFP, under the authorship of Shankar Acharya and Associates. It's heartening to note that, over time, some of our recommendations found their way into government policy, even if our report played little direct role in the process.

With my EA job lined up and a comfortable new home identified, it was time to trade in Manmohan's somewhat troublesome old Padmini for something better. As it happened, an automobile revolution was underway in India, thanks to the pioneering work of V Krishnamurthy, R.C. Bhargava and others. The Maruti–Suzuki 800 had hit the roads to great acclaim and popularity, and had a correspondingly long waiting list. The company ran a government-approved scheme under which those paying in foreign exchange received priority allocation of a car. Early in 1985, I put some of our dollar savings to good use and acquired a Maruti 800 DX (=deluxe!), which came with air-conditioning and a few other features. The Padmini was sold.

So, in early 1985, with two small children, a promising government job, a Kautilya Marg address and a snazzy little car, we started the next phase of our lives.

9

Six Years as Economic Adviser in the Finance Ministry

I FORMALLY SIGNED ON as economic adviser in the MoF in early February 1985, and took over the room Montek used to inhabit. As chance would have it, I was once again inducted by Amaresh Bagchi, by now a good friend. He had, meanwhile, returned to the MoF from NIPFP and had filled the position of the other EA, with a title of officer on special duty (OSD), for some arcane bureaucratic reason. The Economic Survey 1984–85 was about to go to the printer and Amaresh-da requested me to take a quick look, which I did. I tried to make it a little more open-economy oriented, but some of my suggestions were resisted by Bimal as prematurely liberal. I had no role in the process of V.P. Singh's first Budget as the final stages were restricted tightly to the 'Budget group', consisting, traditionally, of the three departmental secretaries—revenue, expenditure, economic affairs (DEA)—and the CEA, serviced by the joint secretary (sometimes additional secretary) heading the Budget Division.

Incidentally, contrary to common misconception, there is no separate post of finance secretary. It is simply a designation accorded to the senior-most of the departmental secretaries in the MoF. By virtue of seniority, and depending on personalities at a given time, he or she sometimes exercises limited coordination functions. Since, under the rules of business, the DEA is charged with Budget policy, monetary policy, capital markets, external finance and much of international economic policy, the overall system works best when the DEA secretary also has the designation of finance secretary.

Within the Economic Division, headed by CEA Bimal Jalan, I took over the areas that Montek used to handle, notably external sector analysis and fiscal policy, with Amaresh-da handling the rest. The other officers in the division were organized into units, each headed by an additional or deputy economic adviser, staffed by senior research officers and research officers. Except for the CEA and the two EAs, all other officers were members of the Indian Economic Service (IES). In effect, the IES officers held no position higher than that equivalent to 'director'. As the years passed, and especially when Montek headed the DEA and I was CEA in the 1990s, we pushed hard, successfully, for reforms allowing normal promotion of IES officers to adviser (=joint secretary) level, and occasionally to AS level.

The rest of the DEA was organized into several 'operational divisions', such as Budget, Fund–Bank, foreign trade, capital markets, UN affairs, foreign exchange/external commercial borrowing, and currency and coinage (that is, looking after the mints). Each was typically headed by a joint secretary (JS), with the department's internal administrative functions being handled by the senior-most JS. There was also an additional secretary for external finance,

AS (EF), for reasons not entirely clear to me. Some of the JSs when I joined were: Jagmohan Bajaj, who handled Fund–Bank and administration, V.K. Sibal (a brother of the lawyer and senior Congress politician Kapil Sibal), Dipak Chatterji (later commerce secretary), Piyush Mankad (later revenue and finance secretary), Madhusudhan Mukherji, and Nripen Misra (the youngest, who much later became principal secretary to PM Narendra Modi). Located outside North Block was the banking division, then headed by an AS, which 'looked after' the public sector banks.

It soon became clear to me that to be effective in the department, I had to win the trust and respect not only of my superiors (the finance minister, or FM, the secretary—then S. Venkitaramanan—and the CEA) but also of my JS colleagues. This I tried to do, not by flaunting any alleged 'superior' economic training, but by being helpful and collegial whenever opportunities presented themselves. My path to acceptance was greatly eased by Bimal's influential position in the department, and my friendly and mutually respectful relationship with Jagmohan Bajaj, an outstanding officer, who would have made an excellent secretary of an economic department but for a spat with his DEA secretary around 1991–92, which came in the way. Importantly, I developed a good relationship with then Revenue Secretary Vinod Pande, who was close to the minister V.P. Singh. He was a bachelor who lived in a government flat in Bharati Nagar. On weekends, I sometimes drove over to have morning tea and a chat with him. Our taste in movies overlapped considerably. I later realized that my closeness to the revenue secretary raised my stock in that department substantially and facilitated productive working relations with senior tax policy officials.

Shortly after I joined the MoF, there was a final meeting in Arusha, Tanzania, of an expert committee on concessional development assistance, headed by Professor John Lewis (of Princeton) set up by the Development Committee of the World

Bank and IMF. On Bimal's instructions, Nripen Misra and I represented India at the meeting. C.M. Vasudev, minister economic in our Washington embassy (and much later secretary, DEA), also joined us. As the issues were mostly economic, I did most of the speaking from our side at the meeting. Its real value to me was the good relations I established with both Nripen and CM which were to last throughout my government career and beyond. I stayed behind in Dar es Salaam for an extra day or two to be with Shekhar and family; he was now our High Commissioner there. One of his remarks from then has stayed with me. What he said was along these lines: 'But for our good luck and policies, we could have been in a soup like Tanzania; on the other hand, with better luck and policies, we could have been like Singapore (his previous posting)!'

A few months after I joined, Amaresh-da was appointed director of NIPFP in place of Raja Chelliah, who had become non-executive chairman. Accordingly, Bimal inducted Dr Prannoy Roy from the Delhi School of Economics in his place. Prannoy led the charge in getting us all familiar with desktop computers, then being promoted within the government by PM Rajiv Gandhi and his technology adviser, Sam Pitroda. Prannoy certainly contributed much to the quality of analysis in the division, but he soon found that government work was too boring for his entrepreneurial spirit. After a year or so, he quit to found New Delhi Television (NDTV), thus making media history in India and adding far more value to the country than he could have as an EA. Bimal took steps soon to bring in Dr Sudipto Mundle from NIPFP in Prannoy's place on an ad hoc basis. Like Prannoy, Sudipto (later a member of the 14th Finance Commission) proved to be an excellent colleague and friend for me. Somewhat unexpectedly, at the end of the ensuing year, when Sudipto's UPSC interview came up, they selected Dr Tarun Das for the permanent position of EA.

V.P. Singh's 1985 Budget speech had promised a long-term fiscal policy (LTFP) document to Parliament. Bimal (who got on very well with the FM) had the overall responsibility to follow through, and tasked me to be the principal 'draft animal' in consultation with senior officials in revenue and expenditure. Together, we all got down to make a good job of it. In the final stages, Venkitaramanan, Bimal, Vinod Pande, Montek (from the PMO) and I had a series of daily meetings, chaired by the FM, to review the document page by page. The LTFP was laid in Parliament in December 1985.

For its time, the LTFP was a remarkable document. First, it was a completely novel initiative, presenting a fairly comprehensive medium-term fiscal policy strategy as a public document. Second, it embedded tax policy intentions within an explicit macro-fiscal framework (and thus, trod on the toes of the Planning Commission!). Third, it promised, in some detail, sweeping reforms of our extremely complex and irrational indirect taxes, both customs duties and central excises. For the former, it proposed a three-tier duty structure. For the latter, it envisaged phased induction of VAT principles (especially crediting of taxes paid on inputs) under the name of 'MODVAT' (short for 'modified VAT'), quite similar to the MANVAT (manufacturers' VAT') recommended in 1978 by the L.K. Jha Committee report on indirect taxes, which had been gathering dust on ministry shelves.

An aside: During the late stages of preparation of the LTFP, Bimal walked into my room one day and asked, in effect, 'Shankar, can we drop this MODVAT stuff from the document?' Apparently, he was getting a lot of resistance from certain quarters. I protested vigorously, saying it was the jewel in the crown of our tax policy intentions. He did not pursue the matter. Not only did the commitment to MODVAT stay in the LTFP, but the FM, in his February 1986 Budget speech, announced its implementation in thirty-seven chapters of the Central Excise, with a clear commitment to extend it over time to all chapters on manufacturing. The reform of customs duties did not, unfortunately, find a place in the 1986–87 budget or in the next four that followed.

On the home front, we were enjoying the charms of living in a spacious flat in one of the fanciest localities of Delhi. Actually, the flat was huge, about 4000 square feet. But it had only two bedrooms (!), one for the kids and their ayah, Jeeva, and the other for us. Both bedrooms opened to a covered veranda, where one could enjoy morning tea and papers as the world went by on Kautilya Marg. On one long side of the flat, there was an eight-foot-wide enclosed veranda, which became a tricycle track for our kids. The large living and dining rooms, in the centre of the flat, were, unfortunately, starved of natural light. The flat would never win any design prizes, but it was more than fine for us. Rabi kaka and Lily kakima lived quietly downstairs and were regularly visited by Pabi from Udaipur, which was nice for us too.

Shortly after I joined the government, all Saturdays (not just the second one) were made holidays and joint secretary–level officers were given the privilege of pick-up and drop from home to office by official cars. Both, especially the former, were very welcome. It meant more time with growing Ta and Nixi and other relatives and friends. Kajal, Nirmal and their three sons stayed in Pandara Road ('Panda' Road to us) in D-II flats till 1988, and Monica, Mrinal and their two little ones in Alipur Road till 1990. In 1989, Shekhar and Twinky (and their son, Sanjay, and daughter, Chitralekha) were posted back in Delhi after Shekhar's posting as deputy permanent representative for India at the UN in New York, and they stayed in Moti Bagh. So, the Dasgupta clan was present in full force, to everyone's benefit.

On my side of the family, Nandita and Sanu (and their two sons) stayed in Delhi till 1987, before returning to Hyderabad. Ma would come at least once a year to stay with us for a few months, when the kids and Jeeva were shifted to the 'long veranda', and Ma took their room. Ta took to calling my Ma 'Thaki' (short for Thakurma). Ma loved that. In late 1988, Dada made a visit, basically to pick up Ma and take her to Canada for a long stay. Unfortunately, that didn't work out and I had to bring her back to India after a couple of months. There was also my older cousin Ranjana Ray and her two grown children, Ronesh and Kaninika, who were in Delhi and whom we saw often. Newly discovered distant cousins included Sujit Gupta, the direct scion of the Kaoraid Gupta zamindar family in East Bengal (see chapter 1), then senior director with Tata Sons, and the Baig family, comprising brothers Murad, Zahid and Khalid, sons of the very warm and hospitable writer and social reformer Tara Ali Baig (husband Rashid, who used to be our Ambassador to Iran in the 1960s, had passed away).

During those years, Gayatri and I experienced the joys and tribulations of having small children to nurture, play with and worry about. Their flashes of unintended humour could be hilarious. Once, Gayatri asked a typical mother-to-son question: 'Nikhil, when I grow old, will you take care of me?' Nixi looked genuinely puzzled and then responded, 'What are you now, Mama?' On another occasion, we woke up one morning to find Nikhil suffering from a very high fever. When Gayatri asked him why he hadn't woken us up during the night, he looked pained and said, 'Mama, you had told us never to disturb you at night unless I was sure I was dying. And I wasn't sure I was!'

A couple of memorable episodes from our early interactions with Delhi's 'high society' may be worth mentioning. Shortly after I joined the MoF, Sujit Gupta kindly invited Gayatri and me to a small dinner in his home near Taj Mansingh. J.R.D. Tata was there and regaled us with stories of his early flying. When he learned it was Gayatri's birthday, he stepped aside for a moment. Twenty minutes later a large cake arrived with 'Happy Birthday,

Gayatri' iced on top! The senior Tata management, led by JRD, sang 'Happy birthday' to her cutting the first piece. For me, it was a fine example of the generous and charming character of that grand old man.

On another occasion, Tara Ali Baig had invited us to a small dinner at their home, including a couple of Ambassadors. While we sat in the living room over drinks, Gayatri attempted small talk with the tall, rugged-looking foreign diplomat on her right and asked if he had visited the famed hill stations in the Himalayan foothills. He responded warmly that he loved the mountains. At that point, one of the younger Baigs on her left said, 'Gayatri, let me introduce you to Sir Edmund Hillary, New Zealand's High Commissioner to India.'

Aside from family, our circle of friends continued to expand, with Pikoo becoming a close friend, and Surjit Bhalla and wife, Ravinder Kaur, returning to Delhi. Our closeness with Pikoo meant that we often visited 10, Janpath with our children, where L.K. Jha and Mekhala lived until his untimely demise in January 1988 and Mekhala's two months later. And, of course, we had a steady and welcome stream of old friends visiting from our days in America. The Banerji family from Orange, Connecticut, also visited us one year, as did Sunethra from Colombo. We also had a fair bit of social contact with the head of the World Bank's large resident mission and its principal economist. Former colleagues and friends like Gene Tidrick, Oktay Yenal and Roberto Zagha come readily to mind in those capacities.

One good thing about being a senior officer in the DEA was the opportunities to visit Washington DC on official matters relating to the Bretton Woods twins (Bank and Fund) and Indo-US bilateral economic relations. They allowed me to stay in good touch with our close friends in the area from our eleven years of living there. On several of those occasions, I travelled via New

York and enjoyed the warm hospitality of Shekhar and family in their lovely flat on 91st Street in Manhattan, overlooking the East River. Shekhar was then the deputy head of our permanent mission at the UN.

The two-day weekends gave me ample time to take Ta and Nixi out to neighbourhood recreation spots like Nehru Park, the Railway Museum, the Nehru Planetarium, Nirula's at the Chanakya complex and, of course, the homes of their cousins. I developed a particular fondness for Nehru Park, where Lenin's statue may be one of the last ones standing in the world. Once Nixi crossed two, we ventured out on family trips outside Delhi, including Ranikhet, Nainital, Shimla, Sariska and Goa.

The first of our many trips to Goa was in 1986. We stayed on Baga beach, at the north end of Calangute's long sweep, in a charming little hotel, Baia de Sol, right across the beach, with the picturesque Baga river flowing into the sea on the north side. The room was small and the bathroom tiny. But very conveniently, we could swing our children over the balustrade of the little balcony of our room on to the small private beach, on which they could happily gambol in the sand. One day, in the shallow part of the sea, an unexpected wave knocked me over and, for a few seconds, I lost my grip of Nixi's hand, allowing the wave to tumble him over on to the beach. After that, he would insist on being in the '*chhota pani*' only; a little trauma may have been born that day.

As the children grew older, first Ta and then Nixi were enrolled in Bimla Bissell's playhouse kindergarten on Tughlak Road, where they were conveyed daily by a colourfully painted little van along with a few other kids from our neighbourhood. Every Christmas, John and Bim Bissell (she with the World Bank resident mission and he with his start-up, FabIndia) would host a marvellous Christmas brunch for some of Delhi's 'A list', into which we had slipped in accidentally. John Bissell had come to India in 1960 as a young buyer for the American retail behemoth Macy's and then got involved in the khadi movement. Realizing that marketing was the key weakness here, he set up FabIndia to overcome the lacuna and bring quality handloom products to a higher-income bracket. He was a remarkable and lovely person. At these parties, for the children, there would be camel rides and other distractions, while the adults chatted and drank punch on the lawns, and everyone partook of a wonderful repast. That tradition still continues, with son William now taking the lead, John having passed away in 1998. On New Year's Eve, there would be the traditional evening party by Romesh and Raj Thapar at their house on Kautilya Marg, a few doors down from us, with sister, Romila, a famous historian, sometimes serving the punch. At one time, Romesh, founder-editor of the journal *Seminar*, had been a close adviser to PM Indira Gandhi. After his demise in 1987, his daughter Malavika carried on the tradition.

Aside from tax policy, I had a keen interest in India's external sector developments and policies. They were a part of my regular economy monitoring responsibilities. I continued the extant system set of half-yearly medium-term balance of payments forecasts. This greatly improved my understanding of the data, international economic developments and the underlying economic forces at work. I soon found some 'trade secrets', like the sizable forex reserves held by the government with its India supply mission account in Washington and elsewhere. While the RBI knew and operated these, they were carefully left out of the public records of the officially released balance of payments data. The view of the mandarins, apparently, was that it would be better to keep some forex balances in reserve, and undisclosed, to expand room for manoeuvre during difficult times.

Our external goods trade account was not at all healthy in 1984–85. Export earnings covered a little over half our import

The author's parents, Bejoy and Nilima
Acharya, after their marriage, 1938.

The author as a card sharp at the age of nine.
Kolkata, 1954.

With brother Sanjoy (Dada) in St Paul's
School, Darjeeling, 1955.

With Gayatri Dasgupta at Oxford, 1966.

Teaching Aung San Suu Kyi to punt on Cherwell River, Oxford, 1965.

(L-R): Chris Verity, Ray Tallis, Lydia Pasternak-Slater (the landlady), author and Rick Kean at 20 Park Town, Oxford, 1967.

With Sunethra Bandaranaike at Oxford, 1966.

Registration marriage to
Gayatri Dasgupta in Bern,
Switzerland, 1968.

(L-R): Sachindra Nath
Dasgupta, Ma, the author,
Gayatri, Renu Dasgupta
and Baba. Bern, 1968.

(L-R): Monica
Dasgupta, the author,
Gayatri, Dada and
Nandita Mukherji.
Bern, 1968.

The author with Gayatri,
Nixi and Ta, at Kautilya
Marg, New Delhi, 1988.

The Budget Group 1994 (*L–R*): Expenditure Secretary K. Venkatesan, Minister of State for Finance Chandrashekhara Murthy, Revenue Secretary M.R. Sivaraman, Finance Minister Dr Manmohan Singh, Finance Secretary Montek Singh Ahluwalia and Chief Economic Adviser (the author).

Finance Minister P. Chidambaram (*seated*) with the Budget Group 1996 (*standing L–R*): Revenue Secretary M.R. Sivaraman, Expenditure Secretary N.K. Singh, Finance Secretary Montek Singh Ahluwalia and Chief Economic Adviser (the author).

Washington friends, after thirty years (L-R): Ranu and Anupam Basu, Gopal and Radhika Yadav, Gayatri and the author, 2000.

With Michael Minton atop the roof of Merton College chapel, Oxford, 2000.

Reunited after thirty-three years (L-R): the author, Chris Verity and Ray Tallis. England, 2000.

With Gayatri in the Ta Prohm temple at Angkor Wat: Ficus trees versus temple stones, 2003.

Dr Manmohan Singh (*left*) and Dr C. Rangarajan (*centre*) releasing the author's first collection of columns, 2003.

With Gayatri, Nixi and Ta at San Gimignano, Tuscany, Italy, 2005.

Book release (*L-R*): Dr Isher Ahluwalia, chairperson, ICRIER; the author; Montek Singh Ahluwalia, deputy chairman, Planning Commission; and Manzar Khan, MD, Oxford University Press, 2006

Old friends (*seated L-R*): Gayatri, Parvati (Pabi) Wadhawan, Liz Minton; with Michael Minton and the author standing behind. Udaipur, 2009.

At a Neemrana Conference (circa 2010): Prof. Anne Krueger, Honourable Vasundhara Raje Scindia and the author in the foreground, with Dr Raghuram Rajan and Surjit Bhalla just behind.

Hanging on for dear life at Devil's Pool, Victoria Falls, Zambia, 2011.

With Daw Suu Kyi in Lodi Gardens, November 2012.

The author with Gayatri at Rockefeller Foundation's Villa Serbelloni, Bellagio, in their suite, with Lake Como in the background, 2013.

Kotak Mahindra Bank board of directors: Front row (*L–R*) N.P. Sarda, Uday Kotak (Executive Vice Chairman and Managing Director), the author (Chairman), Farida Khambata, Dipak Gupta (Joint Managing Director) and Amit Desai. Second row (*L–R*) Prof. S. Mahendra Dev, Mark Newman, C. Jayaram and Prakash Apte. Mumbai, 2016.

Dr Sudipto Mundle (*left*), Prof. Amita Batra (*second from right*) and the author with State Counsellor Daw Suu Kyi (*second from left*) at her residence in Myanmar, December 2017.

The author's portrait hanging in Keble College's special 150th Anniversary exhibit, Oxford, 2019-20.

Celebrating the author's seventy-fourth and Dada's eightieth birthdays. (*Seated L–R*): Shekhar Dasgupta (Gayatri's brother), Kajal Jhala (Gayatri's sister), Sanjoy (Dada), Gayatri. (*Standing L–R*): Devika Dasgupta, Manjula (Dada's younger daughter), the author, Ta, Lalita (Dada's elder daughter) and Nixi. Gurgaon, October 2019.

Celebrating the author's seventy-fifth birthday quietly at home in the year of Covid-19, October 2020.

payments. In a market system, such high-trade deficits should normally lead to currency depreciations, which would help correct the imbalance. But our exchange rate policy then was a fixed peg against an undisclosed basket of international currencies. The policy had been substantially improved in 1983, with Montek's close involvement, to allow for de facto incremental depreciation. Some had occurred, but our real effective exchange rate (allowing for differential rates of inflation with respect to major trading partners) still remained way too high. I chivvied Bimal often on the need for further depreciation. He sometimes agreed and we took fresh notes to the Cabinet a couple of times in those years to facilitate this. Interestingly, notes on exchange rate policy went to the Cabinet committee on political affairs rather than the usual Cabinet committee on economic affairs, underlining the sensitivity of the subject. While exports (in dollars) did rise at over 10 per cent a year over 1985–90, this growth was on a low base and not enough to prevent mounting pressures on our balance of payments (BoP). Much of this pressure emanated from rising fiscal deficits, which 'spilled' into external ones.

Aside from the exchange rate, our foreign trade policy in those times was hugely messed up by astonishingly high customs tariffs, and a complex and comprehensive system of import licences and other trade barriers under the rubric of 'quantitative restrictions' (QRs). The post-war General Agreement on Trade and Tariffs (GATT) among contracting nations disallowed these, except under temporary bouts of extreme BoP pressure, as outlined in its Article 18 (b). We, of course, had liberally interpreted the notion 'temporary' to extend to over forty years, perhaps because of our habit of referring frequently to 5000 years of history since the Indus Valley civilization! Anyway, we had to defend our indefensible policies to the GATT in Geneva every alternate year. Since the matter related to trade, it was handled by the commerce ministry, which would send a small delegation, led by the commerce secretary or the chief controller of imports and exports (yes, we loved controls then). However, since it involved the BoP, the dealing senior DEA official had to go along. That meant me. When we turned up in Geneva, the usually turf-conscious commerce officials were quite content to sit back and let me argue our extremely weak case! So, I had to curb my economist instincts and adopt the garb of a nit-picking lawyer to defend our continuation of QRs with a straight face. Still, Geneva was a pretty nice place, and it allowed me to form collegial bonds with senior commerce colleagues (like Tejinder Khanna and Anwarul Hoda) over fondue and good wine. Tejinder later became lieutenant governor of Delhi and Anwarul served as the deputy director general of the World Trade Organization and, after that, Member, Planning Commission.

After the first two years of the Rajiv Gandhi government, its crucial axis between the PM and a reformist FM ruptured. V.P. Singh was an excellent tax-reforming FM, but part of his strategy of reduced income tax rates was stricter compliance requirements and expectations. This meant closer scrutiny of the accounts of big companies, including their dealings in forex. To ensure this, he shifted the Enforcement Directorate under the DEA to the revenue department, led by his trusted Vinod Pande, and appointed Bhure Lal as its director. Sure enough, the pips began to squeak to the PMO as the pressure of raids and investigations mounted. Singh was shifted from finance to defence in January 1987, with the finance portfolio being temporarily assumed by the PM. He oversaw the Budget of that year. Then came the famous Bofors scandal in spring 1987, followed by V.P. Singh's resignation and his subsequent formation of the opposition Janata Dal party.

The Rajiv Gandhi government never really recovered from these upheavals. As a consequence, the finance ministry lost its reforming zeal, with the portfolio being held, in succession, by veteran politicians like N.D. Tiwari and S.B. Chavan, who had little interest in pushing economic and financial reforms. Of course, government work went on, but for me, the excitement and involvement of the initial two years diminished with time. At my level, we continued to produce the annual Economic Surveys (mostly delegated to me by Bimal) and our increasingly gloomy medium-term BoP projections, with little discernible effect on the government's economic policies. Luckily, several important, reform-oriented official reports got written then by various committees led by reformist senior civil servants like Abid Hussain and M. Narasimham. These were to come in very handy when reform winds revived strongly after the 1990–91 BoP crisis. Oddly, as economic policy became more somnolent, the tribe of well-trained government economic advisers expanded, with the induction of Rakesh Mohan in the industry ministry and Jayanta Roy in commerce. This improved the quality of inter-ministerial economic interactions as well as our off-duty social lives.

With our children growing up, Gayatri decided to resume her teaching career in 1988. She was offered a temporary appointment in St. Stephen's, which she took for a term or two before shifting to her old Miranda House, which offered her a permanent position. We engaged a driver, so that she could commute to Miranda from our home in our Maruti 800. Unlike the snobby, privileged youngsters in St. Stephen's, she found the students in Miranda to be at least as good intellectually, and with far more diverse social and economic backgrounds.

Sometime in 1987, on Bimal's initiative, we instituted a system of monetary targets agreed between the MoF and RBI, and formalized it through a note to Cabinet. It made more sense to target quantities in a system where prices, that is interest rates, were controlled. My work on monetary targeting and external sector issues took me to Mumbai fairly regularly to interact with Deputy Governor C. Rangarajan and Executive Director S.S. Tarapore. I established good a rapport with both and a warm, enduring friendship with Ranga. These good relationships were to become very important in ensuring close coordination between the MoF and the RBI in the 1990s, by when Rangarajan, Montek, Tarapore and myself had all moved up a notch in the technocracy: Rangarajan had become governor, RBI, Montek was finance secretary, Tarapore was deputy governor, RBI, and I was the CEA. Aside from the cordiality of relations among us, our continuity of engagement with the same broad area of economic policy was a major benefit.

It was during this period, the late 1980s, that our old friend from Washington, Anupam Basu, and his family moved to 'Bank House', Mumbai, as special adviser to the RBI on leave from the IMF for a couple of years. My Mumbai visits thus gave me very welcome opportunities to spend time with Anupam, Ranu and their daughter, Alo. They also visited us in Delhi. It was also during that time when my Oxford friendship with Kumar Advani, now a senior partner at A.F. Ferguson Associates, a leading chartered accountancy partnership, grew strong, and I came to know some of his Mumbai friends, like Nasser Munjee of HDFC and Camila Punjabi of Taj Hotels. Mumbai was never again the same for me after Kumar's untimely demise in the early 2000s.

It was in the latter half of the 1980s that the MoF cleared the way for State Bank of India and Industrial Credit and Investment Bank of India (ICICI) to seek credit ratings from international rating agencies, Moody's and Standard and Poor's. This was essentially to smooth the way for greater external commercial borrowing by Indian entities. It was in this context that I recall accompanying ICICI CMD N. Vaghul, and State Bank of India CMD D.N. Ghosh for road shows in the USA and Europe, to make pitches on the country's economy and policies. It was a novel and educational experience. As per the policy of these premier international rating agencies, their ratings for entities in developing countries were typically capped at that assessed for the relevant country even if the nation did not float sovereign bonds. We did manage to get satisfactory credit ratings for these entities, at least a notch higher than the one assigned to India in 2020.

Late in 1988, Bimal Jalan moved to Washington as our executive director to the IMF, and he was replaced in the CEA position by Nitin Desai from the Planning Commission. He too was a very pleasant and capable senior colleague. Further changes occurred in my local environment in early 1989. Rajiv Gandhi's trusted special secretary, Gopi Arora, was appointed as finance secretary in place of Venkitaramanan. As soon as he was apprised of the rather parlous situation of our BoP, he authorized Jagmohan Bajaj and me to go to Washington on an 'informal official' visit to hold preliminary discussions with the IMF on a possible loan, together with an associated programme. We held discussions with Hubert Neiss, director of the Fund's Asia department, and his team, trying to agree on an indicative programme. They wanted more fiscal adjustment than we thought might be feasible. We came back and reported to Gopi. By then, he had assessed a total lack of appetite at the political level, and the initiative was abandoned. Instead, the necessary BoP financing was obtained through a variety of channels, including use of unconditional IMF facilities, drawdown of our undisclosed reserves (see above) and getting our government oil companies to take short-term commercial loans. No reforms were undertaken to address the underlying structural weaknesses.

Towards the end of 1989, Congress lost the general elections to the Janata Dal and V.P. Singh became the prime minister. He summoned Bimal back from Washington to be his finance secretary, while Madhu Dandavate was appointed FM and Vinod Pande became cabinet secretary. The 1990 budget promised, amongst other things, a generous farmer loan waiver programme. Generally, economic policies lurched towards populism, as did the policy on expanding caste-based reservations in government jobs (the implementation of the Mandal Committee recommendations).

As fiscal policies became increasingly loose and pressure on the BoP rose, it became more and more difficult for MoF officials to manage the economic situation. Against this deteriorating background, and with negligible forward movement in corrective policies, I began to think of a break from the MoF. Even though I had been promoted to senior adviser, with the rank of additional secretary, the job essentially remained the same. I had resigned from the World Bank some years ago. Nevertheless, I was still often sounded for possible positions back in the Bank. Hitherto, I had politely demurred. When, in late summer of 1990, Johannes Linn, by now director of the development economics department, offered me the position of chief of the public economics division, I decided to accept. Stanley Fischer was then holding Hollis's old job as vice president of the DPS.

Gayatri was not at all happy, as she felt settled in Delhi and did not relish the prospect of life in the American suburbs with two small children. She made any return to the Bank conditional on my keeping a lien on the MoF job and proceeding only on deputation. Fortunately, Bimal agreed and the paperwork was sorted out. Just to be sure that she had a little place to return to in case I got 'stuck' in the Bank, Gayatri purchased a small flat in a college cooperative in Patparganj. I had to join the Bank by December, which was in the middle of the academic year. So she and the kids stayed on in Delhi, and she put in her application for long leave for two years from Miranda, beginning July 1991. Of course, we informed our mothers in Kolkata, who were understandably unhappy.

10

Washington Interlude

I ARRIVED IN WASHINGTON at the end of November 1990 to take up the reins of my new assignment. The first few weeks were spent with Anupam and Ranu in their comfortable guest bedroom in the spacious basement of their Falls Church house. They, along with Gopal and Radhika, provided not just material help but also unbounded affection, which helped smooth the transition back to the Washington area after nine years, especially in a cold winter month. After carpooling with Anupam for some days I bought a Honda Accord for ourselves—perhaps the best car I have ever owned. Towards the end of the month, Gayatri came over for a few weeks to help us settle down in our old Airlie Way townhouse, while Monica and Mrinal very kindly babysat Ta and Nixi in Delhi. As it happened, Gopal and Radhika had recently moved into the same development for a couple of years, for school-district purposes. This proved to be a tremendous support for us, especially after Gayatri returned with Ta and Nixi in June 1991.

I reported for work on 1 December, and got to know my new division of ten or so professional economists. Thankfully, they were a very capable group with diverse skills within the broad ambit of public economics. The two stalwarts were Emmanuel Jimenez (aka Manny), a Filipino-Canadian, and Zmarak Shalizi from Afghanistan. They would be my two right hands over the next two years, with Manny being my de facto deputy and becoming a good friend Over the next few months, I recruited Christine Wallich (American, from within the Bank) and Shanta Devarajan, a Sri Lanka–born American, who was an associate professor at Harvard. In the last case, the 'recruitment' was really done by Larry Summers, who had, in the meantime, come from Harvard to replace Stanley Fischer as vice president, DPS and the Bank's chief economist, with the latter having been 'promoted' to become deputy managing director of the IMF. After a few months, I also enticed Amaresh Bagchi to join as a 'long-term consultant' for a year.

Rather like twenty years before, when I had worked in the domestic finance division of that time, led by Stanley Please, as a YP, our work programme comprised a combination of research and operational support, with an occasional policy paper thrown in. Amongst our flagship products during my two years was a policy paper (later monograph) on 'Lessons of Tax Reform' (1991) and a conference volume on 'Public Spending and the Poor', which focused on the efficacy of 'targeting' public subsidies and benefits. For the conference in mid-1992, I recall persuading Amartya Sen to come down from Harvard to give the keynote address on 'Theory of Targeting'. Outside the division, Johannes provided very good leadership and support as the department director, until he got promoted, perhaps eighteen months after I joined, to be a vice president in the finance complex and was replaced by Nancy Birdsall.

Actually, returning to the Bank after nine years, I felt a bit like Rip Van Winkle waking up. Much had changed and much had remained the same. The institution was still full of talented staff, but it was still an inward-looking organization—too preoccupied with its processes, procedures and promotions. Coming from the more real world of Delhi and India, I couldn't help thinking that the Bank was like a 'dark star', a black hole where the high density of its matter exerts such strong gravitational pull that light not does not escape! But perhaps such negative views may have been influenced by my own sense of displacement and disorientation, which sometimes led me to wonder what I was doing there. Over lunch one day, Oktay Yenal, who had been a former chief of the Bank's domestic finance division, told me he had faced the same questions and unease when he first returned to headquarters after a stint overseas.

Towards the end of May 1991, I went to Delhi to wrap up the household in Kautilya Marg, and bring back Gayatri and the kids with me to Washington. I flew in shortly after the assassination of Rajiv Gandhi in Tamil Nadu, while he was on the campaign trail for the elections that summer. The mood was sombre. While we proceeded with the wind-up of our household, another, more personal, blow struck us. I got a call that Ma had had a major asthma attack and had passed away. She was seventy-four. We flew to Kolkata to mourn her passing, deal with the practical matters and be with what remained of her family on Darga Road. After a couple of weeks, we returned to Delhi and then caught a flight to Washington.

Ma was a remarkable person, very loving with her family, highly intelligent, well-educated, modern in outlook, charming and beautiful. Had she been born a couple of decades later, she would very likely have developed as a very successful professional woman in whatever area she chose to pursue. But the prevailing sociology of her times came in the way.

Annandale with small children was quite a different life than during our earlier incarnation as a young professional couple. A fair bit of our lives revolved around their routines. We registered them in the primary school, Columbia Elementary, located behind our development. It was a five-minute walk from our front door. Our weekend activities now were much more oriented to destinations like Pet a Pet Farm (where you could pet various baby animals of domesticated species), the National Zoo (where you were advised not to pet even the baby hippopotami) and Busch Gardens with its joy rides. There were also Hindi classes in the 'India school' on Saturday mornings in a school building in Bethesda (later in Fairfax). Of course, some of our old destinations were also fun with the kids, like the National Aquarium in Baltimore, Shenandoah, Williamsburg and Chincoteague, where wild horses roamed free on the Atlantic beach. And, of course, there were the wonders of McDonald's and lots of reasonably priced Chinese, Thai and Vietnamese restaurants in the Virginian suburbs. One very successful Thai restaurant, not far from our home, was Duangrat's, opened by one of the secretaries in my WDR 1979 unit, Pookie Duangrat!

The best thing about being back in Washington was the rebonding with all our old friends, including Jayati and Gautam, Teresa and Viguen, Suman and Maitreyi, Armeane and Mary, Gene and Kathy, and so on. Our centre of gravity remained our 'Virginian friends', especially Anupam and Ranu, and Gopal and Radhika. Gayatri also had her circle of ex-colleagues from the GMU English faculty.

Dada had come down with Ann from Ontario in September 1991 to Gaithersburg (later Germantown) for fifteen months to do a project for Bechtel. That allowed us to get together quite often, including, sometimes, with their now grown children when they visited their parents. During Christmas–New Year of 1991, we had a marvellous get-together in our home for several days, with Monica and her two kids, and Twinky and her two children (she and her daughter, Bibi, were in America to visit Sanjoy, who was attending Harvard College). It was wall-to-wall family in our little townhouse, but great fun. Monica had, in the meantime, parted from Mrinal and was now with Devraj Ray, an economics professor at Boston University, whom she soon married.

Meanwhile, the news from Delhi was exciting. Narasimha Rao had become the prime minister in June 1991, Manmohan Singh had been appointed as finance minister, and sweeping economic reforms were being undertaken against the backdrop of a serious balance of payments of crisis—of the kind I had predicted year after year as economic adviser in the MoF. Montek became secretary, DEA, that November.

Around April of 1992, I got a call from S. Venkitaramanan, by now governor of the Reserve Bank, sounding me for the position of deputy governor in place of somebody who was retiring. I said I would give it serious consideration and revert in a couple of days. I discussed it with Gayatri and she was opposed to it, since it would involve moving to Mumbai, settling down in a new city and looking for a new job for herself, not to mention the upheaval of another transcontinental move in less than a year. I called the governor back and indicated our reluctance. He was sorry, but also a bit distracted by the major securities scam that had just exploded in the Mumbai markets (the Harshad Mehta scandal). I also had an inkling that sometime soon I might be invited to take the position of chief economic adviser (CEA), which had become vacant. Nitin had left for the UN in 1990 and V.P. Singh had inducted Deepak Nayyar into the job in the latter half of that year. But Nayyar had reverted to Jawaharlal Nehru University at the end of 1991, as he was apparently uncomfortable with the market-friendly reforms underway. The MoF was making do with a stopgap in the form of Dr Ashok Desai as 'chief consultant'.

A little later, I went on my first official mission to China with Shahid Yusuf, then the senior Bank economist on the country. Shahid, a few years my junior at Harvard, was a warm and erudite guide on China. He regaled me with offbeat 'reform stories', such as the year when Mao-era tunics were shed and the legs of Chinese women cyclists became visible! For me, the visits to Beijing, Tianjin, Shanghai and Guangzhou (formerly Canton) were eye-openers. The cities were booming. As I remember writing to Gayatri about my train ride from Guangzhou to Hong Kong, the 'countryside on the way seems to be sprouting factories on either side of the train track'. That, incidentally, was the year of Deng Xiaoping's famous swing through southern China to revive the momentum of market-oriented reform.

In July that year, we went on our home leave, stopping to visit Mike and Liz (and their children) in Oxford for some days on our way, and looking up Stanley and Margaret Please, who had retired from the Bank to a cottage in Marsden, a village suburb in north Oxford. Aside from spending time with them, I wanted our young children to meet the most important mentor in my professional life. In Delhi, we stayed at the IIC, and caught up with all our Delhi friends, and the gossip in the MoF and other parts of the government. We also met with Sunethra, who was visiting from Colombo and had recently parted from her second husband. We proceeded to Kolkata to look up our relatives. Darga Road without Baba or Ma seemed very empty to me. Gayatri's Ma joined us on our return trip to Washington to spend a few months with us in Annandale. On the way, we stopped in Geneva and Bern, the old Dasgupta 'home town'.

Back in Washington, the American presidential election campaign was in full swing, our children had settled into their new environment and we were enjoying reconnecting with our old friends. We had the pleasure of several visits from the Bannerjis of Orange, and from Linda Bamber, and her husband, Fred, from the Boston area. Of course, we continued our fairly frequent interactions with Dada and Ann in Maryland. I also made a trip to Minneapolis to visit cousin Atashi.

At the Bank, Larry Summers was getting increasingly involved as a policy adviser in Bill's Clinton presidential campaign, which ended with his election in November and Larry's subsequent appointment as an assistant secretary of the US Treasury. A couple of months later, I got a call from Montek informing me that the UPSC had cleared my appointment as CEA and urging me to return as soon as possible. After consulting with Gayatri, I committed to returning in the first half of April 1993. I informed Nancy and Larry, and submitted my formal resignation from my permanent job in the Bank—for the second time. I daresay not many Indians may have done that. At the senior policy level of CEA, the question of seeking LWOP from the Bank did not arise. We decided that I would return in April, while the rest of the family would take a more leisurely route back, with an extended stop in Beijing, where Shekhar had recently become the Indian Ambassador. There was some last-minute juggling of dates to accommodate Ta and Nixi getting chicken pox!

11

Chief Economic Adviser for Eight Years

IN THE SECOND WEEK of April 1993, having checked into a room in the IIC, I reported for duty at the stately North Block of the Central Secretariat on Raisina Hill for duty. Little did I know then that I would serve in that post for eight years as India's longest-serving CEA, advising three very talented finance ministers: Manmohan Singh, P. Chidambaram and Yashwant Sinha.

I was welcomed to my office by then Joint Secretary (administration and Fund–Bank) Nand Kishore Singh (aka NK, or Nandu), a man of many parts, with whom I was to develop a good working relationship as well as a lasting friendship Among NK's great assets were his ability to get things done and to collaborate productively across the full range of players: Politicians, fellow IAS officers and government economists. These capabilities were to stand him in good stead over a long and distinguished public service career, including, most recently, as chairman of the 15th

160

Finance Commission. Soon enough, I met with Montek (secretary, DEA), Manmohan (now FM, and to be addressed unfailingly as 'sir'), and other senior officers in the MoF. The other two departmental secretaries were K. Venkatesan, heading expenditure, and M.R. Sivaraman, in charge of revenue. Siva, a very bright, upright and hard-driving head of revenue (with a hobby of flying planes!), would spearhead our tax reforms for the next two years. Among the joint secretaries in the DEA were, aside from NK, old friend Venu Reddy in charge of external commercial borrowing and capital markets, Deb Mukherji handling foreign trade, Janaki Kathpalia heading budget, and D. Subbarao, the youngest, in charge of UN affairs, currency and coinage. Years later, two of them would become RBI governor (Venu and Subba) and two would become Finance Commission chairmen (Venu and NK). A strong team by any standards.

Among the officers in the economic division, the two EAs were now Dr Tarun Das and Dr Rajiv Kumar (who, in 2018, became vice chairman of Niti Aayog); the other advisers included Dr Arvind Virmani (later CEA in the late 2000s) and Dr S.N. Kaul. My first task was to get to know them and resurrect some of the standard economy-monitoring systems that seemed to have suffered some entropy in my absence.

Manmohan Singh was a great pleasure to work with. His knowledge of the Indian economy and governmental systems was unmatched, having held all the key economic positions, including CEA, secretary, DEA, RBI governor and deputy chairman, Planning Commission, before becoming finance minister. As minister and senior colleague, he was always warm, courteous and generally supportive. In meetings, he listened carefully, rarely raising his voice, but when he spoke, his wisdom and substance shone through. He took his government responsibilities very seriously and was often more knowledgeable on a subject than the senior officer briefing him. Generally, he was reserved and slightly formal as a personality. That made the flashes of informality and wit even more charming. On rare occasions, with his guard down in the company of close colleagues, he could indulge in a little gossip and even giggle. In formal situations, both within India and abroad, he was the epitome of dignity, high seriousness and soft-spoken wisdom.

During his years as FM, it was quite clear to everyone that Montek, as secretary, DEA, and finance secretary, was his closest confidante and trusted senior officer. Both were brilliant and accomplished economists, who complemented each other in style and substance. Montek was the highly articulate extrovert, always pushing the boundaries of reform possibilities, sometimes moderated a little by his more experienced and cautious minister. On the other hand, the FM needed Montek's eloquence, drive, commitment and team-building skills to push through reform measures which were often both technically intricate and politically challenging. Looking back, it is clear to me that without Montek's relentless drive, persuasive advocacy and focus on both the big picture and the details, some of the reform successes of the 1990s may not have happened.

For me, it was both professionally and personally rewarding to work with both of them. Of course, it helped greatly that Montek was an old friend from my Oxford and Washington years, with whom I could be completely frank on any work issue.

Gayatri and the children had arrived in Delhi by late May 1993, and we were staying in two rooms in the IIC, waiting for our allotment of government housing. We got one eventually, a ground-floor D-I category flat (recently classified as C-II because of an extra room) in the pleasant locality of Satya Marg in Chanakyapuri, close to Yashwant Place and its Chanakya complex, Nehru Park and Sarojini Nagar market. Compared with our earlier Kautilya

Marg address, this was on the 'poorer side of the tracks'. The flat
was reasonably spacious, but not comparable with a decent private
one. I recall Armeane Choksi once visiting us on home leave from
Washington, looking askance at our rather basic accommodation
and asking, 'Shankar, why are you living in abject poverty? Why are
you doing this?' I had to respond with sanctimonious humour: 'To
serve my country, Armeane!'

As regards our children's schooling, Ta reverted to Sardar Patel
Vidyalaya and Nixi was placed in Junior Modern School, with a
helpful introduction from Isher. They both relied on school buses,
to commute to school. After a couple more years in Sardar Patel, Ta
shifted to the British School in Chanakyapuri. They both missed
their cousins immensely, with Monica's kids in America and Kajal's
in Kolkata. One consolation was the arrival of Kajal's middle son,
Ranjit (aka Doopy), to attend the five-year programme at the Delhi
IIT. He soon became a regular weekend guest. Overall, Ta and Nixi
seemed content to be in India. When Gayatri once asked Nixi
whether he preferred to be in Virginia or in Delhi, he recounted
all the delights and bounties of America but still said he preferred
to be back in Delhi. When pressed as to why, he replied, 'Because
everyone here has black hair like me.' Such are the foundations of
tribalism!

Soon, I was asked by the FM and Montek to prepare a short
progress report on the economic reforms, entitled 'Economic
Reforms: Two Years After', which would detail the major economic
reforms undertaken thus far and provide a record of the 'early
harvest' in terms of economic outcomes. This we did and placed
in Parliament as a DEA booklet and had it distributed widely. At
about the same time, an external report had been commissioned
to be done by US-based leading academics Jagdish Bhagwati and
T.N. Srinivasan. That too was made into a booklet and distributed.
One day, the FM took me aside and said, 'Shankar, I think ours is

better.' That pleased me, but I was experienced enough to know that he may have paid similar compliments to Jagdish and TN.

Sometime in 1994, Rajiv Kumar left for a position in the Asian Development Bank. I managed to persuade a bright young economist, Bibek Debroy, to join in his place as a consultant for a year. In 2018, Debroy was to become chairman of the Economic Advisory Council to Prime Minister Modi. Later, Dr Ashok Lahiri came from the IMF to fill that position. He was to become the CEA a couple of years after I demitted the office.

At the MoF (and ministries of commerce and industry), much of the big-ticket reforms had been launched in 1991–92, including: Virtual abolition of industrial licensing, similar dispensing of import licensing for capital goods and intermediates (but not, importantly, for consumer goods), transition to a market-based exchange rate system, the beginning of customs tariff reductions, an opening to foreign investment (both direct and portfolio), and some reforms in the financial sector. A great deal still remained to be done, including defending and nurturing the reforms already undertaken, all of which would occupy us fully through the rest of the 1990s.

Some reduction in the fiscal deficit had already occurred, but by late 1993, we feared breach of the IMF's fiscal conditions for 1993–94. Since our balance of payments situation had markedly improved on the back of a surge in exports and higher capital inflows, we made a virtue of necessity by not drawing the last tranche of the extant IMF loan and terminating the associated programme prematurely. Thus, we were never in default of our programme obligations, while the loan itself had provided valuable and timely emergency support to our stressed balance of payments. Both sides felt good about this. It was, in an important sense, an excellent example of how short-term BoP support from the IMF should be deployed, as temporary bridging finance, while the underlying problem is solved through good policies. Interestingly, studies show that such successful examples are somewhat uncommon in the Fund's history.

We resumed the necessary fiscal consolidation for our own good in 1994–95, helped by the measures in the 1994 February Budget, which included large-scale elimination of the hundreds of end-use-related exemptions in our customs and excise duty structures. We also continued the phased programme of reducing our very high customs duties. Both moves were in line with the recommendations of the excellent, recently published Raja Chelliah report on tax reforms.

As our external finances improved further, we moved, in 1994, to accept the responsibilities of 'current account convertibility' of the rupee under Article VIII of the IMF charter. So, members of the MoF–RBI delegation that attended the Annual IMF–World Bank meeting in Madrid that September (the fiftieth anniversary of the Bretton Woods conference that established these institutions) could hold their heads high. As usual, the delegation from Delhi included the FM, the RBI governor, a deputy governor, Montek, NK and me. With such a strong team, and with the set piece FM speeches drafted, I felt little guilt in sneaking off one afternoon with an Indian embassy official to see my first (and last) live bullfight! In the evenings, our ambassador took us (minus the FM and the governor) to see flamenco dances and partake of delicious Spanish cuisine. More substantively, on the Sunday, we, including Rangarajan, made a day trip to see the beautiful medieval city of Toledo, during which we agreed on the outlines of the bank interest rate liberalizations that were announced by the RBI shortly after our return to India.

That same month, a historic agreement was signed between Rangarajan, on behalf of the RBI, and Montek, on behalf of the MoF. This was the agreement to phase out, over three years, the ad hoc treasury bills system in operation since 1955, which effectively permitted the central government to borrow at will from the RBI to finance its deficit. That, in turn, meant that monetary policy was hostage to the government's fiscal deficits. Rangarajan had been pressing for this major reform, and Montek backed him. A former RBI governor himself, the FM agreed and the deal was done.

A very distinctive feature of that period was the closeness of consultation and collaboration (and personal friendships) between senior echelons of the MoF and RBI. Frequent informal dialogue was the norm. I took it for granted that I would be speaking to the governor, RBI, or the concerned deputy governor at least, a couple of times a week. There was a strong sense of team, which helped not just in the conception and execution of various reforms and policies, but also in their concerted projection to the media and external interlocutors. I mention this because it is my sense that such close interaction may not have lasted beyond the 1990s. If true, that is a great pity. A few years ago, there were well-publicized reports of an FM stating that he 'will walk alone' when the concerned RBI governor did not accede to his wishes for a lower policy interest rate. Two years back, there were widespread reports of a running feud between the secretary, DEA, and the RBI brass on a range of issues, including the possible transfer of 'excess capital' from the RBI to government coffers. (The relevant secretary was transferred soon thereafter). This sort of thing would have been simply inconceivable in the far more cooperative decade of the 1990s.

That year, 1994, confronted us with the unexpected 'problem' of a surge in foreign capital inflows as the world outside gained confidence in India and its economic management. The IMF gave us the conventional advice of letting the rupee appreciate as foreign funds poured in. Instead, we chose to build up forex reserves, partly because it was necessary, but more because we didn't want a currency appreciation to slow the ongoing export boom or fan domestic resistance to our ongoing programme of reducing high customs duties. A stronger currency would have cheapened imports and done that. Our shift to currency convertibility and lifting of quantitative controls on imports of some consumer goods, such as sugar and edible oils, also moderated the extent of forex build-up. This accumulation could have led to surging money supply, thus fuelling inflation, but we moderated that by selling government bonds and mopping up liquidity. Economists call this 'sterilization'.

Our pursuit of trade liberalization was resolute, with peak customs duties being reduced from 300 per cent (!) in 1990–91 to 50 per cent in 1995–96 to make cheaper investment and intermediate goods imports for our industry, making it more advantageous for our exporters. But these reductions were in the notified, applied tariffs, not in the GATT-bound rates, which we were prepared to reduce only as part of a multi-dimensional package in trade negotiations under GATT (later WTO). The phased reduction of effective customs duties met with resistance in some quarters of Indian industry, epitomized by the so-called 'Bombay Club'. However the policy was stoutly supported by the leading industry association, the Confederation of Indian Industry (CII), superbly led by its reformist secretary-general, Tarun Das.

Our capital markets were also reformed and strengthened greatly after the 1992 Harshad Mehta scam. The nascent Securities and Exchange Board of India (SEBI) was bolstered through legislation; the government-sponsored National Stock Exchange (NSE) was established, which soon outpaced the hoary Bombay Stock Exchange (BSE); and a law was enacted to ensure trading and issue of securities in paperless (dematerialized) form, with digital systems as the backbone of these operations. As the markets modernized and regulation improved, foreign institutional investors (FIIs) pumped in funds. This had the collateral benefit of improving the governance of listed companies. Later, between

1997–2000, I got the opportunity to get more deeply into capital market issues as the government member on the board of SEBI.

The fruits of wide-ranging reforms came soon, and were tasty. For the first time in India's history, overall economic growth (in GDP) averaged 6.5 per cent a year over 1992–97 (the highest in our post-Independence history for a five-year period)—in several of these years exceeding 7 per cent—and industry grew faster than GDP. Exports (in dollars) surged at over 15 per cent per year, and the average current account deficit in the BoP remained comfortable, at about 1 per cent of GDP. The fiscal deficit (centre and states combined) came down from over 9 per cent of GDP in 1990–91 to 6 per cent in 1995–96. Inflation during this period was a little high, at 7 per cent, but well below the 40 per cent average for developing countries in this period.

All this could not have happened without the sustained support of Prime Minister Narasimha Rao, probably our best PM ever in terms of economic policy and performance, and his PMO, ably led by Amar Nath Varma, who maintained strong, productive links with the MoF and other economic ministries. My contact with the PM was limited to attending a few Cabinet meetings and the Budget-related interactions each year where FM, the three MoF secretaries and myself would hold discussions with the PM and his principal secretary on the broad outlines of the budget proposals, and, later, the contents of the Budget speech. He always listened carefully, but was generally fairly taciturn at these meetings, preferring to convey any specific reactions or suggestions to FM separately or via Amar Nath Varma. It must also be acknowledged that during these years, India benefited much from a buoyant world economy (the 'Clinton boom'). Nevertheless, a great deal of credit has to go to FM Manmohan Singh, and his team at the MoF and the RBI, especially Montek and Rangarajan. I have always felt privileged to be a member of that very special group.

One important area where we did not make progress was labour reforms. Both Montek and I were fully convinced about the need for reforming our exceptionally rigid and complex labour laws, which worked to protect hardly 10 per cent of our labour force, who held regular jobs in the organized sector, and discouraged employment of the 90 per cent of workers, who toiled for very low earnings in the informal sector. Around 1993, the labour secretary had a draft Cabinet note ready to amend the Industrial Disputes Act in order to make it more friendly towards fresh hiring. However, there was no political appetite for taking this forward. Successive governments ducked this knotty problem of labour policy reforms over the ensuing quarter century, with profound negative consequences for the country's burgeoning labour force and its parlous employment prospects.

Our own social life continued pretty much as before, with the noticeable difference that my average daily office hours were significantly longer than when I had been an EA. In the spring of 1994, Mike and family visited us and took a trip around India. That began a tradition of frequent visits that have, thankfully, continued since over the past quarter century. The same was true for Sunethra, from Colombo. This was at a time when her younger sister, Chandrika, was winning elections in Sri Lanka and soon became president of the country for the next ten years. As a family, we undertook short holiday trips whenever our work and school calendars permitted, mostly to Goa, Rajasthan, Rishikesh, various hill stations in Himachal and Uttarakhand, and, of course, Kolkata. Sometimes we made car trips with friends like Surjit Bhalla and family.

A very special trip towards the end my tenure as CEA was our family visit to Sri Lanka around Christmas 1999. Sunethra organized the whole thing, and very kindly lent us her car and driver to convey us around the many beautiful natural and historical sites of her country, including her charming country home in Horagolla designed by Geoffrey Bawa, the great Sri Lankan architect. It was during this decade of the 1990s that I also got to know Su's mother, Sirimavo, then prime minster, and her sister, Chandrika, then president, and formed a deeper understanding of the twenty-year civil war that was tearing the country apart. Chandrika was always confident, articulate and persuasive. Given the demonstrated ruthlessness of the Tamil Tigers, especially in assassinating political opponents, she was also extremely courageous in steadfastly pursuing a negotiated settlement to the civil war. The obduracy of the Tigers, led by their charismatic leader, Velupillai Prabhakaran, frustrated a peaceful solution. A week before we arrived in Colombo that December, an assassination attempt on her at the Town Hall left her half-blind in one eye. It was also around this time that Sunethra established her Sunera Foundation to set up a network of more than thirty 'workshops' across the country where skilled trainers deployed the therapy of theatre activities to motivate and give meaning to the lives of thousands of disabled children in Sri Lanka in the two decades since then.

Throughout the 1990s, I made a special effort to stay in sporadic telephonic contact with another good friend from Oxford, Aung San Suu Kyi, who was in and out of house arrest in Rangoon for twenty-two years between 1989 and 2011. It was only in the relatively short periods when she was out of house arrest that her phone was activated by the Burmese military government. Nevertheless, we managed to speak from time to time. As her phone was certainly bugged, our conversation was limited to personal and family news, sprinkled with memories of Oxford. Many years later, she told a mutual friend, 'Shankar was the only person in India who always kept in touch with me.'

With the high pressure of work and having no viable place of our own to stay in, we decided to look for a flat for ourselves, just in case I had to quit government service. Gayatri took on the burden of looking at nearly a hundred options, mostly in south Delhi, with me joining her only to check a few of the 'probables'. I had insisted that payment had to be fully in cheque, with none in unaccounted cash, which we didn't have anyway. That ruled out 99 per cent of the places we were shown by brokers. Finally, we found a small flat that met our rigorous condition, in Greater Kailash 2, through casual word of mouth at a social occasion. That's the one we bought, raising the funds by selling our townhouse in Annandale. And that's where we have stayed in since 2003, when we left government housing. In the interim, we rented it, first to Amaresh Bagchi, and then to a young, upcoming journalist, Rajdeep Sardesai, who came to discuss terms on a scooter. Later he became a major figure in serious media, perhaps a household name.

Good things do not last. In 1996, Congress was voted out of office and the motley United Front government assumed power for two years, the first with H.D. Deve Gowda as PM and the second with Inder Kumar Gujral. It was really a period of marking time. The best that can be said is that the reforms implemented in the previous five years were not reversed. Credit must also go to the finance minister, P. Chidambaram, for ensuring that there was no serious backsliding in reforms already undertaken. He was a very clever and articulate lawyer, often charming and sometimes arrogant. His so-called 'dream Budget' of 1997, which cut income tax rates, was predictably popular with the media and the well-off segments of society, but also contributed to a stalling in fiscal consolidation.

The bigger test came with the east Asian financial crisis, which began with the collapse of the Thai baht in July 1997 and spread quickly to the rest of south-east Asia and Korea. It was the world's first, multi-nation capital account BoP crisis, which set back the impacted economies by several years. By September, the gales of contagion had reached the shores of India. Our BoP came under significant pressure, with some flight of footloose capital and pressure on the exchange rate. Fortunately, thanks to our own painful experience with the 1991 BoP crisis, we had well-prepared defences. These included: Deliberate reduction of short-term external debt levels; maintenance of a competitive real exchange rate; keeping the current account deficit to moderate levels; explicit reluctance to deploy massive amounts of forex reserves in defence of any particular level of the exchange rate; a reasonably strong financial sector with little exposure to speculative markets such as stocks and real estate; and a willingness to tighten monetary policy as and when necessary.

Despite our favourable starting point, coping with the contagion was not easy. The RBI, in close consultation with us in the MoF, intervened actively in both spot and forward currency markets for the rupee, allowing some depreciation but with 'brakes on'. Monetary policy was substantially tightened from November onwards, culminating in a 2 per centage point increase in the Bank Rate and higher cash reserve requirements in January 1998. I recall helping to finalize this difficult decision with Bimal (recently appointed governor of RBI) and Montek in a long discussion in the former's Lodi Estate bungalow before he moved to the governor's mansion in Mumbai.

In those difficult autumn months of 1997, I was in almost daily telephonic touch with Governor Rangarajan, who described his role in that period as that of a 'desk officer' on India's exchange rate. Our long conversations did not reflect advice from the MoF to RBI. Ranga knew better than any of us what to try and what to do. He just needed someone to talk to, often and at length. So, my role resembled that of a psychoanalyst, listening to his problems as he thought through the possible solutions. When his term ended at the year's end and Bimal Jalan took over, my job as a personal 'shrink' to the governor ended. Bimal was more self-contained and preferred to play his cards closer to his chest. Fortunately, I continued my close communications with his deputy governor, and my old friend, Venu Reddy.

For India, there was one clear side benefit from the east Asian crisis. Between 1995 and 1996, the US Treasury had mounted increasing pressure on all countries to support an amendment to the IMF Articles of Agreement, which would make full capital account convertibility a desirable goal for all member nations, which the IMF would then chivvy them into fulfilling. We, and several other developing nations, were strongly opposed to this, as we felt it would make our economies vulnerable to massive volatility, stemming from the whims and developments in the huge international capital markets. Larry Summers, the US Treasury assistant-secretary, was the articulate point man for the American view in all official multi-nation meetings on finance. These pressures abated swiftly after the east Asian crisis!

This crisis also gave birth to a new international formation, the annual G-20 finance ministers' meeting. Following the Interim and Development Committee meetings in spring 1998 in Washington, the US Treasury convened a meeting of twenty-two finance ministers and central bank governors, representing about 90 per cent of global GDP, in the Willard Hotel, to strengthen the international financial architecture. FM Yashwant Sinha and Governor Jalan represented India, with Vijay Kelkar, Deputy Governor Reddy and I also present. US President Clinton gave a rousing speech in favour of stronger international financial cooperation. By the following year, this had become the G-20, with Canada's finance minister, Paul Martin, as the first chairman. The first meeting of the G-20 was held in Montreal in autumn 1999. Much of the agenda focused on moving towards common standards and codes in the international finance and capital markets, with the Bank for International Settlements (BIS) the principal locus of the analytical background work. The FM and Bimal represented India, with Venu and myself supporting. The same cast attended the next meeting in Berlin, in late 2000. While some progress was made, over time, these meetings lost momentum as the east Asian crisis receded into memory, degenerating into just another international talk shop. Perhaps the key advance for us was India's routine inclusion in such a group. A decade later, following the global financial crisis, the G-20 mechanism would be upgraded to a summit-level conclave.

Lest I give the impression that my working life as CEA meant just long hours at North Block, and a myriad meetings with ministers and officers, I should rectify that. There was plenty of interesting and pleasant official travel. Twice a year, I went to Washington as a member of the FM's delegation, once to attend the Bank–Fund annual meetings in the autumn and once for the meetings of the Development and Interim Committees of these organizations in the spring. The annual meetings were sometimes held outside Washington, taking me to places like Madrid, Hong Kong and Prague. Each June, when the weather was lovely in Europe, we would go to Paris to attend the meetings of the Aid India Consortium, chaired by the World Bank, where we would dutifully make our pitch to mid-level officials from donor nations. Once, Gayatri came along too and got temporarily misplaced in some museum by the official car, with the driver telling me in a distraught state, 'I have lost your woman' (in French 'la femme' can mean both wife and woman)! Luckily, 'my woman' was soon found. Later, we renamed this exercise as the India Development Partnership, with the first meeting in Tokyo, thanks to NK's long-standing good relations with the establishment in that country. Then there were the annual Commonwealth finance ministers' meetings (typically just before the Bank–Fund jamborees) held in a Commonwealth country. On three occasions, I had to deputize for the FM, twice for Chidambaram at Mauritius and Bermuda and once for Yashwant Sinha at Malta. Yes, the Commonwealth had a lot of lovely island nations.

In all these places, we were put up in swanky hotels, had chauffeur-driven limousines at our disposal and ate well. On the other hand, it was not uncommon for senior Indian officials to be found shopping for mundane items in a grocery store in Washington, late in the evening, to fulfil his wife's shopping lists from Delhi, and then getting into a large black sedan to be driven back to his plush hotel.

In September 1996, we shifted to better accommodation at CI/1, Lodi Gardens, basically on Amrita Shergil Marg and just across from the beautiful Lodi Gardens. It was a two-storeyed semi-detached house, with a lot more space for our growing children, small studies for Gayatri and me, a usable guest room and spacious lawns. We would stay there for the next seven years, the first five during my time as CEA and the last two while I was on study leave (sabbatical) before, as it so happened, taking early retirement from the government at the age of fifty-six. It was a much nicer home in every way and even Armeane may have approved! The proximity to Lodi Gardens and, with a short walk through them, to the IIC, were great boons, not to mention nearby Khan Market. I only got to enjoy the full benefits after I proceeded on leave in January 2001 and ceased to observe the long hours at the MoF. Dada and family visited us from Canada when we stayed there, as did Atashi from Minneapolis and the Bannerji tribe from Orange, Connecticut.

During this period, I was often invited by universities and colleges to speak on economic policy and reform. I accepted invitations whenever I could find the time to be away from official duties. I recall giving talks at the Delhi School of Economics, JNU, St. Stephen's, Hindu College and Miranda House. My most treasured invitation for giving a talk came around 1997 from my 'Rakhi sister'Vasundhara Nath, who was principal of the Bal Vikas School in Panipat. She had built this school from scratch, starting in 1985. By the time I went as chief guest at the annual day function to give a talk, it had matured into the premier school in Panipat, catering to over 1000 students. Later, to keep class sizes manageable and maintain its high quality, Vasundhara developed another school of comparable size under the auspices of the same Raj Trust. When I look back at what my Oxford peers accomplished, I think Vasundhara may have done the most to directly improve the human condition.

In March 1998, the National Democratic Alliance (NDA) came to power, with the Bharatiya Janata Party (BJP) as the dominant party in the coalition and Atal Bihari Vajpayee as the prime minister. He appointed Yashwant Sinha as finance minister. I was away at a conference in Colombo when news of the ministerial appointments came through and confessed to some misgivings to a colleague. All I knew about Sinha was that he was a member of Parliament from Bihar, and had served as finance minister in the short-lived, and somewhat forgettable, Chandra Shekhar government of 1990–91. I called on him on my return to Delhi. He was extremely courteous and straightforward and asked, 'Shankar, will you be able to work with us, the BJP?' I replied, 'Sir, I am a civil servant; it's my duty to offer the best economic advice I can to whoever is my minister.' That seemed to satisfy him and, fairly soon, we developed a good professional and personal equation.

The new FM knew his way around the government as he had spent many years in the IAS before resigning to join politics. He was knowledgeable, intelligent, extremely hard-working and unfailingly courteous to civil servants. In Parliament, he performed very well in both English and Hindi. More importantly, it soon became apparent that he was a strong and effective supporter of economic reforms, who was able to stand up to the inward-looking predilections of some groups like the Swadeshi Jagran Manch.

Within days of the new government gaining office, the 'Buddha smiled', when India carried out several underground nuclear tests in the Rajasthan desert near Pokhran. The action was immensely popular in India, even though it was followed, a few days later, by similar tests by Pakistan. Western countries and Japan deplored the move as an example of nuclear proliferation and against the spirit of the Nuclear Non-Proliferation Treaty, of which India was not a signatory. Economic sanctions in the form of aid suspensions were initiated. In the MoF, actions were taken to persuade major donors of our legitimate strategic needs and our legal rights under international law. I recall flying to London to persuade the head of the Overseas Development Department in the UK of the justness of our actions. Our diplomatic missions abroad mounted a comprehensive campaign. More practically, the State Bank of India was mobilized to market Resurgent India Bonds to non-resident Indians (NRIs) and raised about $5 billion to shore up our forex reserves. Over time, the initial sanctions, not harsh to begin with, were eased and India's nuclear weapons status was accepted as normal.

By November 1998, three of us from the early 1990s, Montek, NK (now revenue secretary) and I had become relative fixtures in the MoF. That month, matters changed. Montek was made member, Planning Commission, NK was shifted to the PMO as secretary, where Brajesh Mishra ruled as Vajpayee's trusted principal secretary, and I remained the last man standing in the MoF. Vijay Kelkar replaced Montek as head of the DEA and finance secretary. I had known Vijay in the brotherhood of government economists for many years, and was quite friendly with him. As the senior officer in the DEA, I had the pleasure of welcoming him to his new office in the MoF. The transition was smooth and we worked very closely together during his tenure at the DEA—also greatly strengthening our friendship. Vijay clothed his prodigious intellect behind an affable, slightly absent-minded exterior, but was very effective in gaining cooperation and commitment from fellow officers and the minister.

On the home front, our household had acquired a new member. One summer morning, as I read the newspapers in the living room, I heard a pathetic mewling sound from the garden just outside the window. Investigations revealed a little 'desi *kutta*' puppy in the flower bed, perhaps six or seven weeks old. Soon she had adopted us quite effectively. We called her Poochy (pooch for dog and 'y' for gender), and had a sizeable kennel built for her in our backyard, which Shekhar described as 'D-II accommodation'. That soon became surplus housing as she inveigled her way to the status of 'indoor pet'. Of all the family, she made the most use of the Lodi Gardens at our doorstep.

Vajpayee's NDA government pushed through a broad and deep range of economic reforms, with FM Yashwant Sinha and the MoF often playing a leading role. These included: A sustained reduction in import duties; removal of import restrictions on consumer goods; the New Telecom Policy of 1999, based on revenue-sharing, which triggered the astonishing and sustained boom in mobile telephony; the phasing out of 'reservation' of several hundred specified products for small-scale manufacturers; reduction of administered interest rates on some government savings instruments, which had tended to bias the prevailing interest-rate structure upwards; a shift to a single-modal rate for the central government's complex structure of domestic excise duty rates; the ushering in of value-added principles in state sales tax systems; successful completion of several real privatizations (as distinct from disinvestment of minority stakes); opening up to private providers of life insurance and general insurance with foreign equity up to 26 per cent; establishment of the National Highways Authority alongside a major new road-building programme, the 'golden quadrilateral'; and the passage of a pioneering fiscal responsibility law.

Unfortunately for the NDA, most of the fruits of this impressive array of reforms were not reaped until the 'golden age' of 2003–04 to 2010–11, when India's growth accelerated significantly to an unprecedented 8 per cent-plus. Growth during the actual NDA years, 1998–04, was relatively lacklustre, compounded by the bad luck of several poor monsoons. Thus, despite 'India shining' in the final year of this period, it proved insufficient for the NDA to win the 2004 election, when the Congress-centred United Progressive Alliance (UPA) won power. From my perspective, looking back over the last fifty-five years, I would rate the six years of economic policy and reforms under Vajpayee's NDA as second only to Narasimha Rao's five-year stint of 1991–96.

At the personal level, my last two-and-a-half years in the MoF with the NDA government was a fulfilling period, with close involvement in some of the reforms mentioned above. In particular, I played an active role in the tax policies of the two Budgets of 1999–2000 and 2000–01, especially with respect to the continued reduction of customs duties and the overhaul of the complex excise duty rate structure. A big breakthrough came in the 1999 February Budget, when eleven excise tax rates, ranging from 5 per cent to 40 per cent, were clubbed into just three (8, 16 and 24 per cent) and, in addition, two non-MODVAT-able additional special excises (at 6 and 16 per cent) were levied on a handful of luxury consumer goods. I recall suggesting the 'algorithm' to achieve this conflation in a politically acceptable form in our super-secret tax policy meetings in the office of the commissioner, Tax Research Unit (then the diligent and highly capable T. Rastogi), deep in the innards of the revenue department, where the FM and the Budget group finalized these sensitive rate decisions. In the next Budget, we conflated the three excise rates into a single CENVAT rate of 16 per cent, buttressed by three non-MODVAT-able special excise rates of 8 per cent, 16 per cent and 24 per cent. I was quite sad when these hard-won reforms were squandered, unnecessarily, by then FM Pranab Mukherjee at the back-end of 2008–09 as part of the government's response to the global financial crisis.

During this time, I often played bridge on weekends with a group centred on Sudhir Mulji and Tiger Pataudi, usually at Sudhir's elegant home in Malcha Marg or Tiger's Lutyens bungalow on Kamaraj Road. Sudhir was a businessman linked with Great Eastern Shipping, who had great and genuine interest in economics and economic policy. He and his warm-hearted wife, Rosaleen, often hosted dinner parties with varied and interesting guest lists, ranging from Amartya Sen to General K. Sundarji. Sudhir loved good conversation and bridge. At Tiger's home, we often had the unusual honour of being served tea by Sharmila Tagore (aka Rinku) during our bridge games. At times, a young Saif Ali Khan would slip in to help himself to a cup. Sadly, Sudhir passed away in his mid-sixties in 2006, and Tiger some years later.

During the Kargil War of the summer of 1999, Vijay and I were asked to brief the Cabinet committee on political affairs (CCPA) on our economic situation. Conscious of our high fiscal deficits, we suggested (with prior clearance from FM) the need for a temporary surcharge on income tax to finance the additional costs of the conflict. PM Vajpayee looked a little uncomfortable, and FM Sinha quickly suggested that we could take up the matter at a subsequent meeting. Luckily, our armed forces ensured a quick victory and we did not have to cause any further discomfort to the CCPA!

My interactions with PM Vajpayee, as with his predecessors, were limited to a few Cabinet meetings, and the much smaller group discussions on the contours of each annual Budget and the associated Budget speech. Somewhat like Narasimha Rao, Vajpayee tended to be an alert listener, rather than a close interlocutor of the FM and his team as they presented their proposals. Sometimes, when he was uncomfortable, he would interject, '*Yeh kaise ho sakta hai?*' and sit back to listen to FM Sinha's advocacy or explanation. Compared to the rather inscrutable Rao, Vajpayee generally conveyed a more friendly and avuncular demeanour. In Parliament, of course, he was a much more eloquent speaker whenever he chose to intervene.

Seen in a broader perspective and with the benefit of hindsight, Vajpayee's political achievement in greatly advancing economic reforms was perhaps even more admirable than Rao's, since the former had to work with a much more unwieldy political coalition, and without the benefit of the urgency and necessity imparted by a grave economic crisis like that of 1991. What cannot be gainsaid is that when their achievements are taken together, these two prime ministers from two very different political parties bequeathed a legacy of almost thirteen continuous years of economic reforms, which laid the foundations of India's exceptional growth spurt between 2003 and 2011.

In autumn 1999, Vijay Kelkar sounded me for the position of India's executive director to the IMF, which was falling vacant. We discussed this in our family, giving two members decisive 'casting votes'. Poochy could not have come with us and clearly did not want us to go, at least so we inferred. More importantly, Gayatri flatly refused to raise teenagers in America. So I conveyed my 'no thanks' to Vijay. A few weeks later, he himself accepted the post and proceeded to Washington. He was replaced in the DEA secretary-ship by E.A.S. Sarma, a very able, upright and warm-hearted IAS officer, with whom I soon bonded well. Though a physicist by training, Sarma had a thorough grasp of economic policy issues. Sometimes he would relax by reading books or papers on string theory!

One of my duties as CEA was to be the key drafter of the FM's annual Budget speech, certainly Part A of it and often Part B too, dealing with tax policy changes. In the latter case, the draft came to the FM from the revenue secretary. However, in most instances, the FM turned to me for ensuring that sufficient economic rationale was woven in and that the language flowed easily. During the two years of the United Front government, my drafting role was somewhat reduced as Chidambaram also called on the skills of his adviser, Jairam Ramesh. Putting the Budget speech and the 'Budget at a Glance' finally to bed, before the print order was given, was also an onerous task; the documents were usually triple checked by the secretary DEA, the CEA and AS/JS for Budget. All that was typically done late in the wintry evenings around 25–27 February, down in the Budget Press in the basement of the MoF, access to which was very strictly controlled. Over my eight years as the CEA, I played this role for seven regular Budgets and a couple of interim ones.

Sometime in 1999, I had received an invitation from Merton College, Oxford, one of the oldest and richest colleges, to be Visiting Research Fellow for the summer term of 2000. This was at the instance of Vijay Joshi, the college's long-standing economics don, whom I had known for many years and who was a friend. I obtained three months' leave (April–June) from the ministry, starting after the 2000 Budget session of Parliament had concluded. After seven years as CEA, and with no desire to take on the administrative burdens of secretary-ship or governor-ship of RBI, I had been pondering a shift to academia or economic journalism. This Merton stint offered just the right opportunity for me to test life without the routine of the in-tray and out-tray of the last fifteen years. Oxford was also where our old friends Mike and

Liz were well settled, and a three-month stay in England offered me the chance of renewing old, close bonds with Chris Verity and Ray Tallis (my old Keble College friends) after an interregnum of thirty years.

So off I went in early April, with Gayatri to follow after a few weeks. Oxford, as a Fellow, turned out to be an absolute delight, in so many ways. I was allotted a charming two-bedroom flat in a renovated fourteenth-century cottage just opposite Merton's Lodge. All meals were available at the college, with dinners at the 'high table' for Fellows in the dining hall and lunches in a separate dining room adjacent to the Senior Common Room. The food was incomparably better than what we had got as students (at Keble), and there was always good wine with dinner from the college's cellars, with port to follow. I had no teaching or other duties and could do what I wanted, which I proceeded to do. I used most of the time to see and savour Oxford as a well-heeled tourist during the week, and visited with Chris in Cambridge, Ray in Manchester or the Mintons nearby over the weekends. And they, in turn, would visit me. After Gayatri joined me, we would rent a car, and drive to lovely villages and abbeys in the Cotswolds area near Oxford, or go down to London. It also gave me time to read widely on anything that interested me. The rebonding with Chris and Ray was a special highlight, and we have refreshed our bonds with them through visits every year since.

After returning to the MoF, and resuming my duties as CEA, my thoughts turned increasingly towards moving to a think tank to research and write about India's economic policies and performance—armed with the knowledge and experience of an insider, and also to fulfil a long-held ambition of being a regular economics commentator in the newspapers. I had already given a couple of memorial lectures and turned them into scholarly papers, and had enjoyed doing that. It so happened that Isher

Ahluwalia had taken over the directorship of the Indian Council for Research on International Economic Relations (ICRIER) in 1998, and was in the process of revamping the institution. She gave me a standing offer to join as professor. My official colleagues strongly advised me against resignation. So, in September 2000, I adopted the middle path of requesting eighteen months' study leave from the government, beginning in spring 2001, preceded by four months of regular leave. The government kindly agreed to this. So, my last day in the CEA's office was 31 December 2000. I left one tangible legacy, the board on the wall behind the CEA's desk listing the CEAs (and their dates) since 1955, when the office was created. I had it made and mounted half-way through my tenure. I had been the 'tenth guru'. There have now been nearly that many since my departure.

Looking back on my sixteen years in the MoF since February 1985 (with a two-year deputation to the World Bank in between), I marvel at my good fortune. After twenty-three years abroad, and another couple at NIPFP, the Indian government had given me the opportunity to serve at its highest levels as a professional policy economist in the nerve centre of the MoF. I had learnt a great deal, enjoyed the comradeship of many fine officers, and, above all, had been accepted as 'one of us' by the 'system'. Perhaps, I had even managed to contribute a little to making our economic policies better. As CEA, I had also been blessed with the good luck of working for three of India's finest finance ministers. Manmohan Singh was the best, with Yashwant Sinha a close second. I was also fortunate to have worked with three outstanding DEA secretaries, Montek, Vijay and EAS. What more can a policy economist ask for? Without question, my eight years as CEA were the most professionally fulfilling period of my life.

12

New Horizons

THE FIRST DAY OF 2001 found me in the garden of our Lodi Gardens home, relaxing in a chair with my feet up, a mug of steaming decaf coffee in my hand and playing with Poochy, as she gambolled around the garden. There was no rush to head for North Block, though Budget season was upon us. What I savoured most was the sense of relief and freedom. Relief, because as a senior MoF official, there was always something to be done: Files to clear, meetings to attend or organize, notes to dictate, special initiatives to undertake or nurture, Parliament questions to answer, telephone calls to return, urgent summons from the FM or secretary, and so forth. It was all very busy and sometimes fulfilling, but it was also stressful. All that was behind me. And the sense of freedom came from shedding the responsibility to speak on and defend government policy. For senior serving officers, it was their incumbent duty, when interacting with the media or other interlocutors, to make the best possible case for any particular policy, no matter what their private assessment was. Now I could speak my mind—even write it—without fear or favour, within the limits of the Official Secrets Act, libel laws and common decency. The government was now somebody else's headache. It really was like shedding a load one had carried implicitly for many years.

I had left matters in the MoF in good order. Work on the year's Economic Survey was well advanced. For obvious reasons, I had not been participating in the Budget group discussions. A few weeks before I left, FM Yashwant Sinha had sought my views on an appropriate CEA candidate to replace me. I had unhesitatingly recommended Rakesh Mohan, who was then rebuilding the National Council of Applied Economic Research (NCAER) as its director general. Others I mentioned for consideration included Isher Ahluwalia and Partha Shome, the well-known fiscal economist. As I had expected, Rakesh was appointed as acting CEA within a fortnight of my departure.

Formally, I was on regular leave till April, with my study leave at ICRIER as honorary professor only starting on 1 May. This was to prolong our incumbency of the Lodi Garden home to cover the period up to Nixi's class twelve boards in spring 2003. But Isher had kindly allocated an office and support staff to me at ICRIER from the beginning of the year. I began to go there regularly fairly soon. I could come and go as I pleased, and work (or not!) on whatever I wanted. There was no boss to report to; I only had to keep the director, Isher, informed of my broad academic activities as a matter of courtesy. As it happened, she sought my advice and inputs on matters big and small quite frequently. My most pressing set of commitments that spring was to help Nixi prepare for his class ten board exams in science and mathematics, as he was an average student in these subjects. Another preoccupation was binging on bridge!

During that spring, Mythili Bhusnurmath, a senior journalist with the *Economic Times* (*ET*), approached me about writing a monthly column. I happily accepted, as this was something I had long aspired to do. I postponed starting the column till May, when my study leave formally started, to avoid having to seek any official clearance while I was on regular leave. Thus began my 'third' occupation or career (after the World Bank and government) of being a regular columnist on economic matters. That was twenty years ago, and I still write.

In ICRIER, I focused on writing a set of 'scholarly' papers targeting the well-known *Economic and Political Weekly* (*EPW*), India's best social science journal. Predictably, my subjects included economic reforms, macroeconomic management, tax reform, external sector issues and growth performance. Generally, my approach was to write analytical economic history of the recent past, explaining the government's policies and their outcomes, including successes and failures. Krishna Raj, the long-standing and superb editor of *EPW*, was very welcoming of these efforts. Later, I collected them in a volume, *Essays on Macroeconomic Policy and Growth in India*, which was published in 2006 by Oxford University Press (OUP) in hardback. There were enough sales for them to issue a paperback edition two years later.

If my ICRIER work focused on the recent past, my columns dwelt on economic policy issues of the present and future. After a couple of years, I had written enough to publish a small collection, which Academic Foundation was happy to do in 2003, under the title *India's Economy: Issues and Answers*. Dr Manmohan Singh (then Leader of the Opposition in the Rajya Sabha), kindly released the volume at a well-attended launch in the India Habitat Centre. That was my first published volume after the study on the black economy published in 1986. It was a fun event.

In the late summer of 2003, T.N. Ninan invited me to shift my column to the *Business Standard* (*BS*), along with playing an advisory role in their regular Monday morning brainstorming sessions for edits for the week. I was happy to do this as I considered *BS* to be the better financial paper, with one of India's finest editors and a strong stable of op-ed writers. The edit brainstorming meetings turned out to be a special pleasure, with the top-notch *BS* journalists present, including Ninan, Ashok Bhattacharya, Sunil Jain, Kanika Datta, Surinder Sud, Mihir Sharma, T.C.A. Srinivasa Raghavan, as well as a few outsiders, like Subir Gokarn, Deepak Lal (when in Delhi), Laveesh Bhandari and (later) Shyam Saran. These meetings inevitably started with gossip on cricket, crony capitalist shenanigans and, occasionally, the personal peccadillos of prominent politicians and media folk. But once the discussion turned to substantive matters, it was usually of high quality. It was a great way of staying abreast with what was really going on in India's economic and financial world. As in the case of *ET*, I followed the practice of collecting my *BS* columns every three or four years and republishing them as a book. By now, there have been six of these books.

The year 2002 turned out to be one of much change at ICRIER, and some changes in our lives too. Montek had proceeded to Washington in 2001 to become the first head of the IMF's new Independent Evaluation Office, with Isher to follow in a year. Both Isher and I.G. Patel, ICRIER's chairman, pressed me to accept the directorship. I declined politely but firmly. I was paying heed to my father-in-law's old adage: 'It is better to be the guest of a prince than the prince himself.' As I pointed out to IG and Isher, I had avoided becoming head of DEA or some other government economic department essentially to dodge too many administrative headaches. I was not prepared to assume those of ICRIER now. Finally, Rakesh Mohan was induced to accept the post, but within a few months, he was hijacked by Bimal Jalan to be a deputy governor at RBI. I minded the store for a few months before Arvind Virmani came on board as director.

My portfolio of activities expanded to include a couple more. For some time, Anne Krueger had been head of the Centre for International Development in Stanford, and had initiated an annual India seminar series there each June. I had already attended a couple of these. Towards the end of 2001, she invited me to spend a couple of months there as a Senior Visiting Fellow, and I was happy to accept this for the late spring of 2002. As in the case of our Oxford interlude in 2000, I went on ahead, with Gayatri following after her lectures at Miranda were completed. We spent a very pleasant couple of months enjoying life in one of the richest campuses on the American west coast, at Palo Alto, a short train ride away from San Francisco. As at Oxford, we would often rent a car, and drive around the beautiful countryside of hills and ocean. One of the less-known treasures of Stanford is a wonderful collection of Rodin sculptures, displayed mostly outdoors, in a somewhat secluded part of the rambling campus. Our life in Palo Alto was enriched by the proximity of three of Gayatri's nephews and a niece—all pursuing careers in Californian universities or major Silicon Valley tech companies.

The other new activity in 2002 stemmed from an invitation from the International Advisory Board (IAB) of Toyota Motor Company in Japan. This involved, other than a generous 'sitting fee', flying (first class) to two meetings a year in Japan, with the spouse accompanying on one, and spending three days on meetings and excursions with Toyota's all-Japanese executive board. This was certainly a novel and educational experience. The IAB was designed to give the Toyota leadership a sense of ongoing major global economic, technological and political developments. Obviously, they already knew how to build excellent cars! Members included an ex- prime minister of Thailand, the famous Canadian environmentalist Maurice Strong, the well-known American public official, author and investment banker Robert Hormats (later an under-secretary of the State Department in the Obama administration), a couple of Silicon Valley notables, a British ex-deputy head of Shell, myself and Martin Lees, the coordinator and a former under-secretary general of the UN. My predecessor from India had been S. Venkitaramanan (former governor, RBI), and three years later, I was succeeded by R.K. Pachauri, then head of The Energy and Resources Institute (TERI).

Several features struck me about these Toyota IAB meetings. First, everything was meticulously organized and largely pre-programmed. Even our statements at the meetings (on the pre-sent agenda) had to be emailed ahead to them. One evening was left genuinely informal, with no prior choreography except for a broad topic. I recall, at one of those, just before the American invasion of Iraq in 2003, I stated that such an action would be bad for Iraq, bad for the US, bad for relations between the West and the Islamic world and bad for the world economy. The Toyota folk listened carefully and made dutiful notes, as they did for differing opinions of other IAB members. Second, there were no women executives in sight. Third, among the executive leadership, hierarchy was strictly followed, with no one speaking out of turn. Above all, what astonished me most was that at our lavish dinners (including numbered ducks from a particular French château-farm on one occasion!), my bilateral chats with Japanese colleagues seated next to me never unearthed any ill-will towards Americans, who had dropped two nuclear bombs on them in the final fortnight of WWII. Practicality clearly trumped everything else.

Back in Delhi, C.M. Vasudev, then secretary, DEA, requested me to give a clear signal on whether I intended to return as CEA at the end of my sabbatical in October 2002 or resign from government. Apparently, the uncertainty was impeding their recruitment of a CEA to fill the vacancy after Rakesh's departure. It was an easy request to fulfil. I sought early retirement from the government effective end August, thus freeing up the position early and yet allowing us to stay for a further eight months in Lodi Gardens, enough time for Nixi to complete his twelfth standard CBSE board exam. Ta had meanwhile completed her GCE 'A' levels from British School in the summer of 2001, and joined Miranda House as a college student.

That winter, Gayatri and I went on a marvellous five-day trip to Siem Reap in Cambodia to see the great temples of Angkor, which I had last visited as a child nearly fifty years before. It involved flying to Bangkok and switching to a hideously expensive, short flight on Bangkok Airways, which had monopoly control of the route to Siem Reap. I reconfirmed my view that the Angkor complex is the single greatest historical site in Asia, with the possible exception of the Taj Mahal. Siem Reap town had a large number of young folk with a limb missing, reflecting the enormous toll taken by the still active land mines from the many years of conflict in the 1970s and 1980s, when all sides to the civil war laid millions of such mines all over the little country. Visitors to Angkor were still strongly advised to stay on designated roads and pathways as they toured the great complex. The stoicism and cheerfulness of the Cambodian people, who had been bombed, secretly, by Americans during the Vietnam War, who had suffered the genocidal regime of Pol Pot and then over twenty years of civil conflict, was simply extraordinary.

In May 2003, I began my 'fourth occupation', as a banker of sorts. That spring, Uday Kotak had sounded me out about joining the board of their new bank as a member. They had received their final licence from the RBI in February. I had met Uday a couple of times in the MoF during the late 1990s, when he headed a successful non-bank financial company (NBFC), which he had established and nurtured as a twenty-five year old, and found him very upfront and knowledgeable about the sector. But I think it would be fair to say that at that time we knew each other more by reputation. After some deliberation, I conveyed my acceptance and attended my first board meeting of Kotak Mahindra Bank (KMB) in Bhaktawar building in Nariman Point, Mumbai, just behind the Oberoi, in May. Actually, it was my first board meeting, not just in Kotak, but in any private commercial organization. I still recall that at the end of the meeting, we all walked down to the new KMB branch at Nariman Point. In fact, it was not just new; it was KMB's only full-fledged branch at the time! Thus began a relationship with a person and an institution that was to endure for many years, providing me with an amazing learning experience, great professional satisfaction and a very strong friendship with an icon of Indian finance.

That May we also had to bid fond farewell to CI/1 Lodi Gardens after seven years, just after Nixi completed his twelfth-standard board exam, and shift to our little flat in Greater Kailash 2. We had built a house in Gurgaon DLF Phase 3 in 2001, but it was too far for Gayatri and Ta to commute to Miranda House, to teach and study, respectively. We thought we would move to Gurgaon after Gayatri retired in 2006. Well, as of 2021, we are still in GK2! The timing of our shift to GK2 was fortunate in one important respect. Until then, the area, like many Delhi colonies, suffered from long and frequent electricity outages under the aegis of the public sector Delhi Electricity Supply Undertaking. In late 2002, the government took the initiative of privatizing electricity distribution in Delhi, and south Delhi was taken over by the private BSES Rajdhani Power Ltd. Within months, residential power supply improved dramatically, and we became the beneficiaries.

After living in the heart of Lutyens Delhi, adjusting to GK2 took some time. However, we soon found the nearby parks, the Jahanpanah forest and other amenities to compensate for it. The local market specialized in bank branches, restaurants, hair salons and sanitary fittings shops. Referring to the abundance of eateries, Suman Bery once remarked, 'Shankar, you are living in the heart of downtown Soho!' The driving time to IIC and Habitat Centre, our most frequent destinations, was a tolerable thirty minutes by car. And, increasingly, our retired or semi-retired friends in south Delhi colonies were closer. The biggest adjustment was for our dog, Poochy. No more lawns to gambol in—front, back and side. But adjust she did, with all of us pitching in to take her for three walks a day. Nixi did his adjustment in Aurangabad, where he went for a three-year degree programme in hotel management at the well-known Taj-sponsored institute there.

Amongst the pleasures of being a reasonably well-known 'think-tanker' was that of being invited often for lectures and seminars, both in India and abroad. Some were regular features, such as the Stanford India conference in summer or the annual December NCAER–NBER (National Bureau of Economic Research of the US) conference at Neemrana Fort, set up in the late 1990s by Rakesh Mohan and Martin Feldstein of Harvard. Others were one-off, like an invitation to give a lecture at Australian National University, Canberra, in September 2003. We converted that into a holiday in Australia, which we had never visited before. That included a visit to Sydney, and to our old friends Gopal and Radhika, who were mostly stationed in Brisbane, since Gopal's IMF posting in Papua and New Guinea was a non-family one (aside from a tense political situation, cannibals were still around in some parts!). We persuaded them to join us in an impromptu trip to Cairns and the magnificent Great Barrier Reef, to which one went out in a launch.

As 2003 drew to an end, my semi-retired life was beginning to take shape and structure. At its heart were three constants: My academic work in ICRIER, my association with *Business Standard* and my growing involvement with Kotak Bank. Other assignments came and went without much predictability. For example, I did some consulting with the World Bank, including leading, in the first half of 2004, a significant economic mission and report on Sri Lanka. A couple of years later, I played an advisory role on a Bank economic mission to Bangladesh. Both these exercises helped me gain insights and understanding about the economic history, developments and challenges of two of our important neighbouring countries. Isher's initiative of establishing a South Asia Network of Economic Institutes (SANEI), with ICRIER as its initial anchor, also helped. I was also invited on to the boards of a number of national research organizations, including ICRIER, NCAER, Institute of Social and Economic Change, and Administrative Staff College of India.

In the general elections of May 2004, the NDA lost its majority in Parliament and a new, Congress–centred United Progressive Alliance (UPA) took office with 'outside support' from the Left parties. Congress president Sonia Gandhi chose Dr Manmohan Singh as prime minister, the first 'appointed PM' in India's independent history. Although his PM-ship lasted a full decade, it did not always work very well, with real political power divorced from the head of the Union Cabinet. It was common knowledge that Sonia Gandhi was the final arbiter on ministerial appointments and that ministers often did end-runs to her when they opposed the PM's decisions or views. One consequence of the change in government was that Twelfth Finance Commission (FC) Member Som Pal, who was the Planning Commission link member with the FC, had to resign, along with other members of the Planning Commission. This created a vacancy on the FC (for a part-time member), which was already eighteen months into its work. The FC chairman, Dr Rangarajan, asked me to fill the vacancy for the remainder of the FC's term, up to the end of 2004. I was happy to accept and gain that experience.

It turned out to be a good group, with strong intellectual leadership from Rangarajan and the solid, federal-fiscal analytical background of Dr D.K. Srivastava, a professor from NIPFP, who later became the first director of the Madras School of Economics. Among the states we visited during my tenure as FC were Uttar Pradesh, Punjab, Haryana and Jharkhand. In Lucknow, I remember being seated next to Chief Minister Mulayam Singh Yadav at a state dinner, but our conversation was somewhat constrained linguistically; my Hindi was worse than his English! However, he was an extremely courteous host. On a more substantive matter, I recall the usual discussions in the FC of the formulae for horizontal (across states) distribution of the total tax revenue devolved from the Centre, which, initially, were yielding a significantly lower share for West Bengal than what had prevailed in the Eleventh FC award. I gently pointed out that this would lead to a major political headache for the UPA government in accepting the final FC recommendations, with its existential reliance on the large bloc of Left Members of Parliament from that state. Rangarajan saw the point and arranged for some adjustments to the formulae.

Actually, the Twelfth FC recommendations helped strengthen, together with other developments, the overall fiscal consolidation in the period 2004–08, a key contributory factor in the economic boom of that period. This was because its recommendations for write-off and relief of states' debts were made conditional on adoption of state fiscal responsibility laws, which nearly all of the states enacted expeditiously.

In the latter half of December, I went to Colombo with a couple of World Bank staff members from Washington to discuss our draft economic report with the government there. A few days after my return to Delhi, the deadly 2004 Boxing Day tsunami killed thousands in that island nation, including a member of the World Bank resident mission in Colombo, whom I knew.

Our family social life had improved significantly after Shekhar retired from his last ambassadorial posting (to the European Union) in 2000 and he and Twinky returned to India to settle in their house in Gurgaon's DLF Phase 1. Now, on Christmas day, we had two great repasts to look forward to: the Bissell's lavish brunch in their home in Panchsheel (where they had moved to after John's passing in the late 1990s), followed by Twinky's wonderful home-cooked spread in Gurgaon, with presents for everyone under the traditional Christmas tree (Twinky is Christian). For New Year's Eve, we maintained a tradition of a family dinner at the good old IIC special event each year.

In late May 2005, we went on a rather special family holiday to Florence and Rome, along with Surjit Bhalla and Ravi Kaur, and their two children, a little younger than ours. In Florence we also managed to synchronize with Jayati and Gautam Datta-Mitra (or J&G as they are often referred to) from Washington DC. It was our first family holiday in several years, and being able to do it with the Bhallas and J&G was a very special pleasure. In Florence, we stayed in a spacious, luxury flat about 70 metres from the main cathedral (or Duomo), which we had rented for a few days via the internet. A wonderful tourist-friendly feature of Florence is that most of the top historical and artistic sights are within a 300-metre radius of the Duomo. Gayatri and I were revisiting the city after our hitch-hiking trip in 1967, with significantly more spending power in our wallets. For me, the best of many glorious sights in Florence was the airy, multi-storeyed Bargello National Museum, once a prison, which housed a gorgeous collection of Italian sculpture of the Renaissance by masters like Michelangelo, Donatello, Cellini and the Della Robbia.

One day, the four of us Acharyas took a bus to the famed little thirteenth-century town of San Gimignano, on a hill, with its striking walls and lofty towers. We had lunch there.

Nixi experimented with rabbit and declared it 'delicious', a rare superlative from someone whose usual response was 'okay'. Even now, we occasionally go to the Italian restaurant of that name in Delhi's Imperial Hotel. The walls are covered with beautiful photographs of that little town in Tuscany, which evoke happy memories.

From Florence we took a train to Rome, with the Bhallas driving in their rental car (J&G had to return to the US), and we met up at the Navona Piazza, in the heart of Rome, where we had booked two little flats in an old building, right behind the piazza. The piazza is dominated by Bernini's great 'fountain of the four rivers', the Nile, the Danube, the Ganges and the River Plate. With that as our base, we spent a few days sightseeing the treasures of Rome. One day, as we queued outside St Peter's, we noticed leading BJP politicians Uma Bharti and Govindacharya a little ahead of us in the line, but decided not to intrude on their holiday with small talk. As in Florence, the public squares and tourist spots were dotted with street hawkers selling knock-offs of luxury handbags, scarves and other items. Typically, the hawkers seemed to come from west African nations. On occasion, they hailed from Bangladesh. Recently, when reading Amitav Ghosh's latest novel, *Gun Island*, where he writes about the many Bangladeshi migrants in Venice, I was reminded of my conversations with the Bangladeshi waiters in restaurants on the Piazza Navona fifteen years ago. At the end of this family holiday, I asked Ta and Nixi for their assessment of it and was rewarded by two endearing words: 'Beyond expectations'.

Venu Reddy had replaced Bimal Jalan as RBI governor in 2003. In 2005, Venu instituted a new 'Technical Advisory Committee on Monetary Policy' and asked me to join as one of the external members. This group would serve as a precursor to the more formal, legally backed Monetary Policy Committee that came into being in 2016. I had the pleasure and privilege of serving continuously for eleven years on this advisory committee, through the succession of RBI governors Reddy, Subbarao and Raghuram Rajan.

On 26 July 2005, I had first-hand experience of the potent, toxic cocktail of climate change and associated extreme weather events, mixed with the secular decay of our urban metropolitan infrastructure, specifically, in Mumbai. I had attended a KMB board meeting and was in a rental car taking me to the airport for a flight home to Delhi that afternoon. It had been raining heavily for several days. A prolonged cloudburst dumped 900 mm of torrential rain on the northern half of Mumbai within six hours. The lethal combination of blocked drains, built-over natural water run-offs and adverse tides totally flooded north Mumbai, bringing all forms of transport to a standstill. After seven hours of being stranded in one spot near the Western Express Highway, I persuaded the driver to cut across six lanes of traffic and turn into the relative calm of the Bandra Kurla Complex (BKC). We parked the car on a water-logged street in front of the National Bank for Agriculture and Rural Development (NABARD) and set off around midnight, on foot, towards the Grand Hyatt hotel in the pitch dark. After a few hundred yards of wading through a totally surreal nightscape, and as the water (or sewage?) rose to my chest, I decided that discretion was the better part of valour and returned to our car. Around 1 a.m., and just before my phone battery died, I managed to reach Rakesh Mohan (deputy governor at the RBI) and sought his good offices to be let into the NABARD headquarters for shelter. The next day, after the floods subsided a bit, I returned to the Oberoi in Nariman Point and stayed there for two more nights till flights resumed.

Later that year, in October, I celebrated my sixtieth birthday with a dinner reception for close friends and family on the lawns of the IIC.

13

Life Has Its Ups and Downs

∽

IN EVERYONE'S LIFE, THERE are ups and downs. Some are lucky and have fewer downs. I was probably one of those, or so I thought, until the years after 2005 came along. The year 2006 was actually a good year. My Oxford University Press book on India's macroeconomic policies and growth was published. I became non-executive chairman of Kotak Mahindra Bank. My columns critiquing the UPA government for lack of productivity-enhancing reforms were finding good resonance, and we undertook some very enjoyable trips to new destinations.

Ta had finished her degree in geography at Miranda in 2004, and had been wondering what to do next since then. By the beginning of 2006, she had decided to switch to English studies and was accepted by the University of Canterbury in Christchurch, New Zealand. Off she went in February, full of excitement and apprehension. Within a month of her arrival, she had found a soulmate in Jako, a young New Zealander, and life looked very good. Soon, Gayatri and I found ourselves occasionally chatting with Jako online. His sweetness of temperament came through. His parents had migrated from South Africa. What's more, Dada's son, Ranjan, his wife, Suzanne, and their three children had migrated to Auckland, New Zealand, around the same time as Ta's arrival in Christchurch. So, she seemed all set for a new life.

For the first time in many years, Gayatri and I found our home an 'empty nest', with Nixi still finishing up his final year at Aurangabad. Gayatri would also finish her term's lectures soon, and, along with it, her teaching career at Miranda. To celebrate, we planned a special holiday in Turkey for late spring. Turkey then was off the Indian tourist track. But it was a country redolent with history, going back at least 4000 years, when the Hittites had ruled over Asia Minor. Carved on a stone tablet in Istanbul's Archaeological Museum is the world's oldest surviving peace treaty (of Kaddish) between the Hittites and the Egyptians in 1269 BC. Then came the Hellenic age, with Greek philosopher Heraclitus born in Ephesus and historian Herodotus growing up in Bodrum, followed by the Romans, who, under Emperor Constantine, shifted the centre of the Roman empire to Constantinople (now Istanbul) in the fourth century AD. They, in turn, were supplanted by the Ottoman empire in the fifteenth century, which flourished for 200 years before going into a long decline, until Kemal Ataturk took charge in 1923 and, almost single-handedly, invented modern Turkey.

With so much history, its long Mediterranean, Aegean and Black Sea coasts and the amazing moonscapes of Cappadocia, Turkey had a lot to offer. We proceeded to partake of the offerings. We made Istanbul, the magical 'city of a thousand mosques', our base, and parked ourselves in a hotel right next to the Blue Mosque, with our windows overlooking one of its courtyards. For the next few days, we explored all the beautiful sights—Roman, Byzantine and Islamic. For the sheer beauty of city centres, there are few rivals in the world to the rose-bedecked park in Sultanahmet with the glorious Blue Mosque on one side and the majestic Hagia Sophia, built by Emperor Justinian in the sixth century, on the other. For a contemplative afternoon, it is hard to beat the lovely gardens of the hilltop Süleymaniye mosque (architect Mimar Sinan's masterpiece), from where one can gaze down on the Galata Bridge spanning the Golden Horn to the posh Beyoğlu district. Part of Istanbul's immense appeal comes from the successful marriage of European standards of public infrastructure with Asian culture and hospitality. The city also met my crucial test for successful urbanization: Clean public toilets.

Then it was on to the great Roman ruins at Ephesus on the west coast and thence to the central Anatolian wonders of Cappadocia, where millions of years of volcanic ash sediments have eroded into thousands of conical rock outcrops, with many of these 'fairy chimneys' converted into dwellings in Hittite and Byzantine times, and some of the larger outcrops hollowed out into frescoed churches and monasteries, as in Göreme. In the same general area are the extraordinary underground little towns chiselled out of rock, where inhabitants of past centuries sheltered from occasional invaders.

In 2006, Turkey was 98 per cent Muslim, but seemed more secular, in practice and ambience, than India. The fifteen years of Islamization of politics and society under President Recep Tayyip Erdoğan since then has changed that substantially. It was while we were in Istanbul that I got a call from Uday Kotak asking me to accept the chairmanship of KMB. The previous chair, K.M. Gherda, had crossed seventy, the cut-off imposed by RBI for independent board directors of commercial banks. After some consideration, I accepted, and thus began a twelve-year year innings in that position.

Shortly after our return to Delhi, I had to go to Cape Cod, near Boston, for a conference, where I was billed as a panellist with

Larry Summers on global economic issues. I had my regulation stopovers in England. This time, I added an extra few days to join Chris Verity, Ray Tallis and their families in their holiday cottages at Padstow on the beautiful north coast of Cornwall. In Massachusetts, I looked up old friends, including Linda Bamber, Chitrita and her 'new' husband, Jai.

Sometime that summer, Ta told us the bad news. Jako had been diagnosed with Non-Hodgkin lymphoma and the outlook was bleak. We were in almost daily touch with her on Skype for the remainder of 2006 and the early months of 2007 as Jako went in and out of hospital with Ta and his parents by his side. It was hard for Gayatri and me, and impossible for Ta. It was all over by early April. Ranjan came down from Auckland for the funeral, a gesture that Ta deeply appreciated. Jako had just turned twenty-three. We arrived a few days later to spend time with Ta and meet Jako's parents. It was our first trip to New Zealand, in sombre circumstances. After about ten days, we returned to Delhi, leaving Ta to struggle on. It had been a massive blow, which left an enduring scar.

Back in Delhi, I had to go into hospital for a prostate biopsy, which turned out to be clear after three tension-laden days, during which I had to cope with the high fever of an infection. While recovering back home, all this continuous tension triggered a latent problem of ventricular tachycardia (a form of arrhythmia or irregular heartbeat), in which the heart rate can triple without warning, and, if it doesn't revert to normal by itself, requires an intravenous injection under cardiac monitoring. That makes one want to know the geography of clinics with adequate capabilities. The doctors offered two solutions: A usually successful surgical intervention, or daily medication, which reduces the probability of such episodes. It was instructive that among the six specialists I consulted, the three surgeons recommended intervention, while the regular cardiologists uniformly preferred the medication route. I took the soft option.

Nikhil had got his degree in Aurangabad and returned home in June. He started work in food and beverages in the Hyatt Regency. It was a challenging occupation for someone from his privileged background in our deeply hierarchical society, where servers in uniform are typically not viewed as real people by well-heeled customers. He recalls once serving the son of a close family friend of ours and his companions, but not being recognized by him! Within a couple of years, he had switched to a retail banking job with Axis Bank.

Our life went on, with Gayatri turning to painting as a new hobby and me getting increasingly absorbed in my responsibilities as non-executive chair of Kotak Bank. My professional and personal relationship with Uday grew stronger by the day, and I marvelled at what he and his superb management team were accomplishing as KMB went from strength to strength. Gayatri and I kept up with our trips within and outside India, often with Mike and Liz. They now came every year to India, usually in February, to attend the annual conference of the Indian palliative care association. Either before or after the conference, we would do a little holiday with them. In February 2008, we went on a very pleasant trip to Kerala, visiting Kochi, Kumarakom in the backwaters and Munnar amidst the tea plantations.

By now the Indian economy was on a roll, with growth above 8 per cent, inflation moderate, exports of goods and services booming, the fiscal deficit falling and the stock market going through the roof. As a successful businessman told me, 'Now the politicians don't want to be paid off in cash; they want equity shares!' I kept writing columns pointing to the almost complete lack of productivity-enhancing reforms by the UPA government, which boded ill for future growth, but no one was interested. It was during those go-go years that the notorious scams of the UPA II period (2009–14) mostly took root, including the ones in telecom licences, coal mines allocation, civil aviation rights sales and the Commonwealth Games expenditures. Many of the massive bad bank loans of the later years were also birthed in this boom.

In 2007, I was made a member of the Indo-UK Round Table, a government-sponsored 'track 2' operation between the two countries to strengthen relations. It has always puzzled me as to why we needed a second track with the UK, given the natural density and vibrancy of civil society interactions between these nations. Typically, the annual meetings would alternate between the countries. In the UK, they were usually held in the charming country house of Ditchley Park, a few kilometres outside Oxford and abutting the massive estate of Blenheim Palace, the home of the Churchill family for 300 years. The Indian side was led by Nitin Desai and the British by Lord Christopher Patten, chancellor of Oxford University and earlier the last British governor of Hong Kong. There were interesting members on both sides and the discussions were very pleasant, even though the outcomes were somewhat diffuse. In 2008, we all met in the lovely environs of Wildflower Hall in Shimla, an upmarket hotel run by the Oberoi group. One day, I saw Sonia and Priyanka Gandhi quietly having tea in the main restaurant, without any oppressive cordon of security.

The global financial crisis came to a boil in mid-September 2008, with the collapse of Lehman Bros and the bailout of the giant AIG insurance conglomerate by the US Federal Reserve. In the months that followed, I was called in several times by PM Manmohan Singh for bilateral discussions on the crisis and its ramifications for India. In one of the later discussions, he invited me to join his PMO as a senior adviser. I said, 'Sir, thank you for your kind consideration, but surely, you are a world-class economist yourself and you already have excellent economic advice on call from Montek at the Planning Commission and Rangarajan as chairman, Economic Advisory Council to the PM. Why would you need me?' He said, 'Shankar, I want you here in PMO,' and went on to add that he wanted me to focus on real-economy developments and issues. I requested a couple of days to think it over. Aside from Gayatri, I spoke to only two people on this: Uday Kotak, to alert him of the possibility that I may have to make a rapid exit from the chairmanship of KMB, and Montek, for his advice. Montek advised me to give it serious consideration, but to make sure that the job was at the minister-of-state rank as I had already been member, Twelfth Finance Commission, a few years ago. I did indeed give the matter very serious thought, especially since the invitation came from the PM himself. Ultimately, I decided against it for several reasons: The ones I had already mentioned to the PM; the fact that over the previous four-and-a-half years, political obstacles seemed to have been the dominant constraint on further economic reforms, rather than lack of adequate economic analysis and input; and my instinctive aversion to immersing myself in the world of twelve-hour days in the government system again.

Just before the Lehman crisis of September hit, Venu Reddy completed his term as governor, RBI. He and FM Chidambaram had been having some differences of view on monetary and financial issues, and their relations were somewhat strained. One consequence was that a leading candidate to succeed Venu, Deputy Governor Rakesh Mohan, became a collateral casualty of the frictions between the MoF and RBI. The government chose to appoint then Finance Secretary D. Subbarao, instead of Rakesh, as the new governor. He had been a young JS in the DEA when I joined as CEA in April 1993. Taking charge of RBI when he did meant that Subba had to face a trial by fire in his initial few months. Rakesh continued for another year as deputy governor, before resigning and moving on to an academic appointment in the US. Subba sought my suggestions on a possible successor to Rakesh and I recommended Dr Subir Gokarn, who had been chief economist at the premier credit rating agency CRISIL, and had impressed me with his acumen and judgement in many Monday morning edit brainstorming meetings at *Business Standard*. The suggestion was well received, and Subir was appointed deputy governor. A decade later, he was to succumb to stomach cancer at a tragically young age of sixty in 2019, when he was India's executive director in the IMF.

Sometime in 2008, I had the idea of editing a Festschrift of papers on the challenges facing the Indian economy, in honour of Montek, who had done so much to improve its performance. I ran the idea past Rakesh Mohan, who was also enthusiastic and readily agreed to be co-editor. Within weeks, we had lined up a strong group of contributors, including Rangarajan, Suresh Tendulkar, Isher, Ashok Gulati, Surjit Bhalla, T.N. Ninan, Sunil Jain, Nandan Nilekani, Gajendra Haldea, Rakesh and myself from India. For global perspectives, we had Anne Krueger, Lord Nicholas Stern and Martin Wolf. Of course, it took longer than we had hoped or expected, but it was published under the Oxford University Press imprint with a gala conference launch in 2010. Thanks to the high quality of contributions, it was probably the best analytical volume on the Indian economy for quite a few years. One lesson I learnt was to never again edit a book. It requires the patience, tenacity and doggedness of a sheepdog. Once was definitely enough.

The one big economic achievement of UPA-I had been its successful reduction of the combined (Centre plus states) fiscal deficit from 9 per cent of GDP in 2003–04 to 4 per cent in 2007–08. The pre-election Chidambaram Budget of February 2008 squandered these hard-earned gains in one fell swoop. Although the Budget claimed to target a Central government deficit of 2.5

per cent of GDP for 2008–09, it failed to make provisions for a newly announced farm loan waiver, the wage-bill increases of the already received Sixth Pay Commission report, the massive forthcoming increases in subsidies for food, fuel and fertilizer, and the ramping up of spending on the rural employment guarantee scheme. This unprecedented level of under-funding led to a record overshooting of the Budget target, with the actual Central government deficit exceeding 8 per cent of GDP (including off-Budget items) and the combined deficit touching 10.5 per cent!

Later, all this fiscal profligacy was rationalized as a necessary response to the global financial crisis of 2008–09. But this does not wash for two reasons. First, most of the excess expenditures were already well under way long before the Lehman collapse of September 2008. Second, subsequent professional assessments (including by the RBI) have concluded that this order of 'stimulus' was not required to shore up India's economic growth. What it did achieve was to usher in six years of painful double-digit inflation, which contributed to the UPA's election loss in 2014.

As 2008 drew to a close, we had more bad news in the family. Just before Christmas, my nephew, Ranjan, had a seizure and collapsed on a street in Auckland. Hospital investigations revealed a grade-4 glioblastoma (malignant tumour in the brain). He was forty-three years old. The prognosis offered no hope of survival. Dada and Ann flew over from Canada, and camped near Ranjan's home, with their daughters flying in and out to the extent their jobs allowed. I went over in March 2009 for about a week, partly to see Ranjan, and partly to be with Dada and the rest of the family in this very dark time. Ta also came up from Christchurch. This was my second trip to New Zealand in two years under the shadow of death. The crisis went on with its twists and turns, including experimental surgery in Cleveland, USA. The inevitable end came in March 2010, with lasting damage to the health of both Dada and Ann.

Once again, life had to go on. In June 2009, I was invited to a conference in Venice to speak on the merits and demerits of G-20 vs G-8. We (including Gayatri) were billeted in a luxury hotel on an island a kilometre across from St. Marks Square. It was an eclectic group, including folks like Sam Pitroda, Bruce Riedel (the well-known American south Asia analyst) and Fred Bergsten, the director of the Peterson Institute for International Economics. Conference members were also given a grand tour of the Venice Biennale art festival, which was going on. After the conference, Gayatri and I moved to more modest lodgings behind St. Mark's Square for a few days and explored Venice to our heart's content. Through a happy coincidence, our visit overlapped a bit with that of her California-based nephew Sanjit and his wife Shilpa.

Back in Delhi, I was appointed a member of the National Security Advisory Board (NSAB), then headed by Shankar Bajpai, one of the doyens of Indian diplomacy. It was a fairly large and varied group of retired military chiefs, diplomats, intelligence officers, academics (who rarely retire!) and civil-society worthies, serviced by a small secretariat, headed by the deputy national security adviser. After a couple of years, Naresh Chandra, another highly respected veteran of senior government positions (including Cabinet secretary, Governor of Gujarat and Ambassador to USA) took over from Bajpai. The terms of reference of the group were unclear, at least to me. In the latter half of my four years with the NSAB, we spent a fair amount of time trying to draft a National Security Doctrine, but it never saw the light of day. It was difficult to resist the appellation 'talk shop' for the group. However, for me, it was a welcome opportunity to get acquainted with former stalwarts of our security and foreign policy establishment.

In 2009–10, I became involved with two other part-time activities. The only thing they had in common was that both were headed by the formidable Naresh Chandra. The first was a 'Track 2' dialogue with China, organized by the Ananta Aspen Centre, with the MEA's blessing. We had some meetings in Beijing and some in Delhi. The basic objective of building good relations between both nations was unimpeachable. My sense was that at first the Chinese took it moderately seriously, but with time, as their economic and strategic heft far outstripped ours, their interest in this channel diminished. The best outcome for me was getting to know Naresh better and being very impressed by the depth and width of his experience and knowledge of public affairs. He was also a superb raconteur, as we discovered most tellingly during a six-hour flight delay in Beijing airport.

It was Naresh who got me on to the board of Eros Media International, a major film company specializing in the production and distribution of Bollywood movies. The Indian company (promoted by Kishore and Sunil Lulla) was just going public, and its London-based parent soon listed in the US. Naresh was the chairman of both the parent and Indian companies. Dhiren Swaroop, a former Union expenditure secretary, was, like me, a part-time independent director of the Indian company. During my years on the board, I learnt something about the business. However, unlike at other company boards I had been on, I did not feel that the management desired comparably deep involvement of the independent directors. So, after a few years, I took Naresh's leave to move on, with Rakesh Sood, the veteran diplomat, taking my place.

In 2010, Gayatri's mother passed away. She was in her early nineties and had been a widow for forty years. She had been lovingly looked after by her eldest daughter, Kajal, and her family. Cheerfulness, optimism and unstinting affection were her hallmarks right through to the end. That left Gayatri and me with no surviving parent. We were now truly the elder generation.

Gayatri and I continued to travel a fair bit each year, our trips sometimes linked to conferences and sometimes just because we wanted to go to some specific place. In the summer, we went to England to be with the Mintons and then journeyed up to Edinburgh, where Gene and Kathy Tidrick had kindly lent us their in-town flat, while they were still in their nearby country cottage. The Edinburgh Festival was on, and we saw several shows with the Tidricks. For me, there was a special thrill in seeing the old statues of Scottish philosopher David Hume and philosopher–economist Adam Smith along the 'Royal Mile' in Edinburgh, reminding me of my perusal of their works in my student years in Oxford.

In February 2011, there was a massive earthquake in Christchurch, New Zealand, which killed over 200 people and laid waste to much of the city centre. We were woken in the middle of the night by a phone call from Ta, sounding very scared and shaken. There was little that we could do beyond trying to soothe and comfort her. The quake and its aftermath disrupted normal life in the town and university for several months. Fortunately, Ta and her close friends were safe, though greatly shaken and disoriented. We spoke to her over Skype as often as possible.

In late September, a conference invitation took us to an unusual venue, the Tswalu Kalahari Reserve in the Northern Cape Province of South Africa. It was the largest private game reserve in the world, owned and developed by the Oppenheimer family, who made their billions in mining. The participants, including us, rendezvoused in Johannesburg and then were flown in small planes to Tswalu's airstrip, with ours being piloted by Nicky Oppenheimer, a scion of the family. Apparently, the story of how Tswalu land was accumulated went as follows: When there was a drought, the local farmers sold their cattle; if there was another drought, they sold their goats; and if there was a third successive drought, they sold their land to the Oppenheimers!

After Tswalu, we spent a few days in beautiful Cape Town, under the shadow of the towering Table Mountain, and took a car trip around the Cape Peninsula, circling the Cape of Good Hope, seeing whales and penguins on the way. At the waterfront of the main bay in Cape Town, there is a cluster of four evocative bronze statues of Nobel Peace Prize winners: Albert Luthuli, Desmond Tutu, Nelson Mandela and F.W. de Klerk, which gleam in the setting sun. Then we flew to Livingstone in Zambia, to meet up with our old friends Bob and Ompie Liebenthal, and spend a few days with them in a fancy lodge by the Zambezi river to enjoy daily boat trips to see hippos and elephants, and, of course, the magnificent Victoria Falls. The local name is marvellously evocative, Mosi-oa-Tunya, meaning 'the smoke that thunders', since, at a distance, that's all you saw and heard. I was foolhardy enough to take a small boat (and tour guide) to an island in the middle of the Zambezi, swim the last fifty metres to an outcrop of rock, and then jump into the famous 'Devil's Pool' at the lip of the Falls ... and then hang on to that rocky lip for dear life.

We returned to Delhi around 10 October. Four days later, Poochy returned from an evening walk, had a massive heart attack and died within two minutes, before my desperate call to the vet even went through. It was almost as if she had been hanging on for our return. The next day, Nixi and I took her body to a pet crematorium called 'Paws to Heaven', collected her ashes and scattered them in Lodi Garden, near the northern entrance, close to our old government house. We had lost a family member.

14

My Years with Kotak Bank

I JOINED THE BOARD of Kotak Mahindra Bank (KMB) in May 2003, a few months after it got its licence to convert from the pre-existing NBFC to a scheduled commercial bank. It was the first bank to do so in India. In July 2006, I was voted non-executive chairman, and held the post until July 2018, when I had to relinquish it because of the RBI age restrictions for bank directors. I have to record my enormous gratitude to Uday Kotak and the rest of the board of that time for giving me this marvellous and fulfilling opportunity to learn about banking and grow with India's best private-sector bank for the fifteen years I was there.

It is impossible to overestimate what KMB achieved in those fifteen years and since. Before giving a few illustrative numbers, I must state upfront that none of KMB's extraordinary, sustained success had anything significant to do with me. The best I can claim as my contribution as non-executive chair is that I don't think I got in the way. Now to the numbers, all relating to comparisons between 31 March 2003 and 31 March 2018. The number of deposit-taking bank branches rose from 1 (yes, just 1) to nearly 1400. KMB's balance sheet increased from just over Rs 2100 crore to Rs 2,65,000 crore, of which deposits rose from a mere Rs 257 crore to Rs 1,93,000 crore. The share of current and savings account deposits (called CASA in banking parlance) increased dramatically, from 19 per cent to 51 per cent—thus giving the bank access to rapidly rising low-cost deposits on which it could earn a good 'spread' through loans and advances. Perhaps, more tellingly, the total market value of KMB shares ('market cap' in the jargon) shot up from Rs 936 crore to Rs 1,99,674 crore, making it among the ten most-valuable companies in India. It was also very close to the market cap of the mighty State Bank of India. That is, by 2018, the stock market valued Kotak Mahindra Bank at about $30 billion, whereas it had been valued at a little under $200 million in 2003! Above all, the stellar growth of KMB and its subsidiaries created over 50,000 good jobs.

And all this happened in India's turbulent financial sector, where several private banks failed or had to be bailed out, and even long-established peers like ICICI Bank and Axis Bank underwent serious stress. As for public sector banks, they routinely had to be recapitalized by the government at high taxpayer expense.

It wasn't just a story of monetary success. Throughout this period, KMB was also diversifying into a full-service financial institution by opening up (or consolidating) fresh areas through new 100 per cent–owned subsidiary firms. In 2005, KMB bought out the 40 per cent stake owned by the Ford Company in Kotak Mahindra Prime, an automobile financing NBFC. Next year, KMB bought out Goldman Sachs' 25 per cent stake in Kotak Mahindra Capital Company, an investment bank, and in Kotak Securities, thereby making them 100 per cent subsidiaries. In 2008, KMB promoted the Phoenix Asset Reconstruction Company with a 49 per cent stake. The following year, it launched a pension fund under India's new National Pension System (NPS), being among the few selected from applicants by the pension regulator. In 2014, we launched innovative solutions of Jifi and KayPay for digital and social media. Next year, Kotak General Insurance Company commenced business.

Our biggest inorganic venture was the merger in 2015 with ING Vysya Bank (henceforth IVB), which constituted the largest acquisition of a private sector bank in Indian banking history to date. This was a big, and somewhat risky, step we had been weighing for some time in the board and management. In physical, bank branch network-size terms, the two were fairly evenly matched: We had about 640 branches and ING Vysya about 570. What tilted matters in our favour were two things: First, the ING parent bank in the Netherlands wanted to exit their Indian operation, and second, and most importantly, KMB was much more highly valued by the stock market than IVB, partly because of our valuable subsidiaries and partly because we were better managed. The ratio of market price to book value of our share was about 4.5, and for the IVB share less than 2. Thus, we had by far the 'stronger currency' for the forthcoming stock swap to execute the merger. The merger (or acquisition, which is what it resembled more) had three main advantages for us: It increased our scale in one stroke; it greatly improved our footprint in southern India, where we had few branches, while IVB was dominant there; and it had the collateral benefit of reducing the Kotak promoter group's stake in KMB by over 6 percentage points, in line with RBI's guidance to bring down the promoter share in the paid-up capital of the company. On the downside were the unknown risks of the quality of IVB's asset portfolio and the pension liabilities associated with their significantly unionized work force.

We weighed these considerations over months, and also the price we would effectively pay through the finally agreed ratio of

KMB to IVB shares in the stock swap to conclude the transaction. At the board level, we finally debated matters over two days at an offsite meeting in Dubai in November 2014, before giving the go-ahead to the management to take the matter forward. Of course, the conclusion of the transaction was only the beginning of a daunting fifteen-month project of integration of the two organizations in terms of their human resources, information technology (IT) systems, administrative organizations, processes, and many other matters. I recall the high tension in our management on the day the two IT systems were 'married', and everyone heaved a sigh of relief with the successful consummation.

Other steps followed, with the opening of an International Business Unit in Gujarat International Finance Tec-City (GIFT) in 2016; acquisition of BSS Microfinance Ltd in 2017; buyout of Old Mutual plc (UK)'s 26 per cent share in our joint life insurance business in 2017 and launch of the 811 digital bank app, India's unique full-service digital banking ecosystem, the same year.

What made all this possible? What was the 'secret sauce' behind KMB's prolonged success? There will no doubt be books written in the future on this. I certainly cannot offer a definitive view. I can only suggest some ingredients that appeared important to me. First, and perhaps foremost, there were Uday Kotak's extraordinary talents as an entrepreneur, financial wizard and top flight manager. Uday is one of those very rare people who combine a full grasp of the big picture with an unrelenting attention to detail. His formidable intellect, almost photographic memory, 200 per cent integrity and unflappable cool … all made for a rare and unbeatable combination. Especially when added to Gayatri's description of him as 'one of the nicest people I have ever met'!

Second, and not unrelated to the first, was the very high quality and continuity of the top management team, most of whom had grown with the institution over fifteen to twenty-five years. It included Dipak Gupta and C. Jayaram as joint managing directors, Jaimin Bhatt as chief financial officer, K.V.S. Manian in charge of corporate banking, Gaurang Shah overseeing insurance and asset management, Shanti Ekambaram in charge of retail banking, Mohan Shenoi as head of treasury, Narayan S.A. heading commercial banking and overseeing Kotak Securities, Arvind Kathpalia in charge of risk management and Bina Chandarana as company secretary.

Third, KMB was blessed with a strong and diverse cast of independent board members, including, over time, Anand Mahindra, an icon of India Inc., Cyril Shroff of the well-known Amarchand Mangaldas law firm, Asim Ghosh, former CEO of Vodafone India, Prakash Apte, former managing director of Syngenta India, N.P. Sarda, former co-chairman of Deloitte, Dr Sudipto Mundle, later member of the Fourteenth Finance Commission, Prof. Mahendra Dev, director of Indira Gandhi Institute of Development Research, Amit Desai, noted senior counsel, Farida Khambatta, former vice president of the International Finance Corporation, and Uday Khanna, former CEO of LaFarge India. It was a board where members did not hesitate to express their views, which were generally worth heeding.

Fourth, there was the culture of the organization, permeating down from the top management. Although drive and entrepreneurship were encouraged, cutting of corners was not. Integrity was paramount. Due processes and procedures were expected to be followed. Fifth, there was an overall tilt in favour of conservatism, recognizing the essential fact that banking was a leveraged play. That is, a bank typically held capital equivalent to only about 10–15 per cent of its assets. Such capital could be easily wiped out if a relatively small proportion of the assets went bad. Conservatism was also desirable because of a bank's fiduciary responsibility towards depositors. So, as Uday was fond of reminding us, KMB had to seek returns to make profits, but the returns sought had to be risk-adjusted ones. Sixth, to concretize these guiding principles, the bank had a very strong internal audit organization and an equally robust risk management system. Credit committee decisions could be overridden by the risk management system.

Seventh, the relationship between the board and senior management was always transparent. Uday was a promoter–CEO, but he never tried to brush aside any concerns and issues raised by the board. If board concerns could not be adequately met, management proposals were modified, or even abandoned. In that very important sense, KMB was not run as a 'Lala company', but as wholly professional one.

Finally, what about the non-executive chairman? Personally, I remained sceptical about my value-add, though quite a few board members kindly expressed more generous views. Somebody has to chair meetings, and it happened to be me. I tried to do this as inclusively and courteously as I could, giving everyone a voice, and coming to as balanced a conclusion as seemed possible when, sometimes, the issues were contentious. I also always tried to do my homework on the voluminous agendas conscientiously. But all this seems like matters of basic professionalism, common courtesy and common sense. No rocket science! Of course, it helped greatly that my personal equation with Uday was excellent. Over hundreds of conversations, he taught me the basics of finance, and soon, I found I had no more economics to teach him. More fundamentally, the relationship was founded on complete trust, mutual respect, and, increasingly, strong friendship.

There were a few occasions when my board role may have been a little more than marginal. In October 2010, Coal India Ltd launched an initial public offering of its shares. It was expected to be competitively priced, resulting in high demand for the shares. In such situations, bidders for the stock usually end up with a modest fraction of the amount of shares they bid for. In the KMB board meeting of 20 October, the management suggested that we bid for a high amount of Rs 3000 crore, since we expected to receive a much smaller allocation. Perhaps because of my forthcoming sixty-fifth birthday on the morrow, I was feeling bullish and asked what the maximum amount we were permitted to bid for was. I was told it was Rs 5000 crore. I suggested that we go for it. After due consideration, the board agreed. We were finally allotted around Rs 200 crores' worth of shares, on which we turned a tidy profit of around Rs 70 crore!

A couple of years earlier, in mid-2008, KMB's management was pushing for an aggressive launch of a Kotak credit card, since it was felt that every bank should have one. Given the high default rate on credit card loans, I was somewhat reluctant, but did not resist decisively. The launch went ahead as planned. A year later, after the economic turndown from the global financial crisis, we were licking our wounds from sizeable losses on this business. After that, I insisted that subsequent distribution of cards should be gradual and limited to established KMB customers. My views were heeded and the business slowly gained traction and profitability. In 2009, we had a less happy conclusion with our purchase of a substantial interest in the Ahmedabad Commodity Exchange (ACE) through KMB and our NBFC subsidiary, Kotak Mahindra Prime. Once again, I had been sceptical of the argument that we needed to have a commodity exchange as a necessary part of being a full-service bank, but went along with the general view of the board. Unfortunately, ACE did not live up to its acronym. It turned out to be more of a joker, costing the Kotak group more than Rs 50 crore in losses.

From the mid-2000s, KMB was actively looking for opportunities for branch expansion overseas. In 2011, a new opportunity arose when Bangladesh Bank, the country's central bank, announced that they would permit some fresh bank branches, including a few in collaboration with banks headquartered abroad. We actively pursued a proposal for a branch in Dhaka to be opened under a joint venture relationship with Bangladeshi partners. Given that I was Bengali and had a childhood connection with Dhaka, Uday requested that I be involved. In the autumn of 2011, I recall giving lunch for the governor of Bangladesh Bank when he visited Delhi on some matter.

By December, matters had developed sufficiently for Uday and me to accompany our operational team on the project on a visit to Dhaka. Before going, I briefed National Security Adviser Shivshankar Menon on the matter, to keep him informed and seek the help of our High Commission in Dhaka as necessary. Our potential Bangladeshi joint venture partners advised us that a successful application generally required a blessing from 'the top', that is, Prime Minister Sheikh Hasina. Accordingly, Uday, two of our colleagues and I called on her late one evening at her residence. For the first and only time, I conducted a serious conversation in Bengali with the prime minister of a country! To smoothen the way, I mentioned my early school years in Dhaka and the cordial links my father had in the early 1950s with Awami League leaders, including her father, Sheikh Mujibur Rahman. She listened patiently and was quite friendly during the ensuing substantive conversation. The meeting probably helped our cause, but it was not sufficient. Perhaps that was because we did not go along with a proposal we received shortly thereafter to link up with an alternative set of joint venture partners, about whom we were not comfortable.

One contentious matter took up a lot of the KMB board and senior management's time over the decade from 2008 to 2018. This pertained to the 'promoter issue'. When KMB received its bank licence from the RBI in early 2003, the licensing conditions stipulated that the promoters (the Kotak family and entities controlled by them) had to retain a minimum of 49 per cent of the bank's paid-up capital for the first five years. Nothing was said about any subsequent dilution. However, reacting to the debacle of Global Trust Bank in 2003–04, the RBI issued guidelines on bank ownership, which required private bank promoters to dilute their share of paid-up capital to 10 per cent over time. The initial set of guidelines of 2004 and 2005 were quite flexible in their language and apparent intent. However, as happens frequently in large bureaucracies, the subsequent interpretations and versions became increasingly rigid.

Over time, KMB was pressed to come up with a roadmap to get down to 10 per cent (later changed to 15 per cent). An indicative roadmap was duly supplied, hedged with various qualifications and reserving our legal positions pertaining to the licence conditions. However, in practice, a small, new commercial bank had no option but to bow to the RBI's diktats. So, over time, the promoter share was reduced to 40 per cent, and then, soon after the merger with ING Vyasa, to 30 per cent by June 2017. The next milestone on the indicative guide map was 20 per cent by December 2018.

From 2015 onwards, the board was seriously concerned that a mechanical reduction in the promoter share should not compromise our fiduciary responsibility to our shareholders, 70 per cent of whom (by value) were not in the promoter group. That meant limiting ourselves to options that would not damage KMB's long-term commercial interests and shareholder value. An option that would have done so would have been a rapid sell-off of promoter shares through secondary sales, which would have led to sharp declines in share prices and hurt all shareholders. The main remaining options were, (a) persuade RBI of the rationale for raising the terminal dilution per centage to 20 or 26 per cent; (b) seek another big merger or acquisition, which would reduce the per centage of promoter holdings by a large amount; and (c) undertake a strategic dilution to an outside party, including a foreign financial institution.

We had several meetings with the RBI in pursuit of the first option. I recall my meeting with the then governor of the RBI, Raghuram Rajan, along with two independent director-colleagues, in autumn 2015, to make our pitch for option (a). We gave him a full presentation, which he heard patiently. Our basic point was that public and private interests were better served when bank promoters had sufficient 'skin in the game'. Promoter and institutional interests would be better aligned and non-promoter shareholders would be better served if the maximum permissible promoter holding was raised from 15 to the 20–26 per cent range. Dr Rajan seemed to appreciate and sympathize with this line of thought. However, when revised guidelines were published by the RBI a few months later, it was clear that the bureaucracy had triumphed over any fresh thinking.

As a board, we were not in a position to recommend a sale, strategic or otherwise, as that would run counter to the promoters' legal rights over private property. Besides, given the scale of the transaction and the relative 'thinness' of the domestic capital market, it would almost certainly have led to the Kotak family selling its holdings to a foreign party and thus bringing about the end of the last majority-Indian-owned private bank (banks like HDFC Bank, ICICI Bank, Axis Bank and IndusInd Bank were already majority foreign-owned). Throughout 2016–18, we actively explored the possibility for another big merger, which would reduce the share of promoter holdings. There were discussions, but no viable possibility emerged.

We then hit upon the idea of selling an appropriate quantity of perpetual non-cumulative preference (PNCP) shares in the market, which would reduce the promoters' share of paid-up capital in

KMB, since it would add a sizable amount to the denominator of the ratio too. All guidance and instructions to us from the RBI had been in terms of the percentage of paid-up capital, not equity capital. However, we recognized the possibility that RBI would interpret this as an instance of 'financial engineering' and not accept our literal compliance to their diktats. Therefore, we sought independent legal opinion from top solicitors, counsels and jurists on the legal validity of RBI's instructions to us for reducing the promoter shareholding under the relevant Banking Acts. We were advised that legal backing for RBI's instructions to reduce promoter holdings was fragile and we had a sound legal case.

So, by July 2018, at the time of my last board meeting, we were getting ready to proceed with the PNCP issuance, subject to blessings from independent legal opinions, while accepting that we may finally have to contest the whole matter with RBI in court, something I had long feared as necessary. That would be our very last resort, as no regulated bank wants to file a case against the formidable power of the regulator. None had done so before. I ceased to be chairman on 19 July 2018 and was replaced by Prakash Apte. A fortnight later, KMB issued the required amount of PNCPs and informed the RBI that the 20 per cent benchmark had been complied with. In due course, the RBI rejected this as compliance and retrospectively defined the target requirement of promoter share in terms of 'equity capital' instead of 'paid-up capital'. A few months later the matter ended up in court.

Happily, in early 2020, the matter was settled, with RBI agreeing to a proposal of KMB's to reduce promoter shareholding to 26 per cent of equity capital by August 2020, while capping promoter voting rights at 20 per cent up till March 2020 and 15 per cent thereafter, until such time that RBI regulations might allow for a higher promoter share in equity capital. So, the RBI's legal powers in this matter were not tested in court. Personally, I was very happy to learn about this compromise. It was the main unfinished business I had left for KMB at the time of my departure.

In the larger context, the logic of allowing a 26 per cent promoter shareholding on the grounds of better aligning the incentives of the promoter with those of the institution seems entirely correct. As events in 2018–20 showed, 'professionally managed' private banks with low private-promoter shareholding, such as ICICI Bank and Axis Bank, were quite capable of running into serious financial difficulties; as were promoter-led private banks, such as Yes Bank. The basic issues were not really about the permissible level of promoter share in bank equity capital. They were about the quality of RBI supervision on the one hand, and the probity and integrity of bank management on the other. The fact that in 2018, the government of India turned to Uday Kotak to chair the new board of the failing IL&FS NBFC (and whatever else it was!) was a testament to the government's faith in his long-demonstrated capacity, integrity and probity. And the government chose to extend his tenure in 2019, even when KMB's legal case against RBI was still in court.

Those fifteen years (twelve as chairman) with KMB were a fascinating experience for me. I came to know some very fine people who ran an amazing organization, which created huge amounts of real value to the Indian economy and tens of thousands of good jobs. And they did this with quiet modesty and utter professionalism, day in and day out. It was an immense privilege to see one of India's best private sector firms up close for many years and understand what a really good private-sector organization can accomplish through clear, hard thinking and enormous efficiency in execution. More than any economic textbook I ever read, that experience taught me the power of incentives, competition and accountability provided by markets to bring about socially desirable progress. Yes, the successful managers were well remunerated. But, at least at the higher echelons, a lot of the motivation came from doing challenging jobs well. And there was as much, if not more, camaraderie, here than in the government departments I had worked in earlier.

My one big regret was that I never bought any KMB shares. That was a potentially large monetary penalty I paid for continuing with my old habit, since my finance ministry years, of not purchasing shares of individual companies to avoid any conflict of interest when advising on tax and other public policies. I like to think that despite a lack of direct shareholding interest, I succeeded in keeping KMB interests front and centre during my fifteen years on the board.

While work was central to my relationship with KMB, there was also more. Gayatri and I came to know the board members, senior management and their spouses at the annual two-day off-site meetings. That's how we found out that there were quite a few marathon runners and mountaineers among them, especially among the ladies, Uday's wife, Pallavi, being one. Gayatri, who is a great listener, also learnt some interesting titbits, such as when one of the well-known board members confided that he had to undergo quite a few sessions with a psychiatrist when his beloved dog expired! As a dog lover myself, I could easily empathize. With about six or seven trips to Mumbai each year for board meetings over fifteen years, I became quite a familiar customer at the Trident hotels in both Nariman Point and BKC. The chef at the Italian restaurant at the latter would readily agree to prepare special dishes for me. All of us also enjoyed the overseas off-site meetings in places like Dubai, Singapore and London. That's the only time we got to stay in a suite in the iconic Savoy Hotel in London.

In 2018, when I had to exit the board of Kotak Bank, I felt the pangs of leaving an extended family, perhaps more so than when I resigned from the Government of India. I think the reason was that, in the final analysis, the government is an impersonal organization, whereas the KMB board was far more personalized. I was pleased when they asked me to stay on as a part-time strategic adviser, occasionally attending a board meeting. Of course, my friendship with Uday was by now completely independent of the bank.

15

The Last Decade

THE TITLE OF THIS chapter could have several meanings: The previous ten years; the last decade I will write on in this volume; or the last decade of my life. At seventy-five-plus, with Covid-19 still swirling around, the third is not improbable. Optimistically, I intend the meaning to be confined to the first two alternatives.

Our flat felt curiously empty after Poochy passed away at the age of thirteen-plus. We had got so used to her presence for so long, despite all her idiosyncrasies. Gayatri, who had strongly resisted adoption of the puppy in 1998, now could not bear to have her regular Marie biscuit at midnight, which she used to share ritualistically with Poochy. She clearly needed a special distraction. So, in the early summer of 2012, we went on a week-long trip to the Kashmir valley, which she had never seen. Kashmir was going through a rare lull in cross-border terrorist activities and associated counter-measures by our security forces. Tourism was recovering strongly. We based ourselves in a lovely little family-run hotel on the banks of the secluded Nagin lake in Srinagar. It was called Dar-es-Salaam, evocative of our visits to the capital of Tanzania in the 1970s. Twice a day, we would take hour-long shikara rides from the little private dock at the foot of the hotel lawns, either just around the beautiful lake ringed by hills, or sometimes, through the lotus-choked, narrow strait to the larger and busier Dal Lake.

Of course, we visited the famous Mughal gardens of Srinagar, including Shalimar Bagh, and other well-known sights, before making a two-day trip to Pahalgam, being driven alongside the swirling waters of the Lidder river. In Pahalgam, we were in a hotel perched over the rushing Lidder and would spend twilights seated contemplatively on the rocks at the river bank, sometimes being chatted up by little groups of local schoolgirls. After returning to Srinagar, we made a day-long foray to Gulmarg, with its gorgeous spring flowers and long, snow-streaked mountain slopes, which were so popular with skiers in winter. Pahalgam and Gulmarg were the last places where Gayatri and I mounted ponies for short rides. Throughout the trip, my mind was often flooded by memories of the earlier visit I had made here with my parents and Dada in 1958. Today, I wonder about the look and feel of these beautiful places after the political turmoil of the recent years.

Towards the end of 2011, I had joined the governing body of a charity called CanSupport, founded and chaired by the inspirational Harmala Gupta, who was herself a long-time cancer survivor. This organization provided home-based palliative care to cancer sufferers, especially from poor households in the National Capital Region. My six-year association with them taught me a great deal about the critical importance of good palliative care for patients coping with serious incurable ailments. In most people's minds, cancer treatment is associated with painful and expensive medical interventions, such as surgery, radiation and chemotherapy.

Few understand and appreciate the very important role of palliative care, which can substantially reduce suffering, and sometimes even substitute for the more intrusive interventions. Unsurprisingly, but unfortunately, our public and private healthcare systems have developed only limited capability in this area. Thanks to a few pioneering practitioners and the example and advocacy of organizations like CanSupport, the situation is slowly improving.

In late September 2012, we went to our first (and perhaps last) full-scale, real-world Bollywood wedding. Kishore and Manju Lulla's daughter was getting married, and the multiple ceremonies were held in Mehrangarh Fort and Umaid Bhawan Palace in Jodhpur. As an independent director of Eros, we were kindly invited by the family. It was a grand affair. The first evening, we were treated, on the lawns of a palace, to a stand-up comedy act by Priyanka Chopra, who had flown in from Los Angeles. The next evening, at the sangeet, we were wined and dined on the rooftop of Mehrangarh Fort, with a floor show MC-ed by Shahrukh Khan. The guests included many of the big names of Bollywood, some of India Inc. and some politicians. For us, it was quite a novelty to be rubbing shoulders with the likes of Ajay Devgn, Kajol, Karan Johar, Sridevi, Shilpa Shetty and Anil Kapoor. When introduced to the last, I cheerily greeted him with a 'Hello, Ajay, I really loved *Slumdog Millionaire*', to which he smiled weakly. I managed to get the name right when greeting Mukesh Ambani with a hug!

A few weeks later, a very different kind of celebrity, an old and dear friend, visited Delhi. Aung San Suu Kyi (henceforth referred to as Daw Suu; 'Daw' is an honorific for 'lady') had been freed from house arrest in late 2010, shortly after a 'managed' election in Myanmar, uncontested by the National League for Democracy (NLD), brought to power a government headed by former general Thein Sein, at the head of the military-sponsored majority party. In the April 2012 by-elections to Parliament, she and her party, NLD, swept forty-three out of forty-five seats, making her the de facto leader of the Opposition. She came to a very smoggy Delhi in mid-November of 2012 to deliver a superb Nehru Memorial Lecture in Vigyan Bhawan and stayed for a semi-official five-day visit. The MEA was coordinating her visit and, responding to wishes from her side, got in touch with me to set up personal meetings with her old Oxford friends. She had also expressed a desire to walk in Lodi Gardens. So, five of us (Bika and her husband, Nalini Jain, Gayatri and I) arranged to meet Daw Suu in Bika's centrally located flat in Sujan Singh Park, have a walk in Lodi and return to the flat for a celebratory meal. It was truly wonderful to see her again after twenty-five years and spend quality time together. The walk in Lodi Gardens (emptied of usual walkers by our security folk) was special, with security maintaining an unobtrusive presence. I also had a couple of separate bilateral discussions with her when she educated me on the complexities of Myanmar politics at that time.

Sometime that year, I received an invitation from the Rockefeller Foundation to spend a month in their Villa Serbelloni in Bellagio (Italy) as a resident scholar. We opted for May–June of 2013. The Villa, with its hundreds of acres of forested hillside, is located fabulously on a promontory jutting into the inverted Y of Lake Como, perched above the lakeside Bellagio town. From our two-roomed corner suite, we could look out at the lake on one side and the forested hillside on the other. All meals were provided, including dinner, served formally, with other scholars and partners. They were a remarkably eclectic group, including a national park manager from Namibia, a former attorney general of Singapore, a musician from the UK, a poet from California and a dynamic agricultural economist from Ethiopia. The most work I did in the beautiful surroundings was to write my monthly column for *Business Standard*. The rest of the time was well spent by Gayatri and me, on long walks on the 15 kms of pathways in the gorgeous estate, ferry trips to other picturesque little towns on Lake Como and occasional croquet on the nearby lawns. I seemed to have retained some skills from my England years since I won a little informal tournament among us resident scholars.

When our stay in Bellagio was over, we flew to Helsinki, spent a couple of days with an old friend from our World Bank years and proceeded to St. Petersburg in Russia. There we met with up with Mike and Liz for our pre-planned five-day holiday together in this great city. Anyone visiting St. Petersburg (formerly Leningrad) for the first time should first read at least one of several available histories of its astonishing past, including the murderous two-and-half-year siege of the city during WWII by the German army, which led to hundreds of thousands of deaths from starvation, bitter cold and desperate cannibalism (Pulitzer Prize winner Harrison Salisbury's *900 Days* is a good choice). We spent long hours in the famous Hermitage art museum, in the former Winter Palace of the Russian Czars, took boat rides on the city's network of canals and visited other iconic sights, including Peter the Great's Peterhof, the eighteenth-century summer imperial palace on the Gulf of Finland.

Back in Delhi, Nixi had become ambitious, had quit Axis Bank and enrolled for a two-year MBA programme in the ICFAI Business School in Hyderabad. Ta returned in July after her long sojourn in New Zealand, somewhat worse for wear than when she had left a few years earlier. After a couple of months, she took a position in a local NGO in our neighbourhood, which provided supplementary teaching to children of poor families. That same month, Dada, who had been suffering from a congestive heart failure syndrome since his son Ranjan's tragic demise, had a quintuple heart bypass operation, fortunately very successful. In August, cousin Atashi from Minneapolis, cousin Nandita from Hyderabad and I met up in Dada's hometown of Grimsby, Ontario, to spend some days with him to help with his recuperation. It turned out to be a very good visit—both from the viewpoint of support and comfort to Dada and family and for a bout of rebonding among the far-flung Acharya family cousins. Dada had recuperated well enough to take us wine-tasting in the vineyards in that region. On the return journey, I stopped over for a few days in the Washington DC area to reconnect with many of our old friends. That was the last time I visited America.

Meanwhile, as I wrote in a series of articles in the *Business Standard* from end 2011, later collected in a volume, *Towards Economic Crisis (2012-14) and Beyond* (Academic Foundation, 2015), the Indian economy was lurching towards a crisis. In my August 2013 piece, 'A Crisis Foretold', I pointed out, 'Economic growth has collapsed, industrial output has stagnated for two years, jobs are being shed, consumer inflation is close to 10 per cent and the current account deficit in the balance of payments is nearly 5 per cent of GDP at last count, investment is fleeing abroad … and the rupee is touching new lows (or highs against the $!) each week.' The same article summarized the principle causes to include: The fiscal blowout of 2008–09, the allowing of substantial real exchange rate appreciation since 2009–10, the supply shocks of 2010–12 (from the eruption of serious scams in telecom, coal and land allocation, the fiasco of missing coal and gas supply for new power projects, the anti-investment policies of the 2012 Budget and a general 'policy paralysis'), the longer-term neglect of manufacturing and the draconian monetary measures of July 2013.

The tide began to turn with the new RBI Governor Raghuram Rajan's confident stabilizing package of short-term, exchange-guaranteed borrowing, government restrictions on gold imports and the fortunate waning of the 'taper tantrum'. The rupee's exchange rate recovered appreciably as capital flows reversed. But economic growth remained lacklustre, as did investment. As the general elections of April–May 2014 neared, I offered a trenchant assessment in my piece, 'UPA's Economic Legacy: Good, Bad or Ugly' (*Business Standard*, 26 February 2014), closing with:

> Fundamentally, the decade of UPA government has failed to undertake economic, social and administrative reforms to strengthen India's long-term development potential, despite the golden opportunity offered by the years of high growth and investment. It is hard to resist the conclusion that the overall economic legacy is bad, if not ugly.

Rajan was a good and effective governor of the RBI. Aside from his initial success in stabilizing the BoP situation, his biggest contribution was the RBI's systematic programme of asset quality review (AQR), launched in mid-2015, to assess the depth and breadth of the bad loan problems festering in the Indian banking system. This was a necessary precondition to moving forward with solutions. It was also during his tenure that the current, legally mandated system of 'inflation-targeting' and the associated Monetary Policy Committee (MPC) was established. Purely on the basis of his professional performance, it would have been natural for the government to extend his initial three-year tenure. However, Rajan was also given to making public speeches and comments on areas outside the remit of the Central bank, such as the government's industrial policy and wider issues of diversity, tolerance and freedom of expression. These were generally appreciated by the press and public, but they went against the grain of tradition and government's comfort level. The government did not extend his term

I recall an interesting conversation one day with a favourite author, Amitav Ghosh, on this matter. He was showering fulsome praise to Rajan's 'off-field' utterances. I suggested another viewpoint:

When the head of a prominent governmental organization makes public statements on subjects outside his recognized domain of responsibility, he runs the risk of inviting pushback, criticism and controversy, which may weaken the effectiveness of the very institution he heads. I was not surprised when Rajan's term was not extended, though I was sorry that the RBI lost a good governor.

In mid-February 2014, along with the Mintons, we made our long-planned trip to Myanmar, starting with Yangon. Daw Suu was in Myanmar's new capital, Naypyitaw, discharging her onerous duties in Parliament. But she had kindly arranged for a party colleague to show us around her inherited home on the shores of Inya lake in central Yangon. This was the house where she was incarcerated for fifteen of the twenty-two years between 1988 and 2010. While in Yangon, we spent an evening with our Ambassador, Gautam Mukhopadhyay, who was generally very friendly and educated us on the fast-changing political situation in that country. We then proceeded to Bagan, the tenth-century capital of the old Pagan Kingdom, which first unified the area of modern Myanmar. With its 3000 temples and pagodas by the Irrawady river, it's a fabulous sight, especially at sunset from atop one of the taller pagodas.

Unfortunately, on our second day in Bagan, Gayatri and I came down with a bad case of viral flu, which confined us to our hotel room overlooking the Irrawady. As if that wasn't enough, I was afflicted by a long and scary episode of tachycardia, which only subsided after ten hours, helped by Mike's ministrations. The next day, I reached out to Gautam, who very kindly had our flights rearranged and generously gave us the warm hospitality of his ambassadorial residence for three days to recover enough to catch our scheduled flight back to Delhi (the Mintons, meanwhile, completed the original itinerary with a trip to the famed Inle

Lake). Throughout our stay, Daw Suu very kindly monitored our progress over the phone.

When we returned to Delhi, we got the bad news that my co-brother Nirmal Jhala, (Kajal's husband), had suffered a major vehicle accident in Orchha while they were vacationing there. A broken hip, and subsequent operation, was to lay him up for nearly two years. His three ex-IIT sons all rallied behind him and took turns to visit from America.

Across the country, the election season was in full swing, with the charismatic new BJP star, Narendra Modi, leading the charge. By May, when the votes were counted, the BJP had won an unprecedented absolute majority and, with other members of the NDA, a commanding hold over the Lok Sabha. A new political era had dawned. The new government restored a sense of economic confidence, helping a significant recovery in growth and investment. However, that lasted for barely three years. The draconian demonetization experiment of November 2016 dealt a heavy blow to the informal sector of the Indian economy, which accounts for over 40 per cent of total output and over 85 per cent of employment. Available reports indicate that demonetization was not recommended by either the finance ministry or the RBI. The impetus seemed to come from the PMO on, apparently, the advice of a Pune-based think tank. Of course, once the decision was announced, both MoF and RBI had to implement it. Most mainstream economists, including myself, felt that the measure would inflict high collateral damage, with little progress towards the worthy objectives of reducing black money and tax evasion.

The damage was magnified by the somewhat maladroit implementation of the national goods and services (GST) tax in mid-2017, a major well-meant reform, which went partially astray in the details of its practical design and execution. Since then, economic growth slowed steadily, to barely 4 per cent in

2019–20, and the employment situation worsened considerably. On the plus side, the government enacted the Insolvency and Bankruptcy Code in 2016, and launched some important social programmes, including the Swachh Bharat Mission to eliminate open defecation and generally improve sanitation, and the Jan Dhan scheme to enhance financial inclusion.

In August 2014, when I was in Oxford for my annual visit, I got a call from Nripen Misra, principal secretary to the PM, asking me to come and see him as soon as I returned to India. I did so a few days before Independence Day. He asked if I would be available to serve as chairman of a new Economic Advisory Council (EAC) to the PM, and, if I was, he would take me in to see the PM straightaway. I thanked him warmly for his consideration, but said that I would soon be seventy and had some health issues, which made it unwise for me to take on such a demanding senior government position. I did suggest the names of Vijay Kelkar and Arvind Panagariya for the position. I made it clear that I would be available for any part-time government work, such as chairing a government committee. I also offered the view that the PMO may want to consider appointing a senior economic adviser in the PMO itself, though I was not available for the reasons mentioned. As it happened, in his Independence Day address to the nation, the PM abolished the Planning Commission and created the Niti Aayog as an advisory body, which came to be headed by Dr Panagariya. No new EAC was set up at that time. Nor was a senior economic adviser appointed in the PMO.

A few months later, in early 2015, Nripen called me up one afternoon and asked if I might be interested in being the first head of the new 'BRICs Bank' (New Development Bank), to be headquartered in Shanghai, since China was the largest equity contributor. I said, 'Nripen, many thanks indeed for thinking of me, but I just don't think I am the right person for this job. You need someone who has successfully run a major financial institution for many years, which I haven't. Give me two hours and I will revert with three good possibilities, who would all do a better job than me.' I did call him back in less than two hours with three names, headed by K.V. Kamath. Nripen seemed to like that suggestion. Shortly thereafter, Kamath's appointment as president of the bank was announced.

In the spring of 2015, Bharat Sheth, the dynamic deputy chairman and managing director of Great Eastern Shipping Company (GESCO), and a cousin of my old friend Sudhir Mulji, asked me to consider joining their board. I pointed out that I knew nothing about shipping, to which his response was: 'Never mind, no one does, and I really like your articles in *Business Standard*.' He, of course, was being modest, since he knows everything about the industry and has run India's most successful shipping company for many years. Thanks to his tutoring over the past six years, I have also absorbed a bit. The most important thing I have learnt is that shipping is hugely different from every other industry I know a little about. It's not just about owning tankers and cargo carriers, and leasing them out. Even more important is the art of timely 'trading', in both ships and ship leases. And that requires a peculiar combination of art and science, thanks to the enormous uncertainties which bedevil this industry. Being Greek also helps a lot, but Bharat has done pretty well without that attribute.

As 2015 rolled on, there was growing interest in India on the outcomes of successive state elections, which the NDA had to win to gradually achieve a majority in the Rajya Sabha. On Sunday, 8 November, the nation's eyes were largely glued to TV screens as the results of the Bihar election poured in. I was perhaps one of a handful of Indians also tracking the historic, first reasonably free election being held after twenty-five years in neighbouring Myanmar that day. The results of the last one in 1990 had been annulled by the military government because they didn't like the NLD's sweeping victory. Well, Daw Suu and her NLD won again. The final tally on 21 November showed a massive victory, with NLD securing close to 80 per cent of the contested seats in both the Lower House and the Upper House. This meant that despite the army being directly allotted 25 per cent of the seats under the 2008, military-crafted Constitution, the NLD would have a comfortable majority in both Houses, allowing it to pass all laws except constitutional amendments, which required 75 per cent of all voting members. The NLD also won over 75 per cent of seats in the state and regional assemblies. There was no historical precedent of a leader and her party winning such landslide mandates in two successive free national elections separated by twenty-five years.

Of course, Daw Suu's victory was greatly constrained by the provisions of the 2008 Constitution. She could not be appointed president. Moreover, the key ministries of defence, internal affairs (including control of the civil service) and border affairs remained directly allotted to the army, which also had special powers to declare a National Emergency. In an important sense, even a massive electoral win only gave the party the right to partner the army in ruling Myanmar. Anyway, the new Parliament session would only start in April 2016. This unusual arrangement of dual control became painfully clear in the autumn of 2017, when the army launched its brutal campaign to drive out hundreds of thousands of Rohingya Muslims from Rakhine state into neighbouring Bangladesh. The civilian government was left scrambling to play down or justify this indefensible pogrom.

Early in that winter of 2015–16, I heard separately from Daw Suu and the MEA about her desire for a study of Myanmar's agricultural issues and priorities, which they wanted me to conduct. I did a fair bit of homework on the subject and found several recent studies, including an excellent recent one by a team from the Michigan State University. Through MEA's good offices, I went for a preliminary visit to Yangon and Naypyitaw later in the winter. In Yangon, Gautam Mukhopadhyay kindly insisted on hosting me during my short visit while I had meetings with the heads of missions of all the multilateral agencies in Myanmar, including the World Bank, the Food and Agricultural Organization (FAO), United Nations Development Programme and Asian Development Bank. As I expected, there were several recent major studies already, including a multi-volume one by FAO. Gautam and I then went across to Naypyitaw for a meeting with Daw Suu. I gave her copies of the better reports on Myanmar agriculture I had unearthed, and suggested that her staff could go through them and then let us know what specific further studies they may require, which I could help organize with assistance from our government.

A few months after Daw Suu's government took charge in April 2016, our then foreign secretary, S Jaishankar (later our foreign minister), met me on the subject of Myanmar to broach a new topic. Apparently, Daw Suu wanted me seconded there in a senior economic advisory capacity for quite a few (unspecified) months. I pointed out that I would be seriously handicapped by the fact I didn't know the Burmese language. I was also uncertain and sceptical about the governmental structure within which I, a foreigner, would function. Anyway, I first needed my family's agreement. Given that I was seventy-plus, with some health issues, that clearance was not forthcoming, and I informed Jaishankar accordingly.

In June 2016, Nripen Misra, the PM's principal secretary, called me with the request that I chair a committee to look into the pros and cons of changing the Indian financial year, and present a report within six months. The other members of the Committee on the Change of Financial Year were K.M. Chandrasekhar, former cabinet secretary, P.V. Rajaraman, former finance secretary of the government of Tamil Nadu, and Dr Rajiv Kumar, senior fellow, Centre for Policy Research. Our secretary was the excellent Dr Subhash Chandra Pandey, then AS and financial adviser in the Department of Industrial Policy and Promotion, mobilized through the good offices of Shaktikanta Das, secretary, DEA.

Ours was the first full-scope committee examination of this issue since L.K. Jha's in 1985. We worked hard over the next six months, seeking the views of all significant stakeholders, and doing a great deal of analytical and statistical work. As reported in the press around that time, we concluded, unanimously, that it would be better to stick with the extant financial year. We presented our report to FM Arun Jaitley in late December 2016, and gave him a presentation on our findings. He seemed well persuaded to our viewpoint. We had hoped that our report would be made public by the MoF to stimulate a vibrant discussion. Alas, that did not happen. However, the fact that the government has made no change in the financial year in the five years since suggests that our labours were not in vain.

During these years we continued to enjoy visits from Mike and Liz each February, and from Sunethra from Colombo every October. On our part, I made my annual trips to London and Oxford in August to see top-class theatre in the former, and enjoy the hospitality and company of Mike and Liz in the latter. In those years, we made several trips to Sri Lanka with Mike and Liz, especially to Colombo and the south-western beaches.

In the summer of 2016, after the long recovery from his accident and broken hip, Nirmal was diagnosed with late-stage lung cancer. He passed away in April 2017. As we mourned him, I remembered the many bridge games we had played together during his Delhi posting in the 1980s, and the thoroughly enjoyable joint family trips to Kullu-Manali and, later, Kalimpong in north Bengal. He had always been particularly affectionate to our two children.

During 2016–17, Daw Suu came to India on a couple of state visits in her capacity as State Counsellor, a sort of prime minister. We would meet up as old friends on each occasion, sometimes with other Oxford friends in Sujan Singh Park. The big difference now was that there was a lot more security. I recall one instance when, as we waited downstairs for her cavalcade to arrive, I spotted several snipers stationed, as part of the protective cordon, on the rooftops of Sujan Singh Park. On one of these visits, she complained about the high-priced consultants international agencies thrust on her fledgling government who rarely produced anything useful. She requested me to put together a group of good people who might do some useful work on a pro-bono basis, but with all costs borne by her government. She mentioned that I would be hearing from someone in her office on this matter.

I gathered a team of top-notch analysts, who also happened to be personal friends and who were willing to contribute their time pro bono. They included Dr Sudipto Mundle, well-known public finance economist; Dr Ashok Gulati, a premier agricultural economist; Prof Amita Batra from JNU, a leading trade economist; Ravi Bhoothalingam, former president of Oberoi and a tourism specialist; and Suman Bery, recently returned chief economist from Shell headquarters in Amsterdam. Joseph Fisher, a young British specialist on Myanmar, who worked in Daw Suu's office, contacted me in spring 2017 to work out the modalities of our involvement. The basic idea was for each of us to make a short 'scoping visit' to Myanmar, agree, a detailed but doable work programme with one's counterpart ministry or agency, and then execute it through subsequent longer visits and work from Delhi. Amita Batra was the first off the block, with a substantive contribution to the commerce ministry in Myanmar in the form of a two-week lecture series on trade negotiations for their officials in the latter half of December 2017.

Suman Bery did a week-long scoping visit to the Ministry of Energy and Electricity in early December, which also involved some work while in Naypyitaw. Sudipto and I went there in the third week of the month to have our scoping discussions with the Ministry of Planning and Finance (MoPF), also overlapping with Amita's first week there. Our meetings were well coordinated by an Australian consultant, Leigh Mitchell, an EU senior adviser attached to MoPF (Joseph Fisher had returned to the UK a couple of months before). At the end of the week, based on our meetings, Mitchell sent us a draft work programme for follow-up work, which Sudipto and I slightly edited and returned promptly. Then came the Christmas–New Year break, and communications resumed briefly thereafter. Then, mysteriously from our perspective, the 'line went dead'. I can only surmise that the MoPF bureaucracy found our proposed work programme unhelpful or that there was some sort of 'deep state' decision not to cooperate further with this project of pro-bono consultants. I did not trouble Daw Suu over it as, in my assessment, there was no point 'pushing on a string' if the senior civil service was not interested, for whatever reason.

Early in our visit to Naypyitaw, Daw Suu kindly invited me over one evening to share some home-cooked pizza. We had the usual wide-ranging discussions that are common among old friends meeting after a year. The army's brutal eviction of many thousands of Rohingyas during the autumn months also figured. While she was clearly concerned about the possibility of a militant Islamic sub-nationalism developing in the Rakhine, I have no doubt that she had no part in the army's drastic and sweeping actions. Once they had occurred, she probably had little choice but to defend their actions given the very peculiar Constitution-dictated, forced partnership between the army and the civilian parts of Myanmar's hybrid government. Had she and her party attempted to openly distance themselves from the army's actions a 'red line' would probably have been crossed, resulting in the kind of military coup the world saw in early 2021. Of course, defending the army in public in the ensuing months and years cost Daw Suu her highly favourable international image and standing. A couple of days after our dinner, she invited us (myself and my two colleagues) over for her traditional Christmas carol-singing event in her garden, which included a sizeable number of guests from Naypyitaw's Christian community.

Naypyitaw is a surreal, enormously spread out new capital city of less than a million people in the central plains, over 300 kms north of Yangon. It was built by the military government at an enormous cost in the early 2000s, partly to exert better control over the rebellious border regions of the country, partly to get away from the climatic perils of the Irrawady delta area and partly to be less vulnerable to any external military intervention. It's stand out features, compared with the other Asian capitals, are its very low population density, and very high ratio of newly constructed buildings and infrastructure to people. The deserted twelve-lane road outside the massive Parliament building could easily serve as a runway for large planes. Everything is organized into a handful of zones: For government buildings, government residences, the military, non-government residences, diplomats, hotels (typically with very low occupancy rates), shopping areas and recreation facilities. It's not easy to walk here and feel natural.

At the end of August 2017, I had just returned from my annual ten-day visit to London and Oxford, and was napping on our living room sofa one afternoon to compensate for the usual jet lag. As I opened my eyes, I found myself staring at a tiny little dachshund puppy, about the size of my hand. He had been procured by Ta in my absence. Consonant with his size and fearsome appearance, he was named Leo. That ended our canine-free status for the foreseeable future. Leo does what he likes when he likes; we adjust.

The following year was busy with KMB matters until July, when I bade farewell to the board. Late that month, out of the blue, came an email from the Development Office of my old Keble College informing me that it would be celebrating its 150th anniversary in 2020. One of the celebratory projects would be a special portrait photo exhibition of thirty 'inspirational' individuals selected from Fellows, students, general staff and alumni over the decades. The specially mounted portraits would hang in the Main Hall of the college for about sixteen months, from September 2019. Apparently, I was among those chosen and was requested to make myself available at the college at a mutually convenient date and time for a photo shoot by the chosen professional photographer, Fran Monks. I confess to being very pleased to get this totally unexpected recognition from my old Oxford college, with which I had only corresponded rarely to inform them about change of address.

I promptly replied that I would anyway be in Oxford for my regular annual visit in late August, and that would be a good time for the photo shoot. So, a month later, I met with Fran in Keble one August afternoon and was duly photographed, perhaps a hundred times in different college locations and poses! I was impressed by her charm, energy and professionalism. Over emails, she had advised me to come dressed in 'red and black', as her internet research showed that that suited me best. Interestingly, Fran turned out to be the wife of Tim Harford, the well-known economist and columnist of the *Financial Times* under the byline 'Undercover Economist'. I only got to see the photo she selected for the exhibition when it opened a year later, and the college sent me a page-sized hard copy. Mike Minton very kindly sent me a number of camera shots of how the portrait actually looked as part of the exhibition. I had planned to see the exhibit in person in August 2020, but Covid-19 nixed that hope. *Business Standard* kindly did a 'Chinese Whispers' on it in October 2019.

During 2018 and 2019, my columns in the *Business Standard* repeatedly drew attention to the slowdown in the Indian economy and analysed the underlying causes. However, right through the summer of 2019, both the MoF and the RBI were still projecting 7 per cent economic growth in 2019–20, despite clear signs of deceleration over successive quarters reported even in the official data. In the event, GDP growth only registered 4 per cent, even below my bearish expectations, with the final quarter slowing to hardly 3 per cent.

In the first few months of 2019, I was troubled by repeated episodes of tachycardia, despite continuous prophylactic medication. I decided to seek the surgical option. On the advice of some good friends who had also suffered from arrhythmia, one Saturday in April, I went to see Dr T.S. Kler, chairman of the Heart Institute at the PSRI Hospital. He looked over my medical history and asked me to check in on Monday morning. By noon, the catheter inserted into by heart was doing the necessary radio frequency ablation in a forty-minute procedure. After an overnight stay, I was discharged, free of the daily medication I had taken for years. More importantly, in the two years since, I have been free of tachycardia episodes. It is a great pleasure to record my heartfelt thanks (no pun intended) to Dr Kler and his team. I only wish I had gone to him earlier.

The general elections of spring 2019 returned the BJP and NDA to power, with the party increasing its single-party majority in the Lok Sabha significantly and winning 37 per cent of the national vote. The election was a thumping vindication of Prime Minister Narendra Modi's personal popularity. Since the victory, the freshly mandated government has pursued its 'core agenda' with vigour. The economy, however, continued to slow throughout

2019–20, for several reasons, including the increasing protectionism of our trade policies and the declining share of our exports in the economy.

In October, we had a very special visit from Dada and his daughters, Lalita and Manjula, from Canada. At the time of their last visit in winter of 2015, Dada had said that given his age and health he didn't expect to come again. But with six good years of decent health after his major heart surgery, he was all set to celebrate his eightieth birthday with his younger brother in India, albeit a month early, under the alert and loving care of his daughters. We spent ten glorious days of family time together; along with Gayatri's brother, Shekhar, and sister, Kajal (visiting from Kolkata), and, of course, Twinky. I also took my brother and nieces for a very enjoyable three-day trip to Corbett National Park, staying at the Club Mahindra resort by the Kosi river. During our two long jeep 'safaris' in the park, we saw plenty of flora and fauna, but not the striped king of the jungle. We did hear him/her roar and saw lots of pugmarks and tiger poop! Back in Delhi, on the eve of Dada's departure, we celebrated his forthcoming November birthday and my seventy-fourth, with the entire family in the private room of the Habitat's Deck restaurant, where sentimental speeches were made and a few tears shed.

In late November 2019, Isher called us with the bad news of her brain tumour. A couple of days later, we spent a morning with them and their extended family in the deceptively bright sunshine of the Sundar Nursery gardens. As we partook of chaat and coffee, we spoke mostly about the final stages of Montek's forthcoming book and bandied around possible titles. That was really our last near-normal time together with Montek and Isher. For the first time in twenty-plus years, they were absent from the December Neemrana conference, as she was recovering from a brain biopsy operation in AIIMS. The results confirmed late-stage glioblastoma. In the months that followed, we wished for the best but feared the worst. Until the lockdown, we visited them fairly often. I remember her telling me in February, just before Montek's book launch, 'Shankar, I am going to write a book too, and it won't be about anything "backstage". It will be about my breaking through from a humble past.' I said, 'Of course you will, Isher,' but with little inner conviction. She confounded my doubts. In an extraordinary assertion of will and tenacity, Isher completed her memoirs in August, with a book launch on Zoom. She passed away before the end of September.

In late February 2020, we were holidaying in Goa with Mike and Liz as the distant thunder of events in Wuhan grew louder and the news began to talk about Covid-19 spreading beyond China's borders. Mike and Liz returned to the UK safely on their flights. In early March, I attended a board meeting of GESCO in Mumbai, despite some rumbles from my family about taking unnecessary risks. On Saturday, 21 March, we enjoyed a very pleasant family lunch with Shekhar and Twinky in their home in Gurgaon. The next day, Delhi and Mumbai were locked down. As was the entire nation from 24 March.

For those of us above seventy, life changed completely. The strong lockdown lasted into June. Even after that, members of vulnerable groups like us self-isolated, partly because of medical guidance and partly from sheer prudence. Gayatri did not venture out of our flat in GK2 for the eight months, up though November, as she has some lung issues, while I went out only for short forays in the locality to buy fruit and vegetables, or for unavoidable medical appointments. Very occasionally, I made a longer trip, like the one in late August to visit Isher one last time and again to see Montek in late September, after Isher passed away. Like many other similarly placed older folk, our daily diet of timepass consisted of long phone calls, plenty of WhatsApp messaging, webinars and Zoom meetings, Netflix, Amazon and reading. Our mobility increased only a little in the next four months till end March 2021, as we waited patiently for our shots from the new vaccines developed since November 2020.

As cases of Covid-19 rose steadily in India and abroad through the spring and summer of 2020, it took its toll among some of our good friends. Deepak Lal, the well-respected economist and member of our *Business Standard* Monday edit brainstorming group, passed away in London in April. In August, it was the turn of our friend Deepak Nath, the husband of my Rakhi sister Vasundhara, on the way to a Delhi hospital from Panipat. Both suffered from co-morbidities. But I have no doubt that in the absence of Covid-19, they would still be with us today. Many other friends and acquaintances contracted COVID but, happily, recovered. By September, officially counted daily cases of Covid-19 in India had soared to around 1,00,000 and deaths to above a 1000, though many independent experts estimated numbers several times higher.

In the four months, November 2020 to March 2021, there was some good news in both India and the world. Joe Biden won the US presidential election in November and was sworn in January 2021, thus ending, at least temporarily, the very dark four years of the Trump presidency, with its much greater social and political divisiveness, heightened racism, disrespect for truth and science, and the across-the-board withdrawal of America from international cooperation and institutions. Second, beginning in November 2020, the world saw the development of several anti-Covid-19 vaccines, which promised much hope for the planet's population. India too began mass production of two vaccines, one wholly indigenous and the other licensed by AstraZeneca, which began to be administered mid-January. Independent of the vaccines, the curves of recorded daily Covid-19 cases and deaths in India had come down steadily from their peaks in September, though it was too soon to declare victory, as we found out in March 2021, when the surging second wave hit the country. The recovery of economic output (GDP) was robust in the second half of fiscal 2020–21, according to official estimates, though job and earnings prospects continued to be bleak for the majority of the labour force.

An important negative development in India's neighbourhood was the military coup in Myanmar on 1 February 2021, leading to the detention of Daw Suu and many leaders of her party, despite their landslide electoral victory in the general election of November 2020. A decade of quasi-civilian government was, at best, under grave threat and, at worst, perhaps extinguished. In the months since, the populace of Myanmar has shown extraordinary courage and commitment through daily public protests in the face of brutal shootings, torture and mass arrests by the utterly callous armed forces. In May, the freshly appointed Election Commission outlawed the NLD and the party's leader, Daw Suu Kyi, faced a number of trumped up charges, all designed to disqualify her from any further political role. As of late May (the time of writing), the world has stood by impotently while this continuing tragedy has played on.

Meanwhile, back in India, the ebbing of the first wave of Covid-19 between September 2020 and February 2021 had bred widespread complacency and serious misjudgments among both the populace and the government. Leading ministers spoke confidently of having conquered the Covid challenge, despite the lessons of global experience and the warnings of many experts. The ordering and stockpiling of available vaccination doses was woefully late and inadequate, and the programme soon ran into serious supply shortages. Beginning in late February, the second wave came roaring in, with exponential growth of both officially tallied daily cases and deaths, which soared above 400,000 and

4000, respectively (and several times higher according to many independent analysts and experts) in May. The surge in cases and deaths was also fuelled by government decisions to persist with state elections and political rallies as well as mass religious gatherings, notably the Kumbh Mela.

This deadly second wave placed intolerable stresses on India's shaky health infrastructure, leading to near collapse in several cities and towns. Inevitably, regional and temporary lockdowns proliferated, with damaging consequences for economic activity. This time, the pandemic hit many of our close friends and relatives. As I write, Gayatri's brother, Shekhar Dasgupta, is in his third week in hospital, and our good friend and economist, Sudipto Mundle, in his fourth. Several friends have passed away in hospital, including Dinesh Mohan (brother of well-known economist and friend, Rakesh Mohan) and leading economic journalist, Sunil Jain. Many others are riding out their afflictions in self-isolation at home. Even as the second wave raged, experts and government spokesmen warned of a third wave. Fear, sorrow and trepidation stalked the land.

In mid-June of 2020, urged by Ta and some friends, and inspired by Isher's example, I began writing these memoirs, armed with only my memory (amplified by Ta's) and family photo collections. Initially, I thought of it as something fun and worthwhile to do while in 'voluntary house-arrest', to see what I could remember and to explore whether I could weave a coherent and readable, account of my life. As the first couple of chapters emerged, and I shared them with family and close friends, I was encouraged by their response and became more motivated. Initially, I had no plans for publication. With time, as the chapters rolled out, friends and some family members urged me to think seriously about publishing. And that's how this book emerged.

16

Covid-19 and the Indian Economy

IT IS IMPORTANT TO understand that when Covid-19 came to India in early 2020, the country's economy was already doing poorly. Economic growth had slowed over the previous three years to barely 4 per cent in 2019–20, only 3 per cent in the final quarter. Employment and unemployment were in the worst shape in four decades, as detailed comprehensively by the government's official labour force survey for 2017–18. Since 2011–12, unemployment had tripled to 6 per cent, youth unemployment had also tripled to 18 per cent and female participation in the labour force had collapsed to a record low of 23 per cent. Investment was slowing. The share of exports in the economy had been falling steadily over eight years. The properly accounted consolidated fiscal deficit of the Central and state governments, that is, the net annual borrowing by the governments in India, was running at a high level of nearly 8 per cent of GDP. The government debt to GDP ratio was over

70 per cent, and rising. The banking and finance sector was under serious stress. Bottom line: The Indian economy's capacity to cope with a once-in-a-century pandemic was low.

Covid-19 had been spreading its tentacles outside China since January 2020. It increasingly became a matter of concern in Indian policy circles from the end of February. By then, its effects were already being felt in Europe, especially Italy. Through most of March, the central government's focus was on screening and restricting international travel to and from other affected countries—notably China. At the same time, the government was mobilizing expert medical policy advice on how to deal with the growing threat. I was concerned that the economic inputs that informed the government's thinking on the pandemic and possible countermeasures were not commensurate with the spate of medical analysis and advice, especially after a strict national lockdown was imposed from 24 March at only a few hours of notice. So, over the course of the next six months, I articulated my views in a set of five articles in the *Business Standard*, which, I believe, have stood the test of time and hindsight reasonably well. Much of what follows in this chapter is drawn from them.

In the global 'war' against Covid-19, lockdowns soon became a weapon of choice in parts of China, the United States and most major European nations. Interestingly, it was not implemented nationally in China, Germany or South Korea, countries with the lowest fatality rates, defined as the ratio of deaths to Covid-confirmed cases. In these, and most east Asian nations, countermeasures to Covid-19 relied heavily on other elements of an evolving strategy, including rapid ramping up of testing, contact tracing, isolation and treatment, bolstered by fairly strict social distancing, hand-washing and mask-wearing. There were at least four important differences between India and the major nations of Europe and the US, which made recourse to a strict, prolonged lockdown a much less desirable approach for India.

First, India is a much poorer country, with average incomes a fifth of even China's and more than twenty times less than in the US or Europe, with about 20 per cent of households living below a minimally defined poverty line, while another 20–30 per cent had incomes only modestly higher. What this meant was that nearly half the population was close to subsistence standards of living, with little reserves to ride out fluctuations in incomes caused by sudden shocks like a strict lockdown. They had little alternative to reducing already low levels of consumption of even basic items like food if the lockdown was prolonged.

Second, over 85 per cent of India's 450–500-million-strong labour force was in the informal or unorganized sector, comprising casual labour and the self-employed—typically with low average earnings, often below recommended minimum-wage levels. In a national lockdown situation, where around half of all economic activity came to a grinding halt, it was these workers who took the biggest hit in terms of job loss and earnings cuts. The millions of migrant daily wagers, seen in the news, trudging hundreds of kilometres to their distant homes in spring 2020, vividly demonstrated this. The concurrent survey data from the Centre for Monitoring the Indian Economy (CMIE) showed massive loss of jobs and declines in labour force participation rates in the last week of March, throughout April, and much of May. And, precisely because this vast labour force was in the unorganized sector, they were difficult to protect or compensate significantly through the ramping up of government income/consumption support programmes.

Third, as in other poor countries, India's patchwork of welfare programmes fell far short of European-style national welfare safety nets, like unemployment insurance and universal public health service provision.

Fourth, our extant availability of health infrastructure and services was incomparably worse than in the countries mentioned above. In those nations, the basic logic of a lockdown was to provide the healthcare sector some breathing space, during which key medical facilities (such as critical care hospital beds, ventilators, oxygen and personal protection equipment for medical staff) could be procured, manufactured and organized to step up capacity to meet the anticipated peak, or near-peak, requirements of Covid-19 patients needing hospitalization and critical care. This was the so-called 'flattening the curve' strategy, while waiting for that time in the future, perhaps twelve to twenty-four months, when reliable anti-viral medicines or vaccines against the virus become widely available. In the Indian context, the goal of ramping up available facilities to meet likely peak Covid hospitalization needs was an awesome challenge, whether the lockdown was maintained for three weeks or three months. What had not been achieved in seventy years simply could not be done in a few weeks.

So, did the initial three-week lockdown achieve much, other than the pervasive shutdown of economic activity and massive job losses, especially among the poorer segments of the population? Well, a few things. First, by slowing the transmission of the disease, the lockdown did buy some time to enhance and organize the availability of hospital facilities and critical medical equipment (though starting from a very low and inadequate base), and to increase capacities for screening, testing and quarantining. Second, it brought home to the general public, in a dramatic manner, the seriousness of the pandemic crisis and the associated need for public action to minimize the perils and costs. This would have increased adherence in the post-lockdown phase to non-lockdown norms, such as 'social distancing', frequent hand-washing, mask-wearing as needed, and proscription of large social and religious gatherings. Of course, much of this was not possible in India's densely populated and poor urban slums, which housed around 100 million people; nor in the thousands of poor rural villages without running water.

In rich countries suffering lockdown, the initial debate on costs and benefits of prolonging lockdowns was soon active. Often, this debate was cast in binary terms: The weighing of likely Covid deaths avoided by 'flattening the curve' versus the economic costs of shutdowns. For India, such a binary discussion was always too simplistic. This was so for the simple reason that prolonged lockdowns would also lead to higher-than-normal rates of morbidity and death, especially among the poorer half of the population, as the loss of incomes and reduced consumption of nutrients and other essentials rendered people vulnerable to a wide array of disease vectors, such as tuberculosis, diarrhoeal diseases, respiratory ailments, cardiovascular diseases, and so on, not to mention Covid-19 itself. Then there was the vulnerability of the poor to death from starvation.

So, it was not just about the GDP foregone in the lockdowns. There were human deaths on both sides of the balance: Those Covid ones saved versus the other extra ones caused by prolonged lockdowns, mostly among the poorer half of the population. No one knew the numbers on either side. It had to be a matter of informed judgement. Mine was clear: I did not favour extension of the strict nation-wide lockdown beyond 14 April. However, the government decided to extend the lockdown in phases, right through to early June.

Those first two-and-a-half months of fairly strict lockdown hammered the Indian economy harder than any other external or internal shock (including wars, harvest failures, oil price hikes and demonetization) experienced since Independence. And it did so with unmatched speed, ferocity and pervasiveness. The damage to the economy, its institutional fabric and livelihoods, was bound to be massive, with long-lasting scars.

The early signals of the enormous economic damage came in soon enough. In the words of poet T.S. Eliot, April was the cruellest month. As the rolling household surveys by the CMIE showed, about 120 million Indians, or 30 per cent of the total employed, lost their livelihoods between mid-March and April as unemployment soared to an unheard-of 23 per cent and participation of the working-age population in the labour force dropped to a historic low. Three quarters of the livelihood losers were daily wagers, small traders and hawkers, the remainder being split about evenly between salaried workers and business persons with some fixed assets. Nothing remotely like this had ever happened in India before. The nation's industrial output plummeted by over 50 per cent in April. Merchandise exports crashed by over 60 per cent that month, the steepest fall in over twenty-five years. India's imports fell 59 per cent that same month. Revenues of the central and state governments collapsed by 50 per cent to 80 per cent in April, bloating borrowing requirements and impairing governmental capacity to carry on normal programmes and responsibilities to meet the rising needs of the jobless and the poor and strengthen public health capacity.

The lockdown was slowly loosened from late May and more aggressively from June, when the central government transferred the responsibility for subsequent relaxations mostly to the state governments. The complex and ever-changing lockdown guidelines created serious difficulties for their consistent, coordinated and efficient implementation across different tiers of government and their multiple departments and agencies. For businesses and economic agents, the challenges were manifold, resembling the bad years of the licence-permit raj.

Given this extraordinary and unprecedented level and intensity of economic disruption, I could not comprehend, let alone explain, the relatively sanguine forecasts for India's economic growth in fiscal year 2020–21, in the range of a *positive* 0–2 per cent, maintained by the IMF, the World Bank, investment banks such as Goldman Sachs, and credit rating agencies such as CRISIL, right up to mid-May, after which they began to gradually revise their forecasts downwards. How could economy-wide employment collapse by 30 per cent and output (GDP) decline by only 3–4 per cent? Frankly, it was a huge puzzle, and I expressed my unhappiness, and even anger, with such Panglossian expectations in TV interviews. Even the finance ministry, through its CEA, stuck to projections of positive growth through most of the summer. The RBI judiciously avoided public growth projections for FY 2020–21 until October.

In this vacuum for realistic projections of GDP, I offered a couple of guesstimated scenarios in an article on 14 May in the *Business Standard*. These were, I believe, the first published projections, quarter by quarter, of unprecedented GDP decline in 2020–21. In scenario A, I expected the GDP to fall sharply by 14 per cent in the full year, with a crash of 33 per cent in the first quarter, April–June, from which it would gradually recover as the year progressed. In a more optimistic scenario B, I projected a full-year GDP decline of 11 per cent, with a steep fall of 25 per cent in the first quarter. When the official National Statistical Office (NSO) estimates for the first quarter (April–June) were released nearly four months later at end August, they showed a GDP decline of 24 per cent, almost identical to my guesstimate of 25 per cent in scenario B! Actually, the first-quarter GDP decline is likely to have been even greater because the initial quarterly estimates fail to adequately capture developments in the informal, non-agricultural sector, accounting for about 25 per cent of the economy, which was hit hardest by the lockdown. This was the largest GDP decline experienced in the April–June quarter by any of the G-20 countries.

Several friends expressed surprise, mixed with congratulations, and wondered how I managed to be so prescient. I readily admitted that I had not got these projections from any sophisticated economic-statistical model that I had laboured over painstakingly. Rather, as I had explained in my May article, they came from an application of common sense and some basic understanding of how the Indian economy works. The steps were simple. Based on discussions with knowledgeable people, I assessed that the strict lockdown of April shut down about 40–50 per cent of national economic activity (GDP), bearing in mind that government services, agriculture and various categories of exempted essential goods and services continued functioning. Thus, if 50 per cent of GDP was shut down in April 2020, then growth over the previous year's April would be minus 50 per cent. This huge, policy-imposed decline would gradually shrink over the course of the year as the lockdown was gradually loosened. It was just a matter of making reasonable guesses about the trajectory of shrinkage in order to arrive at my estimates of GDP decline for each quarter of 2020–21. In the more optimistic scenario B, the initial locking up of economic activity in April was assumed to be 40 per cent, instead of the 50 per cent assumed in scenario A. That was all there was to my 'methodology'.

I also pointed out that recovery from the deep trough of the first quarter was likely to be gradual, as some restrictions were bound to remain for more narrowly defined hotspots and containment areas, and there would also be requirements of social distancing, sanitization and work-from-home procedures, all of which would be costly for businesses and rolled out gradually. Besides, it would take time for disrupted supply chains to be repaired, battered businesses to be revived and migrant labour to be wooed back.

In that May article, I also emphasized two other points. First, the massive job losses in April and May shown by the CMIE household surveys indicated that around half of India's population was likely to be suffering significant economic pain. The loss, even if temporary, of 120 million livelihoods would affect close to that number of households out of the total of India's 270 million households. So the economic hardship and deprivation resulting from the lockdown may have been almost universal among the poorer half of the nation's population. These scars would not heal rapidly. Second, although many economists, including a couple of NRI Nobel laureates, had called for large-scale government spending support in cash or kind to ameliorate the plight of the job losers, such efforts faced two big hurdles in Indian circumstances: The assistance might not reach many millions of those affected; and with government treasuries drained by huge revenue losses, there was a real problem of sustainability. It was, I felt, more important to lift the lockdown swiftly and restore the bulk of the lost livelihoods through renewed employment and economic activity. That would also replenish government revenues and revive the capacity of central and state governments to discharge their manifold responsibilities.

I recognized that lifting of the lockdown would lead to more Covid infections and deaths. That central dilemma remained. As I pointed out in my April article, there were deaths on both sides of the ledger: maintaining the lockdown was also likely to cause many thousands of deaths among the jobless and the poor from malnutrition, disease and starvation. I felt strongly that the balance of uncertain risks and considerations favoured swift restoration of job-intensive economic activity.

The government did begin the process of 'unlocking' formally from early June.

As the summer and monsoon months of 2020 unfolded, various high-frequency indicators of economic activity showed clear signs of recovery. Such indicators included increases in power consumption, urban traffic, rail freight, industrial production, merchandise exports and imports, retail transactions and office attendance. Most importantly, the CMIE employment data showed strong recovery of low-end employment and associated decline in unemployment from June, though some of this may have reflected absorption of migrant labour into sowing and harvesting activity in agriculture. Salaried employment continued to fall.

After the NSO's official estimate of a 24 per cent decline in the GDP in the first quarter (April–June) came out in end August, everyone adjusted their projections for GDP decline in the full year 2020–21 smartly upwards to a range of 10–15 per cent, that is, the range I had foreseen back in May. The international financial institutions were among the last to make their adjustment to grim reality, which they did only in the first half of October, with the IMF projecting a 10.3 per cent fall and the World Bank 9.6 per cent. Around then, the RBI also projected a drop of 9.5 per cent, their first growth projection for 2020–21.

Meanwhile, Covid-19 had not been standing still. Throughout the summer and monsoon months of 2020 the number of confirmed cases rose swiftly as the pandemic spread beyond the metropolitan cities to smaller towns and the rural hinterland. By late October, the total tally of confirmed cases had exceeded 8 million, and new cases were being confirmed at the rate of 50,000–80,000 a day. Confirmed deaths were above 1,00,000. By early January 2021 the toll had crossed 1,50,000. Some respected epidemiologists assessed the actual infection cases to be many times larger and Covidattributable deaths perhaps two or more times greater. There was a marked and steady decline in officially confirmed daily cases from October 2020, down to 10,000–15,000 per day in February 2021, before an ominous uptick at the end of the month.

With the first-quarter debacle in national output known, everyone rightly concentrated on the possible trajectory of economic recovery and on policies to speed such recovery. The finance ministry's CEA confidently foresaw a swift V-shaped recovery. The first, brutal downward stroke of the V had certainly occurred. I feared the upward stroke might be far from linear. For the record, my two scenarios of May foresaw a fairly swift partial recovery in the second quarter, followed by a much more flattish trajectory in the remaining quarters of the year, with GDP still remaining a little below the previous year's level in the final quarter of 2020–21.

In fact, official estimates of GDP that have emerged up through February 2021 indicate that the recovery was significantly more robust and swift than what I and most other analysts expected in June–October of 2020. The NSO's official estimate of growth in Q2 of fiscal 2020–21 was a moderate -7.5 per cent, not the double-digit negative number that many had feared. What's more, in the projections (called 'Advanced Estimates') that were published in January and February 2021, the NSO forecast full FY 2020–21 growth at -8 per cent. That looked a little optimistic, as it suggested that after a 16 per cent drop in GDP (according to official estimates) in the first half of the year, the economy would bounce back to the previous year's level in the second half. One must also remember the initial estimates and projections of the NSO tend not to be based on actual data on India's informal or unorganized sector, where outcomes are typically inferred on the basis of recent trends in the organized segment of the economy. Thus, in a context where the informal sector had been hit disproportionately hard, the early NSO estimates and projections of GDP and its growth, may be especially vulnerable to subsequent downward revisions.

As I wrote in May–June 2020, there were several reasons why economic recovery from the deep trough of April–June was likely to be slower and more halting. First, the immense blow to the economy had come from the supply side because of the central government policy of strict lockdown. Even after it had been progressively lifted from June, fresh, partial lockdowns had been repeatedly imposed by state governments, re-disrupting supply chains. Thus, the trajectory of economic output up to October 2020, and probably for the rest of the year, was being determined more by evolving supply constraints than demand factors. In this context, the chorus of voices calling for large fiscal stimuli was mostly misdirected. Fiscal relief to the poor and the worst hit was a priority, and remained so. A fair amount had been done by government within the limitations of its weak delivery systems and dire fiscal situation. The government had used its limited resources to strengthen existing relief programmes like MNREGA and PM Kisan, and offer a major credit guarantee programme for medium, small and micro enterprises (MSME), while leaving it to the RBI to hugely ramp up liquidity to support economic activity through various channels.

Second, the initial harsh lockdown knocked the stuffing out of the already weak fiscal health of both the central and state governments as revenues collapsed across the board. Absent the Covid-19 pandemic, the combined deficit of the centre and states, properly accounted, would probably have been about 8 per cent of GDP (with the centre accounting for 5 per cent) in 2020–21. Post the Covid-lockdown shock, this was likely to jump to unprecedented levels of 13–15 per cent of GDP. That meant a rise in the government debt/GDP ratio at year-end to dangerously high levels close to 90 per cent. The very high future interest burdens and borrowing requirements would pose a serious drag on future economic growth, stoke inflation and erode financial stability. So, my assessment was that to the extent a fiscal stimulus had a positive role in a largely supply constrained economy, there was plenty of it already being pumped in, perhaps even too much.

Third, risk aversion had become a dominant depressant to economic recovery in various ways. For enterprises, risk-mitigating precautions (often mandated ones) posed additional costs, reducing supply response. In spite of such precautions, risk-aversion by workers remains a dampener, especially against a background of a rampaging pandemic. Furthermore, supply was being weakened as many small and medium enterprises ceased to function after months of struggling to stay afloat. Consumers, especially older, richer ones, were naturally avoiding consumption transactions involving close contact. Amazon and Flipkart could not substitute for barber shops, airline and train trips, restaurants, hotels, tourism and many other items of India's very large service economy. These contact-intensive sectors were likely to remain highly stressed for quite some time. The long-term viability of quite a few businesses and sub-sectors was undoubtedly threatened.

Fourth, the long-stressed financial intermediation sector was under renewed pressure as its extant loans and advances looked increasingly shaky. Regulatory forbearance by the RBI and borrower-friendly court judgements weakened the viability of commercial banks and NBFCs as well as the possible safety of depositors' savings. That naturally damped the flow of new loans and advances, and might continue to do so. More bailouts of banks and NBFCs could loom. But this raised the question of who would do the bailouts and with what resources.

Fifth, as the world economy recovered, and with it world trade, there were opportunities for seeking dynamism from external markets, especially in resilient and fast recovering east and south-east Asia. But to benefit strongly from such opportunities, we needed to reverse our three-year-old lurch towards protectionism in our foreign trade policy and join the Regional Comprehensive Economic Partnership (RCEP). As of early 2021, those necessary policy changes did not look likely.

For all these reasons, I did not foresee such a rapid recovery of GDP to pre-Covid-19 levels as the January–February 2021 official projections indicated. We will have a better idea of what actually happened to the trajectory of economic output during fiscal 2020–21 in a year's time when the revised and more reliable data for this period is made available by NSO. In any case, there is no difference in the basic assessments that GDP fell by a record per centage in the year due to Covid-19 and lockdowns. Nor is there any difference in the view that in new fiscal year 2021–22, GDP would see a sharp rebound in the growth rate simply because of the bounce back from the output trough of 2020–21 (economists call this 'the low-base effect'). I and many others expected growth to be 9–12 per cent, which was echoed in the government's end-January 2021 Economic Survey projection of 11 per cent.

However, this modestly optimistic view of developments in 2021–22 had not reckoned with the virulence and ferocity of the second wave of Covid-19, which hit India in March 2021. As the health infrastructure crumbled under impossible pressures, state-wide lockdowns proliferated to cope with the dire situation. This meant that the reasonably robust recovery seen in the second half of 2020–21 was likely to be significantly dented in the April–June quarter (Q1) of 2021–22, with possible declines in GDP of 5–10 per cent as compared to Q4 of 2020–21. As of May 2021, this suggested that the rebound in GDP in the full year 2021–22 was likely to be constrained to around 6–8 per cent, substantially lower than the 9–12 percent growth foreseen in February. That means the level of GDP in 2021–22 could well be a little lower than that enjoyed in 2019–20. The Covid-19/lockdown toll over the two 'lost' years could well amount to 10–12 of GDP.

Perhaps more importantly, the generally anticipated good growth of GDP (from a low base) in 2021–22 would provide no assurances of sustained rapid economic growth in the future, beyond fiscal 2021–22. The key issue that remained was what would happen to India's economic growth in the medium term, say, the five years beyond 2021–22? From the vantage point of May 2021, it is hard to be optimistic. Covid-19 and lockdowns had clearly damaged an already weak Indian economy seriously. Restoration of high growth at, say, 7 per cent or higher was likely to be extremely challenging. This was so for many reasons. First, both the global economy and India were burdened by enormous uncertainty in many dimensions, including the course of the pandemic, the pace of vaccination programmes, efficacy of vaccines in the face of numerous mutations of the virus, the health of the institutional structure of global economic activity and the pattern of economic recovery across the globe. Early indications were that east and south-east Asian countries had done markedly better at dealing with the pandemic, leaving them with more resilient economies, and with greater potential for growth in output and trade. India, by contrast, had been hit hardest and would have to struggle harder to restore sustained and robust economic growth.

Second, even by the end of 2021–22, India's economy would be weighed down by the burden of historically high government debt and interest obligations, and very high levels of RBI-injected liquidity, which limited the space for more expansionary fiscal and monetary measures. The government's February 2021 Union Budget for 2021–22 foresaw a fiscal deficit of nearly 7 per cent of GDP (which meant about 11 per cent including the states) and continued very high levels of government borrowing. The risks of debt sustainability, financial stability and unacceptably high inflation were real.

Third, the banking system would still be highly stressed, with large proportions of past loans owed to insolvent or battered enterprises, with little prospect for quick recovery. RBI's flagship 'Financial Stability Report' of January 2021 foresaw a sharp rise in the proportion of bad loans in the banking system to a very high 14 per cent by September 2021. The heavy dominance of government-owned banks in the system was an added constraint, given their long histories of inefficiency and governance problems.

Fourth, the eternal problems and weaknesses of most of our infrastructure sectors (like power, railways, ports, roads and logistics) would continue to constrain economic performance significantly, plagued by the old conundrum that publicly owned infrastructure providers rarely met commercial tests of performance, while the regulatory and governance environment to encourage successful private–public partnerships remained elusive.

Fifth, despite significant recent reforms, the markets for labour and land remained clogged by legal and bureaucratic impediments, making it very difficult (or expensive) for entrepreneurs to deploy these resources for efficient and profitable production in a competitive world economy.

Sixth, the unfortunate tilt towards protectionism in our foreign trade policies since 2017 would seriously hinder our ability to gain from the likely recovery in world trade, especially in neighbouring and dynamic east and south-east Asia, thus constraining our aspirations for rapid export growth. In particular, recourse to bouts of import protectionism and continued abstention from the RCEP would make it very difficult to enhance India's desired integration with global and regional supply chains in trade.

Seventh, the Covid-19 pandemic has demonstrated the crucial importance of efficient, technologically equipped and purposeful state capacity and action in dealing with the pandemic. South Korea, Taiwan, China and Vietnam are some exemplars. More broadly, such capacity is also a key determinant of sustained, high, modern economic growth. It's an area in which we will need to do a lot better.

That is why, writing in February 2021, I said, 'we will find it difficult to exceed an average of 5 per cent growth in the medium term'. The economic, social and strategic consequences of such modest growth could be profoundly negative. It is worth spending a little time speculating on the nature of these possible consequences.

On the economic side, the most worrisome dimension relates to employment and unemployment. Despite fairly high economic growth at nearly 7 per cent per year, India's employment–unemployment profile had worsened considerably between 2004–05 and 2017–18, especially after 2011–12, according to official National Sample Survey (NSS) data. The rate of open unemployment had tripled to 6 per cent, youth (15–29) unemployment had also tripled to an unprecedented 18 per cent, the labour force participation rate (LFPR, the ratio of those employed or seeking employment to the working-age population) had dropped from 64 per cent to under 50 per cent and, most depressingly, the LFPR for females had plummeted from 43 per cent to 23 per cent. On all these ratios, India compared very unfavourably with its Asian peers, such as China, Indonesia, Vietnam and Bangladesh. Fundamentally, thirteen years of robust economic growth up to 2017–18 had been far from job-ful. Successive governments had, through their unsound economic policies, squandered a great deal of the much hyped 'demographic dividend' of a large, youthful population.

The more recent data from CMIE surveys showed that slowing growth since 2017–18, followed by the Covid-19-lockdown shock, had reduced the national LFPR by another 4 percentage points or so by the end of 2020–21 and cut the proportion of working-age population actually employed by over 5 percentage points to just 36 per cent. Thus, out of a working-age population of about 1 billion, only 360 million actually had employment of some sort.

With the anticipated slow economic growth after 2021–22, especially in the relatively employment-intensive service sectors and low-end manufacturing, the current massive jobs crisis in the Indian economy is likely to persist and could even worsen in the medium term. This would be a prolonged tragedy, not just from the livelihoods perspective but from many others too.

Slow or negligible growth in jobs and incomes would likely sharpen existing social and political stresses in respect of tensions between religions, castes, classes, states and even genders. Managing India's unparalleled diversity has been a huge challenge for all governments since Independence. Slow economic growth will make those challenges that much greater. Just as a rising tide lifts many boats and usually softens tensions between diverse groups, the persistence of slow growth and stagnant job opportunities will heighten these tensions, raising the probability of unpleasant social and political eruptions, with unpredictable fallouts. Problems of law and order, and crimes against women, could well worsen.

Slow growth would likely exacerbate tensions between the central government and state governments. There would be strains on the federal structure and institutions, which would need to be managed through wise statesmanship on all sides. Otherwise, matters could get ugly.

Slow growth in the medium term could be expected to reduce India's global profile and clout in important ways. Geopolitics is a harsh business. Our robust economic performance in the 1990s and the 2000s was the crucial ingredient in our rise in global affairs, which could be skilfully deployed by our leaders and foreign policy practitioners to enhance our geopolitical profile. A tepid Indian economy could be expected to have the reverse impact on our international standing and limit our geopolitical possibilities. Other nations tend to be more friendly and accommodative when a country is strong and prosperous. The reverse is also true. It is no accident that the civil nuclear deal between the US and India, and the ensuing Nuclear Suppliers' Group (NSG) waiver, which lifted the embargo on India to participate in civil nuclear trade, happened when the Indian economy was booming. Eight years later, India's application to the Nuclear Suppliers' Group for membership did not find favour.

India lives in a tough neighbourhood, with long-standing territorial and other disputes with our neighbour in the west and a rising super-power to our north. With slow economic growth in the medium term, India would find it hard to fund the levels of armed forces, modern weaponry and equipment necessary to successfully deter or counter hostile actions by China and Pakistan, possibly acting in concert in particular areas. Alliances with friendly nations like the US, Japan and Australia could certainly augment our defence capabilities, but only up to a point. It is highly unlikely that any of these nations would commit armed forces to support defensive military actions by India in any combat roles. So, '*Atmanirbhar*' would have to remain the guiding principle in our defence capabilities and postures. But for that, we need a stronger economy and more rapid economic growth. Until we can achieve that, our defence and strategic needs might not be adequately fulfilled.

In the short run, our ratio of defence spending to GDP has to rise from the low level it has fallen to. The challenge would be to secure this vitally necessary increase without significant damage to those categories of government spending that are most supportive of economic growth. That means there would have to be either increases in the share of tax and non-tax revenues in GDP or reductions in the so-called 'non-essential' and 'populist' expenditure categories, such as large allocations for subsidies for major sectors and insupportably high real wage and salary levels of public employees. These would pose tough political choices to the government of the day.

Clearly, everything would be easier if medium-term growth were higher than the 5 per cent, or so I expect. But that would require greater discipline in fiscal, monetary and financial policies, and a programme of sustained strong economic reforms. The government's recent reforms in agricultural marketing and labour laws offer hope, as does the strong commitment to privatization of inefficient public enterprises, even of public sector banks. But these policy commitments are still works in progress and a great deal remains to be done. Furthermore, we need to harness the growth impulses from a recovering world economy, especially in Asia. For that we need to reverse our protectionist policies of the last three years and recognize the benefits of membership in RCEP. Many decades of development experience strongly suggest that sustained high economic growth requires an open economy with rapid export growth. Without an open economy, rapid export growth will not happen. And without that, fast overall economic growth may not happen either.

17

Reflections and Premonitions

∽

LOOKING BACK ON MY seventy-five-plus years, the most prominent feature that strikes me is the dominant role of chance and circumstance in my life. It was great good luck that led me to be born into a well-placed family of India's very small professional class, with the Second World War having just ended and India's Independence from two centuries of British rule only two years away. With my father in the elite Indian Civil Service and my mother a rare woman graduate of physics, it meant I would always have a substantial head start in a very poor country. It also meant that the transmission of ample high-quality human capital to me was almost guaranteed. The country's imminent Independence meant that I would grow up in an atmosphere of increasing self-confidence as my parents' generation took charge of public affairs and went ahead to forge a new nation, gifted with a cohort of talented and dedicated leaders, who had sacrificed greatly to achieve Independence for the country.

What I had no idea about in my early years, and only gradually understood over the succeeding decades, was that the timing of my birth was extraordinarily fortunate in a much wider sense. Ours would be the first generation in many that would enjoy at least seventy-five years of a world free from global conflict. At least as importantly, it would be a generation that would witness the greatest material progress resulting from technological advances and the prosperity that comes from relatively unrestricted international commerce. There is, I think, no other comparable period of seventy-five years in recorded human history with the kind of almost continuous and widespread material progress that my cohort has had the exceptional good fortune to enjoy. Of course, there were, and are, many nasty local wars, famines, disease outbreaks, subjugations of one group of people by another, terrorism, huge inequalities across people and their life chances, and other bad things. But all these have to be seen against a backdrop of unprecedented human material progress.

My generation in India, and across most of the world, has taken such unidirectional progress mostly for granted. Indeed, they have expected nothing less in what has sometimes been called the 'revolution of rising expectations'. However, in the last quarter of the twentieth century and the early decades of the twenty-first, it has become increasingly clear that man's unrestricted exploitation of our planet's natural resources and the associated despoliation of many delicate environmental and ecological balances has been fuelling global problems of adverse climate change, depletion of natural resources, more frequent pandemics, air pollution, water crises and other unpleasant symptoms, clearly signalling the limits of unchecked material human greed. The probability that future generations of the human species will enjoy the kind of material progress and rising healthy life expectancy that my cohort has had for the last seventy-five years is almost certainly less than 100 per cent, perhaps a lot less.

We may end up being not just the luckiest generation to date, but the luckiest generation ever!

Chance also played a leading role at many significant points in the trajectory of my life. It was chance that took me to Europe in my early teens, for school and college in England. It was chance that bestowed the gift of lifelong friendship with Mike Minton in Highgate School. It was chance that I went to Oxford and formed long, close friendships with people like Aung San Suu Kyi, Sunethra Bandaranaike, Chris Verity, Ray Tallis, Montek Ahluwalia and a few others, who continued to figure large in my life for more than half a century.

Above all, it was chance that I broke my arm in Orange, Connecticut, in mid-summer 1966 and arrived back in Oxford with my right arm in a plaster. I had, after all, met Gayatri before, during our years in Oxford. But it was her kind offer to trim my fingernails that seemed to lead down a particular path, including fifty-three years of marriage! And that offer may not have come if my arm had been in its normal healthy state.

Yes, I would have probably gone to a good American graduate school for my economics PhD and thence to the World Bank. But it was surely chance that my first boss was Stanley Please, who turned out to be such an exceptional mentor in my early professional life, and thus helped build a foundation for a strong eleven-year career in the World Bank.

In Delhi, it was that chance meeting with Pikoo in 1983 that took us to Pune and her child welfare agency, and brought two little infants into our lives, who have grown up to be Maya Prajakta Acharya and Nikhil Acharya, our daughter and son. Later, in October 1984, when we were all set to return to the World

Bank in Washington DC, it was the chance assassination of Prime Minister Indira Gandhi by one of her bodyguards that set in train a chain of events that led to my appointment as economic adviser in the finance ministry and the subsequent sixteen-year government career, including the last eight as CEA. And those eight years were really contingent on the Congress party returning to power in 1991 under Prime Minister Narasimha Rao with Manmohan Singh as finance minister. Otherwise, I may have stayed on in the World Bank, where I had gone for a short deputation.

Later still, chance surely played a role in the form of a few meetings with Uday Kotak in the 1990s, which led him to invite me on the board of his fledgling bank in early 2003, and started my fifteen-year association with that extraordinary institution, the last twelve as chairman.

Of course, not everything in my life was due to chance. There were quite a few decisions I made, which had a material effect on my life's journey. I chose to give up physics in favour of politics, philosophy and economics when it came to my choice of subject in Oxford. When Gayatri and I became engaged at the end of our Oxford years, that was a matter of joint decision, not chance. Towards the last third of my Harvard years, while I was still incubating my thesis, I did turn down a couple of academic offers at decent universities, preferring to go to the World Bank instead. After a decade in Washington, we took a deliberate decision to proceed with the LWOP option to spend a few years in India, even though that meant Gayatri had to resign her faculty position in George Mason University and I had to give up my 'fast track' of upward mobility within the Bank.

In Delhi, we did make the decisions to adopt our children, despite reservations from my mother, and specifically chose Ta and Nixi on our forays to Pikoo's child welfare agency, in Pune. It was also our decision, though perhaps a foregone one, that I accepted the offer to become economic adviser towards the end of 1984.

Much later, it was very much my decision to quit the post of chief economic adviser after holding it for eight years and move to a think tank, ICRIER, in 2001. This decision had thoroughly puzzled my colleagues in the government, most of whom considered it a bad one. It was extremely rare in the Government of India for a secretary-level officer in good standing to opt for early retirement five years ahead of his normal retirement date. For me, it was an easy decision, guided by two mutually reinforcing and firmly held beliefs: I had only one life to lead, and, second, a variety of lived experiences contributes to a more fulfilled life.

In the twenty years since leaving the Ministry of Finance, there were two other (related) easy decisions I had to make—accepting Uday Kotak's offer of a board seat in Kotak Mahindra Bank in 2003 and acceptance of the chairmanship in 2006. Saying yes in both cases added greatly to the quality of my professional life and experience. There were, of course, many other little chance events and encounters of daily life, and commensurately numerous small decisions, but they do not merit mentioning here.

The daily stuff of a human life is not just about chance and deliberate decision. There is the more mundane, and yet fundamental, question of what makes one get out of bed every morning to take on a new day? Of course, it comes mostly from habit. But what about motivation? Well, the answer varied with the stages of life. In childhood years, it was about doing well in school, making and keeping friends, and, of course, the love of one's family and, especially, the weekend activities and outings with them. In college, again, it was about learning new things and doing well in performance tests and making friendships as near-adults, especially with those of the opposite sex. Later, in Harvard and Washington, it was the joys (and occasional tribulations) of being part of a married couple, while finding one's feet in the new world of working for a living. I realize that I was among the fortunate, small minority in this world who enjoyed his work, at least most of the time, in environments that were professional, challenging, yet supportive. In those years in Washington, and again in the last twenty years, our travels around the world also contributed significantly to the pleasures of living.

Back in India, our two small children were wonderful new sources of daily joys and worries. They were very good practical reasons for getting up from bed early! Later, especially during my fifteen years in the Ministry of Finance, there were two other important elements of life satisfaction. There was the sense of public purpose, of being engaged in implementing and improving public policy for the greater good. It wasn't always there, but it was there often enough to materially add to life satisfaction. The other more general, and in many ways rather diffuse, ingredient was the comfort and sense of belonging back in one's home country after so many years abroad. There was a much greater sense of connectedness with everything around than had ever seemed possible in the far more prosperous and materially comfortable Washington. When the daily newspapers in Delhi reported good and bad things happening, the connect was much more immediate and personal than it ever had been in Washington or Virginia. Good news was savoured more, while bad news (and there was usually plenty of it) hurt more.

Looking back with a wider-angle lens, I think the thirteen years between 1991 and 2004 were the best for India's economic policymaking, during which there was a degree of coherence and good economic sense, which was perhaps not matched in the years before or after. I refer here to economic policymaking, not economic outcomes, which continued to be good till 2010. That's because the outcomes of good policy choices often take time to work through the economic system, and the same is true for bad policies too. This distinction is typically lost in both daily discourse and political assessments, but it is surely important for thoughtful analysts. In terms of outcomes, the two decades of the 1990s and the 2000s have undoubtedly been the best in Independent India's economic history so far. There are serious questions about how soon that momentum can be restored, if ever.

What about the world as a whole during the last seventy-five years since the Second World War? I can only essay some personal reflections, limited to economic developments. Obviously, a great deal was happening, on many different fronts, in the domain of global economic developments. I would tend to agree with those who point to the increasingly free cross-border expansion of global trade, technology and capital flows (sometimes called 'globalization') that occurred between 1950 and 2009 as perhaps the single most potent force driving the unprecedented increase in human material prosperity during this period. That 'great ascent' went on for sixty years, despite some hiccups in between, until the global financial crisis of 2008–10. To my mind, it is a great tragedy that India did not open up to the global economy till 1991. And even afterwards, our embrace of global economic opportunities was somewhat halting and half-hearted. Had we integrated closely with the expanding global economy earlier, we would have enjoyed rapid economic development for much longer, as many other countries did, including China. We would have benefitted from substantially more growth of national output and employment, and less poverty.

The other key factor propelling world economic growth and welfare was the rapid spread of decent education and skills across the world population. Here, too, very unfortunately, India lagged behind seriously, especially when measured by learning outcomes in her schools. Sooner or later, this was bound to constrain the expansion of the nation's output, employment and incomes.

Since 2010, the world economy has grown, but with less vigour, especially in the Western economies, which were the original locomotors of globalization. In 2016, two major events hastened the retreat from globalization and multilateralism in the major western nations. The first was the referendum result in the UK in favour of Brexit. The second, and more important one, was the election of US President Donald Trump. These two Anglo-Saxon nations, which had come out as victors in the Second World War, had been at the forefront of creating the post-war international economic order, with its major international financial institutions and the General Agreement on Trade and Tariffs (GATT), under whose auspices successive 'rounds' of multilateral trade liberalization drove the journey towards freer international trade and greater global prosperity. The process of Brexit weakened the European Union and the UK. The Trump administration withdrew America from various multilateral institutions and agreements, such as the World Health Organization, the 2015 Paris Accord on climate change and the Iran nuclear deal, and actively undermined the World Trade Organization's crucially important disputes settlement system. The US also launched trade wars against major trading partners such as Europe and China. All this slowed the growth of world trade and output. The election in November 2020 of Joe Biden and Kamala Harris as US president and vice president, respectively, offers significantly higher chances for a better world in the medium term. But the journey back from the Trumpian darkness may not be easy or smooth.

Increasingly, China in particular, and east and south-east Asia more generally, have become the principal source of impetus for growth in world output and trade. The baton was clearly shifting when the Covid-19 pandemic struck the world in early 2020. Despite China being the country of origin of the disease, that nation was one of the first to recover. Other east Asian nations, like South Korea, Thailand, Taiwan, Vietnam and Malaysia, were among the best performers in handling the Covid-19 challenge and containing its economic damage. Thus, by early 2021, they were best placed to lead the recovery in global output and trade. Stronger economic linkages with this vibrant region will improve our own economic performance.

What does the future hold? For me, for India and for the world? It is easy to deal with my case with brevity. I have no idea how many years, or months or weeks, I have left. Enough relatives and close friends have already departed this planet for me to comprehend the fragility and contingent nature of individual human lives. Speculation is both macabre and useless. I always remember one remark from a historical novel about Alexander the Great, where a mentor says to him in words more of less to this effect: 'You have to live this life both as if you will live forever … and die tomorrow.' It may seem a hard dictum to follow, but most of us behave as if the first is true while only intellectually recognizing the possibility of the second. And the global brush with Covid-19 has probably brought the second possibility emotionally closer to most thinking people.

What about the world? In particular, the world economy? Human life and economic activity have survived and prospered on this planet for many millennia. But in the last century, the threats to major global disruption seem to have proliferated beyond the traditional ones of war, famine and disease. They now encompass nuclear holocaust (whether by intent or accident), irreversible and disastrous climate change, pervasive air pollution and uncontrollable pandemics. We have lived with all these threats for decades and have taken some steps to reduce their risks. But, as Covid-19 has brought home, we have clearly not done enough. That has also become the dominant view of climate scientists in recent years. Many believe we have crossed the point of no return in our ability to protect our basic ecological and environmental systems from the perils of a warming planet.

In looking ahead at the nearer term, say the next decade, it is relatively easy to be moderately optimistic. There will be an economic recovery from the Covid-19 triggered global recession, and economic growth will resume as technological progress continues and international economic linkages of trade and capital get repaired. But there are many anxieties. The recovery could be highly unequal across nations and within them. Where will the lost jobs come from? Could the reversal of decades of poverty alleviation progress be recouped fairly soon? Will public health systems be strengthened where the need is greatest? Will governments find the will to undertake the right policies? Will scientists make the near-miraculous technical breakthroughs necessary to reverse the juggernaut of climate change? I don't know the answers, but based on the recent historical record I lean towards pessimism.

What about India's economic future? I have already explained in the previous chapter why I think India's economic prospects in the medium term, up to 2027, are none too bright going by present trends and policies. I have also outlined some darker consequences of slow economic growth for employment, social welfare and cohesion, and our strategic capabilities. Let us hope that our present policies improve soon ... and substantially. Or that my expectations are unduly bearish. The years after 2027 are well beyond my visibility. There are just too many imponderables and uncertainties.

In non-economic areas of the nation's life too the future is fraught with uncertain challenges and perils. Our polity is now quite clearly in a different place compared with the Nehruvian vision which dominated the first half century after Independence when I grew up. The latter valued diversity and pluralism, at least in theory, if not always in practice. The currently prevailing political narrative emphasizes a more majoritarian view: India is mostly about the majority community of Hindus. Whether, in the long run, this more recent and less inclusive guiding perspective will lead to swifter economic and social progress for the people of India, only time will tell. I have my doubts.

Acknowledgements

I N PUTTING TOGETHER THIS book, I have benefitted greatly from the comments and encouragement received from a number of close relatives and friends. First and foremost, my wife, Gayatri, read and commented on every chapter before it went to anyone else. I deeply appreciate that she was a very liberal and benign gatekeeper, never applying the censor's blue pencil. Rather, she enriched the account by suggesting several telling anecdotes and some other ideas. As a self-appointed keeper of family history and photo archives, our daughter, Ta, and her sharp memory were a great asset. She also helped me learn the art of making corrections at the proof stage using Adobe Reader. My brother, Sanjoy, also read every chapter carefully, and made valuable factual additions and corrections, especially for the early years of our shared childhood and the years together in England. Gayatri's siblings, Shekhar Dasgupta, Krishna Jhala and Monica Dasgupta, were extremely generous with their positive feedback, as was my cousin, Nandita Ray.

Amongst friends, a fair number took the trouble of reading and commenting on all (or nearly all) the chapters. They include: Montek Ahulwalia, Sunethra Bandaranaike, Amita Batra, Ravi Bhoothalingam, Emmanuel Jimenez, Michael Minton, T.N. Ninan, Y. Venugopal Reddy, Karan Thapar and Gopal Yadav. I am deeply indebted to them for the time and trouble they took. Even where I may not have accepted all their views and suggestions, I am grateful to them for making me think seriously about the issues they raised.

Johannes Linn and Martin Wolf gave me the benefit of their comments on most of the early and middle chapters of the book. On the chapters dealing with my years in England as school boy and college student, I am grateful for comments and corrections from Sir Robin Christopher, Michael Minton, Raymond Tallis and Christopher Verity. Mohiuddin Alamgir gave me helpful comments on the chapter about my Harvard years, as well as on the first chapter, which included sections on his homeland, Bangladesh. The chapters relating to my World Bank years benefitted from the comments and feedback of Jim Adams, Robert Liebenthal, Ping Loh, Gene Tidrick and Stephen O'Brien. The chapters on my finance ministry years were improved by the comments of Vijay Kelkar, C. Rangarajan, E.A.S. Sarma and, of course, Montek Ahluwalia. I am grateful to Prakash Apte, Jaimin Bhatt and Dipak Gupta for their thorough review and constructive comments on the chapter covering my years with Kotak Bank.

I am indebted to Karan Thapar for introducing me to Krishan Chopra, then in charge of non-fiction publications at HarperCollins (India), who very kindly gave me a swift, positive response on the basis of a synopsis and some chapters. He and his editorial team gave detailed comments on the full manuscript, which improved the book significantly. Much thanks are also due Shatarupa Ghoshal for her meticulous editing and for anchoring the manuscript so ably and professionally in the final months of transformation into a book.

I am grateful to Rupa Publications for their permission to use the photo of finance minister P. Chidambaram's Budget group of 1996 and to Kotak Mahindra Bank for the photo of the board. Special thanks are owed to Fran Monks for the cover photo.

Needless to say, all remaining errors in the book are my responsibility.

Index

About the Author

Dr Shankar Acharya is a renowned Indian economist, and currently honorary professor at the Indian Council for Research on International Economic Relations, Delhi. He was the longest-serving chief economic adviser to the Government of India, a member of the Twelfth Finance Commission and the National Security Advisory Board, and, for twelve years, chairman of Kotak Mahindra Bank. He writes a regular column for the *Business Standard* and has authored a number of books on the Indian economy.